MW01644593

True Stories of Aircraft and Passengers Who Disappeared into Thin Air

---

For many, aviation still brings with it an air of mystery, a century-long magic trick. Though most of us will board an aircraft at some point in our lives, we know little about how they work and the procedures surrounding their operation. It is that mystery that makes these losses, such as the vanishing of Malaysia Airlines flight 370, so terrifying.

Without a Trace explores the most interesting of these disappearances: mysteries that have baffled investigators for years. Occasionally tragic, frequently amusing, *Without a Trace* is unerringly accurate and informative.

The two *Without a Trace* volumes span 150 years and explore mysteries from around the world. Volume One begins just before the golden age of aviation with a manned balloon swept over the English Channel and ends with a top-secret spy plane disappearing at the height of the cold war. Volume Two begins with a 1970s UFO incident and ends with the most recent case of an aircraft disappearing over the Indian Ocean. Each case is laid out in rich detail and presented chronologically, highlighting the historical context, official accident reports and contemporary news surrounding each mystery.

Where did they go?

Sylvia Wrigley introduces the crews, innocent bystanders and rescuers in this collection of true stories. Documenting the popular theories from each case, she uses her knowledge and experience as a pilot and an aviation journalist to demystify aviation jargon and narrow down each disappearance to the most likely explanations.

This collection takes a hard look at the human failings of great aviators, explorers and celebrities who have pushed the limits of flight and ended up at the heart of a mystery. The stories encompass airships, military jets and commercial airlines—all of which have vanished without a trace.

WITHOUT A TRACE

1881—2016

SYLVIA WRIGLEY

Without a Trace I & II: 1881—2016
2019
UUID#49C05BE6-ED0E-48EC-93D3-1782D5C0E681

For information address:
sylvia@planecra.sh

Editing and interior design by:
EQP
EQP BOOKS

CONTENTS

Without a Trace

1881–1968

CONTENTS FOR

WITHOUT A TRACE VOL. I 1881–1968

Acknowledgements

Thank you to Codex and to Vice. Although neither has anything to do with aviation, both offered me unrelenting support.

I owe a huge debt of gratitude to many people for offering your thoughts and feedback as I was writing this book: Laurel Amberdine, TJ Berry, Brenta Blevins, Laurence Brothers, Rick Fisher, Dominic Hall, Debra Jess, Jim Noble, Robert C Otteni, Laura Pearlman, Frances Silversmith, Cliff Stanford, Deborah Walker and many, many more. Thank you, all of you; you know who you are.

Thank you to Curt Mason, Christopher Michel and Ealdgyth for their excellent photographs, along with all the other photographers and repositories who have placed their images in the public domain.

A collection of many incidents like this is impossible without the hard work and good writing of other people. I have included a long list of references at the end and I recommend each and every piece for further reading. But I would specifically like to call out the following websites as extensive and wonderful resources for aviation history and information:

- The International Group for Historic Aircraft Recovery at https://tighar.org/
- Check-Six at http://www.check-six.com/
- 90° North at http://90north.tripod.com/
- National Investigations Committee on Aerial Phenomena at http://www.nicap.org/

- United States Department of Transportation Online Digital Special Collections at http://dotlibrary.specialcollection.net/Home/
- Wikipedia at https://www.wikipedia.org/

I'm also grateful to news agencies around the world for stellar reporting and free access to their archives, in particular the BBC and the New York Times.

1881

The Disappearance of Aeronaut Walter Powell

The fascinating story of Walter Powell, a Welsh gentleman born in 1842, may not be what one expects from a book on aviation mysteries, as it does not seem that difficult to lose track of a balloon, even one on loan from the War Office. However, it sets the tone for the more conventional aircraft nicely: a chain of unfortunate events which individually are not catastrophic but inevitably lead to disaster. We'll see, as the book progresses, that this is a sequence which is typical of aviation accidents. The disappearance of the *Saladin* also features the earliest documented search and rescue operation for a lost aerial vehicle.

Walter Powell, the Tory Member of Parliament for Malmesbury, took up ballooning in 1880 after the death of his wife. He was a well-liked MP, known as "the poor man's friend". He spearheaded a movement to supply 50 tons of coal to those in need every winter. He was interested in technology and, after the death of his wife, he became interested in ballooning. It was an expensive hobby and required the balloonist to have a flexible work schedule, as flying was most dependent on wind and weather. Aeronaut Henry Coxwell, who at the time held the record for the highest ascent without oxygen, initially trained Powell but soon recommended that someone else take him on as a student, complaining that Powell was "rather too enterprising and fresh for an aeronaut at my time of life."

Powell had a dream that, one day, a balloon would be able to fly across the Atlantic to America, a transatlantic crossing unheard of at the time. It began as a hobby but within a relatively short time, ballooning took over his life.

From *Walter Powell—Malmesbury Memories* by David Forward:

> In Malmesbury they looked at their Member's new interest with tolerant amusement. We read how in October 1880 when Walter Powell was to have proposed the election of the town's new coroner he had to send a telegram of apology as he would be up in a balloon then. There was much friendly laughter at the meeting when the message arrived, and jokes were made about the hope that they would not soon be needing to elect a new M.P. as well.

He soon tired of flying other people's balloons and decided that he must have his own balloon made for him. He invited avid balloonist, Captain James Templer, to design a balloon for him.

Captain Templer is considered the godfather of the modern Royal Air Force. He pioneered the British military use of balloons and airships. In 1878 Captain Templer started a British Army balloon school in Woolwich, using his own balloon, *Crusader*. Templer was also the Instructor in Ballooning to the Royal Engineers and commanded the military balloon department at Chatham.

It was in 1881 when Templer came to stay at Powell's house and they designed a custom balloon using Lyons silk. The red- and yellow-striped silk balloon used hydrogen gas and included cork seats and life belts. Sadly, history seems to have forgotten what the balloon was named but it was clearly a beautiful sight.

Captain Templer also used hot-air balloons to make observations for the Meteorological Office. Thus, it was interesting to him when, on the 9th of December, 1881, London was enveloped by a "very peculiar fog". He wanted to ascend into and over the fog to investigate. And, as it happened, the Meteorological Society had been given access to the newly developed military balloon *Saladin* from the War Office. *Saladin*, which was moored at Bath at the time, was not a hydrogen balloon but instead utilised 38,000 cubic feet of coal gas. The Meteorological Society agreed that the captain could use it for an ascent to measure the temperature and atmospheric conditions which had produced the fog.

Walter Powell and James Templer in the basket gondola of the coal gas balloon *Saladin*.

Captain Templer arranged a flight for the 10th of December and invited the 39-year-old Powell to attend to the balloon, which would leave Templer free to make his observations. A gentleman by the name of A. Agg-Gardner was also invited to join them.

Saladin was a green and yellow calico balloon. The aeronauts threw sacks of ballast out to reduce the weight so they would rise into the air. A valve in the balloon neck allowed them to let out the coal gas, reducing the lifting power and bringing the balloon down. Navigation was completely dependent on wind and air currents.

They departed from the field at Bath Gas Works on the 10th in poor conditions and passed over Wells at 4,200 feet. They passed over Glastonbury and then a current of air blew them between Somerton and Langport. Here, they rose to 5,000 feet to investigate a bank of cloud and then sank to 2,000 feet and drifted towards Crewkerne.

Visibility in the fog was poor. Captain Templer only realised their danger when he suddenly heard the roar of waves. He realised they were perilously close to the English Channel, west of Bridport. The balloon was now rapidly drifting towards the sea and Captain Templer felt that the descent was critical.

Captain Templer reported the final moments to the Meteorological Office:

> Crewkerne was sighted when we were at 2,000 feet altitude, and Mr Powell allowed the balloon, at my request, to descend, and we passed Beaminster, where we first heard the sea, and immediately I verified my position, and we prepared to effect our descent. The horizontal velocity was increased to thirty-five miles an hour. The balloon was descending most favourably near Symondsbury when Mr Powell threw out some ballast. On his telling me that he had done so I immediately opened the valve. He then asked me if this was necessary? I answered, "We are nearing the sea," and he replied "I am afraid I rather overdid that last ballast." Glancing downwards I found that our pace had increased.

Saladin touched the ground less than 150 metres (450 feet) from the edge of a cliff. The "landing" was uncontrolled and violent. Captain Templer half-fell, half-disembarked from the balloon as the car capsized, still holding the valve line in his hand. The balloon rose sharply as a result of the change in weight and Agg-Gardner fell out as well, breaking his leg in the process.

Powell was still half in the car which, now much lighter, righted itself and began to climb again. Captain Templar kept a rough hold of the valve line which tore into his hands as he was dragged along the ground behind the balloon. He shouted at Powell to jump down. The car was still just 8 feet (2.5 metres) above the ground but Powell didn't jump. The valve line was ripped from Templer's hands as the balloon rose. He watched the balloon float away, with Powell standing in the car.

Why did Powell stay in the car? Possibly he was just frozen from the surprise. Perhaps he was afraid to jump. Or maybe he believed the balloon—on loan from the War Office, remember—was too valuable to simply cut adrift. Certainly, Templer told the Meteorological Office that he believed that Powell might have stayed with the balloon hoping that he could save it. Powell could have been a hero if he managed to bring it down on the beach, or perhaps, as the car weight was now so much lighter without the other two occupants, he might even be able fly the balloon straight across the Channel to land safely in France.

Powell was last seen waving his hand to Captain Templar as the balloon was swept out to sea. Templer left Agg-Gardner (with his broken leg) in charge of the scene and immediately sent word to the Coastguard and Bridport harbour-master, hoping that one of the boats in the area might have seen something. Meanwhile, he telegraphed the Royal Engineers to have a steamer in readiness for a search, and hopefully a rescue. Once he arrived at Weymouth, where the SS *Commodore* was ready with steam up, he received a telegram from the Bridport harbourmaster. Someone had reported a balloon dropping into the sea to the south of Bridport. Templer rushed to the location and searched, taking wind and current into account, but they found nothing. Templer couldn't have known, as we do now, that false sightings are common in the case of an aircraft disappearing. Still, he realised that it was unlikely that the balloon would have been visible at that distance in the evening sun, let alone that it would have fallen so close to the shore, so soon after floating away. He came to the conclusion that Powell may have thrown part of the gear out to lighten the balloon.

The steamer continued across the channel until the Casquets lighthouse came into view, which meant that they were nearing the Channel Islands east of the French coastline. If Powell could have made it this far, surely he would have made it to the French shore. They turned back and searched again, arriving back at Weymouth at five o'clock on Sunday morning. Templer immediately organised further searches and for three weeks they attempted to locate Powell and the *Saladin*. They only found one clue: a thermometer was discovered on the beach with a single human hair attached.

Over the next three weeks, they doubled the coast guard and continued to search, including dredging some areas of the Channel, but to no avail.

The *Spectator,* a conservative British magazine, ghoulishly pointed out that if Mr Powell was still "floating about" in the balloon, it could only be his corpse, as "the extreme cold would render food and cordials absolutely essential to life".

This did nothing to slow public interest in the mystery, of course. The reported sightings continued to flood in: witnesses from Devon and France swore they'd seen the balloon but reports also came in from locations where, given the prevailing winds, the balloon was unlikely to have reached. The balloon disappeared on the 10th of December but, as the media coverage covered the search internationally, the reports continued to come.

American Charles Fort, who became famous for his research of the paranormal, was fascinated by this and wrote about the reports in *New Lands:*

> A balloon is lost near or over the sea. If it should fall into the sea it would probably float and for considerable time be a conspicuous object; nevertheless the disappearance of a balloon last seen over the English Channel, can not, without other circumstances, be considered very mysterious. Now one expects to learn of reports from many places of supposed balloons that had been seen. But the extraordinary circumstance is that reports came in upon a luminous object that was seen in the sky at the time that this balloon disappeared. In the London *Times*, it is said that a luminous object had been seen, evening of the 13th, moving in various directions in the sky near Cherbourg.

Fort tracked the apparent sightings of the luminous balloon, which he believed to have been the *Saladin.*

The *Times* reported that three customhouse guards in Laredo, Spain, saw something like a balloon in the sky on the night of the 16th. They'd climbed a mountain to get a better view but then it shot out sparks and disappeared. The *Morning Post* had a similar report from Bilbao, just 60 km from Laredo, which described the balloon as sparkling, a luminous display.

The same edition of the *Standard* reported that Captain Mc. Bain of the steamship *Countess of Aberdeen* was just off the coast of Scotland when he saw something in the early morning sky. He looked through glasses to see a large light attached to something that might have been the car of a balloon, moving against the wind (or possibly with the wind of an upper stratum) towards the Scottish coast, visible for about half an hour. The *Morning Post* countered that someone in Dundee had set up a "fire-balloon" which was carried along the coast by a gentle breeze until it collapsed near the coast, although Charles Fort argues that this would not have been visible from the location of the *Countess of Aberdeen*. Finally, Fort reports that in the *Standard*, two bright lights were reported over Dartmouth Harbour.

None of the sightings helped to narrow down where the balloon might have ended up or to come up with any way to rescue its occupant. Despite weeks of extensive searching and following up on many reports, no trace of Powell was ever found.

The searchers eventually dismissed the sightings, concluding that the balloon and its occupant must have come down halfway across the Channel and sunk to the bottom.

Two years later, the mystery took on new life. The *New York Times* reported that the remains of *Saladin* had been discovered. Fragments and shreds of the cloth of the balloon were recovered in the mountains of Sierra del Pedroza in Asturias, on the northwest coast of Spain. This meant that the balloon had travelled some 800 kilometres (500 miles) from the coast where it had escaped Templer's grasp and floated away.

So now it was easy to dismiss the bulk of the sightings, specifically those in Scotland. The balloon clearly *had* made it clear across the Channel and even across the Bay of Biscay. Author Mike Dash of the *Fortean Times* plotted the sightings reported from Spain and found that they showed a clear path of the balloon continuing directly south.

However, there was no sign of any human remains: Powell did not come down with the balloon.

He may have been tossed out of the car in rough weather, which would explain the balloon's ability to continue to fly for such a distance. A *New York Times* article on the find, published on the 24th of January 1883, believes that is exactly what happened:

> The wreck of the balloon discovered in the Spanish mountains settles the dispute as to the strength of that pride of the aeronaut; it undoubtedly did not pitch into the Channel, but half-inflated with gas, sailed through the air for many days. But while the tattered rags and splintered wood which formed it have been rotting among the peaks of Spain, the bones of the intrepid aeronaut have been whitening beneath the waters of the English Channel.

But then, he was safe in the car of the balloon as it flew away and seemingly made no attempt to jump out. Once he was over to the Channel, it seems very odd that he would have fallen overboard *exactly* at the point where he would not be found. There were rumours at the time that Powell might have flung himself overboard on purpose, in order to escape debts at home, but this seems completely out of character of the MP at the time. More importantly, he couldn't possibly have planned the situation as it played out so it would be a rather opportunistic means of committing suicide on what started as a beautiful ballooning day.

Lost in the depths of time, we've little chance now of discovering what happened to Walter Powell, let alone why he remained in the uncontrollable craft in poor visibility and unfavourable winds.

Of course, Powell is not nearly the last to have come to a bad end when the weather has turned. As powered aircraft came onto the scene, it didn't take long before brave pilots began to push the limits of what mankind could achieve. It was in 1927 when the disappearance of two French pilots changed the course of aviation history.

1927

The Last Known Whereabouts of the White Bird

The disappearance of *L'Oiseau Blanc* is one of the enduring mysteries of aviation history. The pilots eventually achieved their goal of changing aviation history, but certainly not in the way that they had hoped.

These days, the case is not well known in the English-speaking world, certainly not compared to the loss of Amelia Earhart fourteen years later, even though the search effort is claimed to have dwarfed hers in terms of money, manpower and area searched.

In fact, the interest was enough that The French Minister of Transport re-opened the case in 1984 and that report, translated and made available for reference as a part of a project to discover more (The International Group for Historic Aircraft Recovery: Project Ghost), gives us a great source of information about Nungesser and Coli's flight, leaning heavily on the original investigation at the time.

Even with modern technology, it is impossible to piece together exactly what happened and, although there are various groups who have attempted to establish the route and find some trace of the aircraft wreckage, so far no one has been successful.

The story starts with the Orteig Prize which was offered by New York hotel owner Raymond Orteig in 1919.

> Gentlemen: As a stimulus to the courageous aviators, I desire to offer, through the auspices

> and regulations of the Aero Club of America, a prize of $25,000 to the first aviator of any Allied Country crossing the Atlantic in one flight, from Paris to New York or New York to Paris, all other details in your care.
>
> Yours very sincerely,
>
> Raymond Orteig

$25,000 would be the equivalent of a prize worth around $350,000 in 2018, enough to pay the debts of an aviator and maybe even enough left over to buy a brand new aircraft.

That year many record-breaking flights were made, including the first non-stop flight between Newfoundland and Ireland and the first crossing from East Fortune Scotland to Long Island, New York. However, the trip from New York to continental Europe was still beyond the capabilities of the aircraft of the time and the reward, which specified New York City to Paris, was not claimed during the five-year period of the prize.

In 1925, Orteig reissued his offer and this time, there was a real chance of an aviator collecting the prize.

The first serious attempt was by French flying ace René Fonck in 1926, who was flying a custom-built Sikorsky aircraft. The attempt literally never got off the ground: the Sikorsky crashed and burst into flames on take-off, killing two of the four on board.

The following year, a number of serious contenders in the US undertook to cross the Atlantic from New York to Paris.

Clarence Chamberlin and Bert Acosta had private funding for an attempt in a Bellanca WB-2 monoplane. In April, 1927 they set the world endurance record, circling New York City for over 51 hours and covering a distance of 4,100 miles. The planned flight from New York to Paris was 3,600 miles. But, before they were able to make their attempt, the pilots and the chief backer (who was also the owner of the aircraft) ended up in contract arguments and an injunction was placed on the aircraft. These arguments caused multiple delays and twice the transatlantic flights were cancelled. In the end, Chamberlin did cross the Atlantic but not until after the prize had been claimed.

Polar explorer Richard E. Byrd, whom we will see again in the next chapter, commissioned a tri-motor aircraft from Anthony

Fokker. The Fokker crashed nose-over during a test flight; Byrd and his two crew members suffered multiple broken bones. The aircraft was repaired but, in May 1927, they were still testing and awaiting favourable weather. In the end, they did cross the Atlantic, but not until after the prize had been claimed. They also didn't quite make it to the finish line; they failed to reach Le Bourget airfield in Paris and ended up ditching on the coast of Normandy.

Back in 1927, Stanton Wooster and Noel Davis planned a crossing in a Keystone Pathfinder named after their primary source of funding, the American Legion. Their aircraft crashed on a test flight, killing both aviators.

At this time, only one team was considering the more difficult east–west crossing from France to the United States. Charles Nungesser was a French ace pilot who had racked up 43 air combat victories during the First World War. Although he was one of the best fighter pilots the French had, he was also regularly put on house arrest for flying without permission. He met François Coli during the war.

François Coli lost an eye in a crash in 1918 but had already solidified his reputation as an excellent navigator. After the war he took part in a number of record-setting distance flights and had already planned a non-stop transatlantic prize as early as 1923. However he and his partner had an accident which destroyed their biplane. Coli still wished to attempt to win the Orteig prize and was on the lookout for another aircraft and partner. Charles Nungesser had planned to cross solo but the aircraft designer, Pierre Levasseur, insisted that he should consider taking Coli as his navigator in the new two-seater version of the Levasseur PL.4. Nungesser and Coli worked with the Levasseur chief engineer and the production manager to design the Levasseur PL.8 biplane, which they named *L'Oiseau Blanc.*

On the 8th of May in 1927, Nungesser and Coli departed Le Bourget Field at 05:17 local time, half an hour after dawn. The aircraft, heavy with fuel, barely cleared the trees at the end of the runway. Four military aircraft accompanied the flight on the first leg. Photographs and films of the time show the aircraft's attitude as normal. The landing gear was released as they flew over the Seine in order to reduce the weight of the aircraft. If they were to make an emergency landing, they would ditch the plane on water, so there was no point in carrying the wheels for the rest of the journey.

Post card of Charles Nungesser and François Coli and their biplane *L'Oiseau Blanc.*

At 06:48, the aircraft was sighted over Étretat on the coast. At this stage, they'd travelled 108 nautical miles in over an hour and a half, an estimated ground speed of 133km/h. This was considerably slower than they had estimated and it is not clear why. The wind was light and they had planned the weight of the aircraft carefully.

The sighting at Étretat was important because this was the decision point. Nungesser and Coli had agreed that they would turn back here if they felt the attempt was unlikely. They continued flying northwest at low altitude, committing to crossing the English Channel.

This is the last point where we can be sure of their decisions.

It's not clear what the weather was like over the Channel. Descriptions of the last sighting of the biplane range varied from "lost to view, far away between the water and the sky" to "arrived at the Channel in the thick fog". Whether they disappeared into the fog or into the distance, that moment is our last piece of reliable information, the last position update clearly confirmed by multiple witnesses.

The military aircraft turned back and *L'Oiseau Blunc* flew on. Now it begins to get odd.

A Frenchman out walking on the cliffs near Étretat that day, M. Joseph Meny, remembers that it was around 6 a.m. when he saw a plane overhead. He said it was low-flying and jolting about as it flew and at the time he thought, "Well, that won't go far." He thought it was almost certainly *L'Oiseau Blanc* but, at the time, he decided it would be better not to tell anyone. There was a wave of proud patriotism in France in the wake of the attempt to be the first to make the crossing and the man believed that such a negative description of the French aircraft would be dismissed. In fact, he did not report what he had seen until 1980.

Aircraft were not a common sight but his timing is wrong or, at least, misremembered. We know that the *L'Oiseau Blanc* didn't reach Étretat until 06:48. If he actually saw the aircraft around seven, then the "jolting" is worrying.

There should have been position updates as the aircraft crossed the Channel but, embarrassingly, it seems that the French Navy were watching in the wrong area. By the following day, they didn't bother with lookouts, presuming that *L'Oiseau Blanc* had already crossed. It wasn't until the 10th, two days after the aces' glorious departure from Paris, that a flurry of telegrams were sent to the ships to search for any sign of the aircraft. By now, the weather had turned bad; the Navy weren't able to carry out aerial patrols and gave up the search on the evening of the 12th of May.

One man thought he saw the wreckage of the aircraft. In 1937, ten years after the famous flight, a fisherman told his wife and his sons that he'd seen *L'Oiseau Blanc* a day or two after the famous departure. He was fishing, piloting a 14-metre cutter from Fécamp, when he briefly saw the wreckage of a white plane off of the coast of Étretat, which the waves then pulled under. He reported it immediately to the Naval Authority, who ordered him not to tell anyone else what he had seen. The man's son reported this conversation when the French aviation authority reopened the investigation.

> He said that his father, who was accompanied by three or four of his fellow boatmen, did not say

> what the weather or the sea was on the day, but that since he was fishing, the weather must have been all right. His father did not see the airplane land and did not hear the sound of the airplane's motor. He was about 150 meters away from the wreckage when it went under. He recovered no debris from the area. The wreckage was apparently empty, but if the members of the crew were prostrated unconscious in the cockpit, he probably could not have seen them. In any case he heard no call for help.

There are no records of this at the Naval District of Fécamp, which is where the fisherman would have likely made his report. Was the fisherman wrong or was his report covered up? It is impossible to tell.

However, there's no way both of these reports could be true. If the jolting aircraft crossed the coastline on the 8th and then crashed, the wreckage would not still be floating for the fisherman to see it pulled under the waves a day or two later. Neither report, made so long after the fact, is compelling evidence that Nungesser and Coli crashed before they flew out of sight of the French coastline.

Then there's a British Naval Submarine who reported seeing an aircraft on the far side of the Channel, twenty miles southwest of the Needles on the Isle of Wight. This sighting, at least, is right on course for their planned flight.

Press release from the British Admiralty:

> London, May 12. — The British Admiralty have published the telegram below received from the base commander of Portland (England): The submarine H.50 conveys an account of seeing an aircraft at 50°29′ north by 1°30′ west at 0745 British summer time on May 8, altitude 300 meters. Course about 300°. Light coloured biplane. The only markings visible were red, white and blue on the tail. The biplane looked like one with a large fuselage. The visibility was not more than two or three miles. Weather too foggy to see other marks.

Aircraft were not commonly crossing the channel and clearly it wasn't a British plane, which they would have recognised. Who else could it possibly be? But this report isn't as reliable as it looks at first glance. There's no mention of the aircraft in the submarine logs, which is very odd. It's possible that the sailors were simply watching for the French flight out of interest and felt no need to log it as an official note of observation, but now we are starting to make excuses. Also, the timing is wrong: *L'Oiseau Blanc* would have had to travel 380 km/h to cross the channel by 07:45 British summer time and we know that the aircraft was barely travelling at half that speed.

Somehow, the press release was never officially communicated to the French Navy even though it was quoted in the Times of London and various French newspapers. It didn't matter anyway. No one followed up on this because, by then, more people had claimed to have seen or heard the French aces flying overhead.

Many of these reports contradicted each other and it's very possible that every single one is wrong. But a combination of sightings could be cherry-picked for a feasible recreation of *L'Oiseau Blanc*'s journey.

One report of an aircraft flying at a height of 1,000–2,000 feet near Exeter at 08:15 fits the timeline, as does a 10:00 sighting over County Clare in Ireland at 1,000 metres, which claims that the French colours were confirmed by telescope. These sightings form a straight line from Le Bourget and heading straight across the Atlantic. If we accept these sightings as true, then the French pilots would have flown over the west coast of Ireland at 11:00 local time (10:00 GMT).

Certainly, the French Embassy in Ireland collected all the reports they could find and confirmed "without possible doubt that Nungesser crossed Ireland from Lismore to Carrigaholt, and was seen for the last time here at around 1100 hours."

One eyewitness was just eight years old at the time but when the case was reopened, he said that he clearly remembered seeing the aircraft with his father.

> I was only 8 years old when I saw the 'plane, and would have been with my father. My recollection is that the 'plane was flying fairly high over the River Shannon and went west over Knocknagaroon Hill towards the Atlantic. Knocknagaroon Hill

> is on the Atlantic coast, 5 or 6 miles south west of Kilkee. The association between that 'plane and Knocknagaroon Hill is very clear in my memory.
>
> I still have a distinct recollection of seeing the aeroplane fly out west over Knocknagaroon Hill. My father was greatly interested in this effort by Capt. Nungesser to fly across the Atlantic, from this side, and the fact that both he and I had seen the 'plane made it a topic of family conversation and interest which lasted for long after the reported loss of the two brave pilots and their aeroplane.

The combined testimony from Ireland led to hope that the aircraft made it across England and Ireland, heading over the Atlantic about six hours after it departed from Paris.

Here was another decision point for the pilots. Once they started the long and dangerous flight over the Atlantic, they would have very little chance if they had to ditch. If they were not sure that they could make it across the Atlantic, now was the time to call it off. If they decided not to continue, then they could either land locally (in Ireland or England) or cross the Channel again and return to Paris.

Although the first aviation radio was installed in 1910 along with the first in-flight radio transmission ("Roy, come and get this goddamned cat!"), that was in an airship, not a plane. In 1927, the weight of a radio system was still well beyond what a little biplane like *L'Oiseau Blanc* could carry, so there was no way for the French aces to interact with the rest of the world unless they landed, which in itself was fraught with danger and could only be done once; remember, they dropped the landing wheels to save weight when they took off.

Their engineer told *Le Journal* about the discussion he'd had with the pilots before they departed.

> The eminent engineer wished to tell us that all of his interpretations had as their base the passage of the white plane over Ireland. Nungesser and Coli were supposed to cross the area in about five hours after departure, at a minimum altitude of

1000 meters; and if, at the moment pinpointed on their progress tables for direction and altitude, they could see that everything was going according to the mathematical checkpoints established before their departure, they could embark over the Atlantic; but only under these conditions. In case of doubt, the aircraft would immediately have reversed course, in order to land on one of the numerous British rivers.

At this point, we have evidence for three possible scenarios:

1. *L'Oiseau Blanc* crashed in the Channel after passing over Étretat (the last solid sighting), flying low, slow and "jolting", and every other sighting is a mistake or a case of wishful thinking.
2. *L'Oiseau Blanc* made it across the Channel, overflying England and Ireland before turning back to return to France, crashing near the coast of France, which would mean that the wreckage seen by the fisherman was in fact the French aircraft.
3. *L'Oiseau Blanc* successfully followed its expected route and the French aces began their Atlantic crossing at around 10:00 GMT that day.

No further sightings were reported that day or that night, not even impossible ones. Would someone have noticed the aircraft returning over Ireland and England in the dark? It's quite likely that they wouldn't, bearing in mind no one was watching for it by now. Certainly no one could have seen it flying over the Atlantic in the dark.

For the moment, let's assume that the mood was bullish in the cockpit and they continued their record-breaking flight. In the original plans, Coli had originally hoped they could follow the Great Circle route from southern Ireland to Belle Isle, passing between Newfoundland and the rest of Atlantic Canada. After seeing the weather forecasts on the morning of their departure, he revised this course. His plans for the new route estimated that they would fly over Belle Isle at around 06:00 GMT.

Many believe that the aircraft and the pilots were lost during those dark hours, flying over the Atlantic. But there are a number of witnesses in Newfoundland and Maine who claim that they heard the aircraft fly overhead above the clouds. And it's true that if they continued on their course and if they did not divert north, then it is quite possible that they next overflew Harbour Grace in Newfoundland.

This is important because *La Presse* published seven reports from residents of Harbour Grace who stated that they had heard an aircraft flying overhead around 9:30 or 10:00. Four of the witnesses recall the aircraft sounds overflying the bay from the north but the other three are just as emphatic that the aircraft was flying towards the north-west. The following day, *La Presse* retracted the article and said all of the reports were erroneous. That same day, the *Evening Telegram* quoted two more reports, including this charming account from a woman who had no idea *what* she'd seen.

> Annie Kelly, a married woman residing in Harbour Grace, South Shore, swore that between 9:00 and 10:00 in the morning of Monday, May 9th, she was working near her house when she heard a buzzing sound that seemed to be overhead. The noise passed over her house, it seemed, and searching to find out what caused it, she saw over her and going south what she took at first to be two big gulls with their wings touching. They were two large white wings on a line with each other, but she knew the object could not be a bird from the strange sound it made. She did not report the matter earlier, because she did not know anything about the missing aeroplane until she saw it in the Harbour Grace Standard on Friday night, and then she thought she should report the matter.

But there was serious question as to whether these reports were trustworthy. On the 17th, over a week after it was clear that the French flight had been lost, *The Times* published an article stating that the witnesses to the overflying aircraft were incorrect and that they could not confirm that the aircraft had ever been there.

> Investigators at Harbour Grace are now inclined to believe that the persons who said they saw or heard an aeroplane there on May 9 were self-deluded.

If *L'Oiseau Blanc* did fly over Harbour Grace that morning, then the French pilots had a serious problem: fuel. Based on the times that the witnesses heard or saw an aircraft, Nungesser and Coli had been flying for over 41 hours, exceeding their initial planned flight time. They could hope for another seven hours, at best, before running out of fuel. They could not possibly make it to New York City. They obviously couldn't make it back to Europe. They needed to divert.

They had discussed this possibility during planning and had a list of possible diversions: Quebec, Nova Scotia, New Brunswick or Maine. Even if one assumes that the biplane made it this far and then diverted and landed, this is an impossibly large search area.

A sighting that might have helped to find the biplane came from a fisherman who inexplicably did not see any reason to report what he had seen until 1930.

> On the morning of May 9, 1927, in a thick fog and white calm, I was finding the fish in an area about a mile and a half south of the black cape, when I heard a noise like the motor of an airplane. . . . The noise increasing, I was quite sure it was an airplane. . . . Suddenly toward the open sea, I heard a great crash like something very heavy fell into the sea . . . then there was total silence. At the same moment, my Newfoundland dog who was sleeping on the motor's casing stood on his hind legs and started to howl; I had a lot of trouble making him be quiet. . . . I went back to the port in the afternoon. It was one or two days later that I heard about the disappearance of the aviators Nungesser and Coli.

This is again not a particularly reliable account. It's hard to explain why the fisherman, who seemed quite clear that he had heard a crash, stayed where he was and continued fishing rather than sounding alarm, and continued to say nothing during the massive searches around St Pierre, waiting until three years later to tell his tale.

The mystery now spans thousands upon thousands of kilometres, with eyewitnesses to vouch for each of the following:

1. *L'Oiseau Blanc* crashed in the Channel after passing over Étretat.
2. *L'Oiseau Blanc* made it across the Channel, overflying England and Ireland before turning back to return to France, crashing near the coast of France.
3. *L'Oiseau Blanc* continued across the Atlantic but was lost at sea somewhere between Ireland and Newfoundland.
4. *L'Oiseau Blanc* reached Newfoundland, overflying Harbour Grace, with a range of around seven hours flight time left to them, and then crashed.

Knowing that clearly not all of the sightings (especially of the wreckage) can possibly be true, and with evidence that many of the witnesses were flat out wrong, it becomes impossible to know who to believe.

There's just one more reported sighting; this one was in the north-east of Maine.

> The crash of this plane was heard by a woodsman, Anson Berry, deceased in 1936. While he was fishing that afternoon on Round Lake, he heard a plane engine that, after some misfiring, ceased to function. The noise of a forced landing followed. The witness did not see the plane because of the fog and low clouds. He did not attempt to go to the area of the crash.

Now, based on the timing, this could have been the same aircraft which overflew Harbour Grace. This sighting has even led to a theory that Maine bootleggers shot down the biplane, fearing police surveillance.

But even if that were likely, which it isn't, then it means that *L'Oiseau Blanc* was still flying towards New York City, despite the fact that both of the pilots must have known that they could not possibly make it there. This makes no sense: Nungesser and Coli were highly competent pilots and by that time had already exceeded their planned flight of 40 hours. No magic wand could possibly have got them to New York to win the prize. They could not magic up fuel. It seems fantastical that they would simply carry on, knowing for a fact that they did not have enough fuel to make it to their destination.

The search for the remains of *L'Oiseau Blanc* has never stopped; although obviously the aircraft would have disintegrated by now, there is one part which is likely to have survived over the years: the 400-kilogramme metal engine.

So far, no sign of L'Oiseau Blanc has been discovered. In 1982, TIGHAR's *Project Midnight Ghost* began searching the area around Round Lake, based on the woodsman's sighting, hoping to find the engine. After ten years, they concluded that further searching was pointless and that L'Oiseau Blanc had not made it to Maine. In 1992, they refocused their efforts to explore the options in Newfoundland. However, there are hundreds of lakes where the biplane might have attempted to ditch and after twenty-five years of searching, Project Midnight Ghost is struggling for further funding to continue the search.

Since 2009, French businessman Bernard Decré has been searching the area around the French islands of Saint-Pierre et Miquelon for the remains of the biplane. In 2013, he took a team to scour the south-east coast of the Ille de St Pierre using sonar and a magnetometer to try to locate the engine. Decré believes that US authorities covered up the disappearance and the crash in order to pave the way for an American victory.

It was just ten days later, on the 20th of May, when Charles Lindbergh departed Roosevelt Field in New York to make the first cross-Atlantic flight from New York City to Paris. He arrived thirty-three hours later, winning the Orteig prize as well as making the first ever solo transatlantic flight.

Over 150,000 people were at Le Bourget to watch him land and he became a great sensation on both sides of the Atlantic. Elinor Smith Sullivan, who was a pilot at the time, described how this success immediately changed American aviation.

> People seemed to think we [aviators] were from outer space or something. But after Charles Lindbergh's flight, we could do no wrong. It's hard to describe the impact Lindbergh had on people. Even the first walk on the moon doesn't come close. The twenties was such an innocent time, and people were still so religious—I think they felt like this man was sent by God to do this. And it changed aviation forever because all of a sudden the Wall Streeters were banging on doors looking for airplanes to invest in. We'd been standing on our heads trying to get them to notice us but after Lindbergh, suddenly everyone wanted to fly, and there weren't enough planes to carry them.

And so ends the "Everest of aviation mysteries" as it has become known. Although it is tempting to believe that someone might one day find the engine, it's just not possible to narrow the search area for any one of the three possible locations (the English Channel, the Atlantic past the Irish shore or in the wilderness of the eastern coast of North America). The reported sightings cannot possibly all be true and so we are left with a ninety-year-old mystery of the French flying aces who "vanished like midnight ghosts".

Knowing where to look, in any case, does not always mean success, as we shall see in 1928 when the airship *Italia* disappeared with six crew still on board.

1928

THE GOLDEN AND DEADLY AGE OF ARCTIC EXPLORATION

TO UNDERSTAND the loss of *Italia*, we need to understand the context of aviation exploration in the late 1920s and, specifically, the flight of the *Norge*.

The turn of the century was an exciting time for aviation and exploration as people learned to take advantage of the ability to cross large distances relatively safely using aircraft and airships.

Dirigible airships were the first aircraft capable of powered flight. The name "dirigible" comes from the French "diriger" (to direct, guide or steer) and differentiated the new airships from the traditional hot air balloons, which were at the mercy of the wind and weather. At the time, however, dirigibles were referred to by many different names, ranging from flying-ships to air yachts.

The idea of combining the lighter-than-air technology with an outside source of power and the ability to steer had its first success in 1852 when the French engineer Henri Giffard developed a hydrogen-filled balloon powered by a 3-horsepower steam engine attached to a propeller. On his trial flight of the *ballon dirigeable*, he successfully travelled from Paris to Élancourt, a distance of 27 kilometres.

Initially dirigibles were very fragile; they did not see much use for travel until the invention of the internal combustion engine. By the start of the 20th century, the Germans, the French, the Spanish and the Italians were all focused on developing airships and in the early 1900s, all three believed that airships would change the face of military strategy. The Italians were the first to use dirigibles as bombers and, by the start of World War

I, the Germans, French and Italians all employed airships for scouting and bombing. However, all of them suffered the expensive loss of their airships as they came to the sad realisation that airships were still too fragile and too unreliable for military operations. By 1917, all three countries had reduced or ceased sending them to the front lines.

However, the airships had advantages beyond their military prowess. At around the same time, a number of explorers made attempts to reach the North Pole and it was with dirigibles that the most progress was being made.

Melvin Vaniman made the first to attempt to reach the North Pole by dirigible. He had previously considered an aerial attempt in 1894 but balloon technology did not offer the steering and propulsion he needed, so he dismissed the idea, leading two ground-based expeditions and making it as far as the 82nd parallel. Finally in 1905, he discovered that recent innovations in France might offer the solution he was looking for. A dirigible was constructed in Paris and shipped to Spitsbergen, Svalbard, which borders the Arctic Ocean, where a custom hangar had been built.

However, when they came to erect the dirigible, the engines self-destructed and the ship was sent back to Paris for repairs. They tried again in 1907; this time bad weather forced them to turn back after travelling only a few kilometres. The dirigible took damage in the storm and was again sent back to France.

Wellman and his crew made one more attempt in 1909 but returned after another mechanical failure. By the time they were in a position to try again, Wellman discovered that they'd already lost the race to the North Pole. However, there were two claims to be the first.

Dr Frederic Cook, along with two Inuit men, declared in the spring of 1909 that they had reached the North Pole the previous year but were unable to report it, as they were cut off and stranded for 14 months from 1907 to 1908.

At the same time, Robert Peary returned from his Arctic exploration, excited that he had reached the North Pole and believing that he was the first to do so. Imagine his disgust when he discovered that Cook was claiming to have reached the Pole the year previous. He stated outright that he believed Cook's claim to be a hoax and launched a campaign to discredit his competitor. Cook was expelled from the Explorers Club when

Copenhagen University rejected his proof of having reached the North Pole. In 1910, the New York Times called him "one of the boldest fakers the world has ever known."

To this day, it is still not clear if either man (or for that matter Richard Byrd, who claimed the prize next) had reached the North Pole.

The first *undisputed* explorers to have reached the North Pole (although without setting foot on the ground) were Roald Amundsen and his 15 crew in the airship *Norge,* in 1926.

Roald Amundsen had previously cancelled his expedition to the Arctic in 1909 when he heard that Frederick Cook and Robert Peary both separately claimed to have reached the North Pole. He went instead to Antarctica, where he and his crew were the first to reach the South Pole, beating the British expedition led by Robert Falcon Scott by five weeks.

There was still plenty to discover in the Arctic, even if the race to the Pole was over, and Amundsen started exploring unknown areas of the Arctic Ocean. He discovered the north-east Passage (now called the Northern Route) by ship in 1918–1920.

Struggling for funds to continue his exploration, he had a change of fortune when he was contacted by American explorer Lincoln Ellsworth, a man who described himself as having "an independent income and a strong thirst for adventure". They agreed to attempt to overfly the Arctic Ocean, flying from Europe to North America. In 1925 they made their first attempt with six men travelling in two Dornier seaplanes. They reached the northernmost latitude ever attempted by aircraft at the time but, unfortunately, they damaged their aircraft when they were forced to land on the ice.

After this experience, Amundsen came to the conclusion that the best opportunity for crossing the expanse was to use a "lighter-than-air" aircraft instead of a seaplane or flying boat. Amundsen sent a telegram to Umberto Nobile, who had designed *N-1,* the Italian army's dirigible, to discuss the possibilities of using the airship for the first crossing of the Arctic Ocean.

Umberto Nobile was an Italian aviator, aeronautical engineer and a colonel in the Italian military. He had been considering a polar expedition himself and rushed to Norway to discuss the possibilities with Amundsen and Ellsworth.

He told them that he would pilot the ship and bring his own crew and most importantly, that the Italian Premiere Mussolini had agreed to donate the N-1 for the trip across the Arctic ice cap if they would agree to fly the Italian flag.

Amundsen refused the offer, retorting that the trip was strictly a Norwegian/American expedition and would not be rebranded as an Italian affair.

Nobile countered that, if they would not fly the Italian flag, then they would have to purchase the *N-1* outright. He would still pilot it, but only if an experienced Italian crew was used.

Purchasing the *N-1* was fine by Amundsen: Ellsworth had put up $85,000 to underwrite the trip and the Aero Club of Norway had already agreed to cover the rest of the cost. He was also happy to take Nobile as pilot along with five Italian mechanics, as long as his own men would have control of the rudder, the elevators and the navigation.

Nobile agreed but only, he said, if he had the authority to turn the airship around in case of trouble.

Amundsen refused, wanting to maintain control of the expedition. He appeased Nobile with a promise that he would consult Nobile on all major decisions. They had finally reached an agreement. Nobile began modifying the *N-1* for the expedition, which was renamed *Norge* ("Norway" in Norwegian).

The Airship *Norge* at Ny-Ålesund, Norway.

Norge consisted of a semi-rigid gas bag with a rigid frame at the bottom which ran from nose to tail of the airship, allowing the crew to move along the length of the craft. Three gondolas were suspended at the rear and side, each holding an engine and a rear-facing propeller. At the front was a fourth larger gondola, the control cabin, which held the steering wheel, the rudders, and the levers to control the gas valves.

They arrived at King's Bay, Spitsbergen, late, their trip from Rome beset with delays caused by weather and maintenance issues.

At King's Bay, they found Richard Evelyn Byrd with a Fokker tri-motor called *Josephine Ford* ready to depart for his flight to the North Pole. The controversy as to whether Cook and Peary had reached the North Pole had come to a head and Byrd was capitalising on this uncertainty, making his own claim to be first to the Pole. He planned to circle the North Pole in his Fokker and then return to King's Bay. Amundsen wished Byrd the best of luck, stating clearly that the North Pole was not their objective.

He may not have seen Byrd as a competitor but Nobile clearly did. He thought they should leave early for their crossing so that they could beat Byrd to the Pole. Amundsen refused, not willing to rush the trip. He believed that Robert Peary had already reached the North Pole in 1909 and so there was no point anyway. The primary purpose of their expedition, he reminded Nobile, was to observe the uncharted Arctic Ocean.

On the 9th of May, Richard Byrd returned from his flight, claiming that he had successfully circled the North Pole. He received a hero's welcome upon his return to the US, with many believing that he was the first to reach the Pole. However, once again, controversy abounded, with some suspicion that he had turned back early. His Fokker, said detractors, could not have flown the distance that Byrd claimed in the time that he was away. This controversy continues to this day: Byrd's notebooks from the trip were published in 1998, with various navigational calculations erased, along with the words *"How long were we gone before we turned around"* which could imply that he had not in fact reached the Pole.

But this was all still to come. At the time, Amundsen and Ellsworth simply restated that the purpose of the trip was the continent-to-continent flight across the Arctic Ocean. Nobile, it seemed, was more interested in getting to the North Pole and making a name for himself. The tension between Amundsen and Nobile grew.

The *Norge* departed King's Bay with Amundsen, Ellsworth, Nobile and eleven further crew, and on the 12th of May, Ellsworth's 46th birthday, they crossed the North Pole. Amundsen threw a Norwegian flag mounted on a weighted spear out of the window. Ellsworth released the Stars and Stripes to fall down alongside Amundsen's. The flags were small, "not much larger than a pocket handkerchief" as everyone was concerned with keeping the weight down. So both were quite shocked when Nobile appeared with an armful of mounted flags to drop.

From Amundsen's memoirs:

> For a few moments, the Norge looked like a circus wagon of the skies, with great banners of every shape and hue fluttering down around her. Nobile produced one really huge Italian flag. It was so large, he had difficulty in getting it out the cabin window. There the wind struck it and it stuck to the side of the gondola. Before he could disengage it we must have been five miles beyond the Pole. When it finally flew free, it hurtled back to the rear gondola and there for an instant it seemed that it would become entangled with the propeller and give us serious trouble. At length it fluttered free and sank swiftly to the surface of the ice below us.
>
> Fortunately, I have a sense of humour, which I count one of my chief qualifications as an explorer.... Scornful as I was at Nobile's overreaching in this matter, irritated as I was by his selfishness and presumption, I could still be amused at his childish pleasure in feeling that he had "put something over" and had gained a greater honour for his country by the size and number of its flags deposited in the unseeing vastness of the Arctic. That a grown man and a military officer could have so little imagination as to measure the value of such a moment by the physical size of its symbols rather than the depth of the sentiment behind it struck me as so grotesque that I laughed aloud.

> . . . Nobile still boasts that he dropped overboard at the Pole the banner of the Aero Club of Italy. He will not know until he reads these lines that one of the Norwegian boys discovered this banner among the baggage unloaded in Alaska after we had made our descent at Teller!

The *Norge* continued on its way and successfully flew to Alaska where the expedition was recognised as the first crossing of the Arctic Ocean. Interestingly, the dropping of the flags means that Roald Amundsen and his crew also hold the position of the first *undisputed* explorers who can be verified as having reached the North Pole.

The relationship between Nobile and Amundsen disintegrated completely upon their return to civilisation, with Amundsen accusing Nobile of attempting to steal credit for the trip, publicly describing Nobile as fatuous, overreaching, selfish, presumptuous, boasting, impudent, insolent and vain.

Meanwhile, Nobile accused Amundsen of cutting him out and dismissing his importance to the expedition which, Nobile claimed, was *only* a success because of his airship and his leadership. Amundsen accused Nobile of not understanding the difference between the skipper and the commander and that he, and the other Italians, did not have the skills or expertise required for Arctic exploration.

It's hardly surprising under the weight of these accusations that Nobile began planning another expedition to explore the Arctic Ocean, this time as the commander.

Backed by Mussolini, he designed another airship based on the *Norge*, adding enhancements based on his trip with Amundsen two years previously. It was powered by three Maybach engines allowing it to reach a top speed of 120 km/h, quite an improvement over *Norge's* top speed of 70 km/h. Polar exploration was also driving the use of short-wave transmitters and receivers, which had undergone rapid technical advances during World War I. Radio operators used Morse code for communications. The new airship included a Marconi RA8 transmitter and RA6 receiver, radios developed for military transport.

Nobile was never one for subtleties: the new airship was called *Italia*.

Airship *Italia* overflies Stockholm.

The expedition was to be the first scientific aerial exploration of the Arctic, whereas the Norge did only limited research, focusing on aeronautics.

The crew consisted of fourteen Italians, one Czech, one Swede and one dog, Nobile's pet fox terrier Titina. They departed Rome with 1,500 kilos of equipment, 2,000 kilos of ballast, 350 kilos of oil and 4,300 kilos of fuel. The Navy accompanied them with a base ship, the *Cittá di Milano*, which would travel with them as far as King's Bay, the expedition base, providing support and a radio watch during their trip.

The trip to King's Bay was slow. It took them 30 hours to cross the 1,900 km of the Baltic Sea in difficult weather with severe hailstorms and lightning. They had to stop for ten days for repairs and were later forced off course to avoid more bad weather. When they landed in Finland for refuelling, a blizzard struck and *Italia* suffered structural damage. They departed Finland for the final leg of their flight on the 5th of May. When they arrived at King's Bay the following day, Nobile radioed the *Cittá di Milano* to inform them that the *Italia* was approaching and asking for 50 men for the ground crew to assist the landing. The captain of the *Cittá di Milano* responded that he would not be providing assistance unless he received orders from Rome and that his crew were not required to perform chores on land.

The Norwegian authorities were able to collect 150 miners to help haul the ship down and drag it to the shed. It took two hours to safely get the ship down and anchored to the mast.

Nobile had also requested access to two seaplanes for rescue work in case it should be necessary, but they were not there: the Italian Minister of Air had vetoed the request. It was becoming clear that Nobile did not have the military support that he thought he had.

The *Italia* was repaired at King's Bay and the expedition was ready to begin. They planned five flights, each starting and ending at King's Bay, to explore five different areas of the Arctic Ocean. The first expedition did not go well; the *Italia* had to turn back early because of extreme weather conditions. The second expedition, however, was a great success, lasting sixty hours as they travelled over 4,000 kilometres (2,500 miles).

The third trip was planned to cross over the North Pole, a moment that Nobile had long waited to recreate.

They departed King's Bay on the 23rd of May, taking advantage of the tailwinds that sped their progress along the Greenland coast. They carried a winch to lower scientists to the Pole along with survival packs and an inflatable raft. The weather was poor but the wind was with them as they journeyed towards the pole for the next nineteen hours. They arrived just past midnight, the polar sun shining on the thick bank of fog below.

They used the sextant to confirm their position and then descended to get a view of the ice. The winds were too strong for them to dare to land, or even to drop the scientists onto the ice pack. Nobile once again dropped the Italian flag from the airship's window, this time hopefully landing a bit closer to the Pole. Then he dropped the city flag of Milan and a small medal depicting the Virgin of the Fire from the Italian city of Forli. Finally, he dropped a large oak cross, received directly from the Pope Pius XI. Inside the cross was parchment declaring that the cross was "to be dropped by the leader of the expedition, flying for the second time over the Pole; thus to consecrate the summit of the world."

Noble then sent a radio message to say, "The flag of Italy again flies above the ice at the Pole." He had achieved his dream: the glory of crossing the North Pole to belong to Italy alone.

They had two possible routes: they could return back to King's Bay or cross the pole and use the prevailing winds to fly to MacKenzie Bay on the Canadian coast. The Swedish meteorologist recommended turning back to base and the others agreed, possibly concerned about the risk of landing in the Canadian wilderness.

They had spent twenty-two hours in the air when they turned back towards King's Bay. But the strong winds that had hurried them along their way to the Pole were now against them, slowing their progress. Their fuel consumption doubled. As they flew south the wind and the mist increased and the airship's frame and fabric began to show signs of strain. After another twenty-four hours, they were still only halfway to King's Bay.

Nobile became concerned that the expedition was in danger. He'd been awake for over 48 hours when he sent the message through the wireless operator to say "If I don't answer, I have good reason." The meteorologist believed that they needed to press through the storm as quickly as possible, sure that there were calmer winds ahead. They did not dare land in the storm anyway. Ice formed on the propellers and the crew began to struggle to maintain control of the ship. By the morning of the 25th of May, the fuel situation was serious. "Wind and fog. Fog and wind. Incessantly," wrote Nobile in his journal. They had travelled 36 hours since leaving the pole.

They had released some of the gas when something failed: perhaps the valve was stuck or maybe the fragile fabric of the skin had developed a hole. Or perhaps the ice accumulating on the propellers and the frame had become too much for the airship to carry.

The airship plunged towards the ground.

"We are heavy," shouted a crewman as Nobile ordered the engines brought to full power. As the *Italia* continued to descend towards the ice pack, he changed his mind and ordered the crew to halt all engines, hoping to slow the ship.

Nobile's last recollection was a loud crash as they impacted the ice and something smashing into his skull. He heard his bones breaking. He simply thought, "It's all over," as he drifted into unconsciousness.

He woke up lying on the ice, the wreckage of the control cabin all around him. He could hear the groaning of his men. As he opened his eyes, he saw the *Italia* above him. Having relieved itself of the cabin and most of the crew, it was rising back into the sky. There were still seven men on board.

The Chief Engineer was one of those men. He immediately began to throw everything he could think of to the men on the ice, including the supplies that they'd brought for landing at the pole. Helpless to do anything more, he and the rest of the crew stared at the battered men below as they climbed away.

Ten crew and the fox terrier found themselves stranded on the ice. One crew member was killed in the crash. The rest all suffered various injuries. But they had food, the supplies that the chief engineer had thrown down to them. And more importantly, the radio operator had grabbed the portable emergency radio as they fell, protecting it from impact with his body. And they had a tent, which they coloured bright red using the dye from the emergency flares.

Nevertheless, they were in a sorry state. Nobile had a broken leg, a broken arm, a cracked rib and a head wound. The meteorologist injured his shoulders and suffered from internal injuries that they could not treat. The chief technician broke both of his legs and the navigator suffered severe chest pains from broken ribs. None of them had survival gear for the arctic. They had enough food for 45 days.

The Swedish meteorologist blamed himself for misreading the weather and became suicidal. Nobile stopped him from searching for a break in the ice to drown himself. A few days later, the man shot and killed a polar bear which had approached the camp, greatly increasing their food stores.

Meanwhile, the radio operator focused on getting word to the outside world. He found the batteries had survived the crash intact and would last for about sixty hours. He fashioned an antenna from an aluminium tube recovered from the debris and suspended wires across the ice to act as a ground connection. Every fifty-five minutes, he transmitted an SOS call in Morse code, hoping to reach the base ship still at King's Bay, the *Cítta di Milano.*

However, no one on the base ship was keeping a radio watch, even though the *Italia* by now must have been past due. The distress signals went unheard for over a week.

On the 31st of May, two members of the team who were less injured decided to leave the camp, as there had not been any response to the distress message. They wished to take with them the radio operator and any others who could travel. Nobile put his foot down, knowing that the radio was their only real chance of rescue. The two took with them the depressed meteorologist and headed off to search for the coast.

On the 3rd of June, an amateur radio operator in Arkhangelsk, Russia picked up their SOS transmission. He alerted the Soviet authorities who passed the information to the Italian government. The *Cítta di Milano* finally got the news that the Italia crew were in distress. Two days after the radio operator heard the SOS signals, the *Cittá di Milano* successfully contacted Nobile and the other survivors on the ice floe. But still they did nothing to start the search, instead sending a telegram to Italy to ask instructions as to what to do next.

In the end, the Norwegian government sent the first plane to search for the campsite on the ice floe, on the 5th of June. The search was underway.

Rescue expeditions were sent from all over the world in the first massive air-sea rescue operation consisting of twenty ships and fourteen aeroplanes. However, *Cittá di Milano* had no plan in mind and was not up to the task of coordinating the efforts. Their preparations were limited to having some soldiers with mountaineering experience on hand. There were no seaplanes in Spitsbergen at the time.

On the 20th of June, almost a month after the crash, an Italian seaplane scouring the area finally spotted the red tent on the ice floe. The weather was too rough to risk a landing but the flight crew were able to drop supplies to the team to keep them going for a while longer. It had been almost a month since the crash and they only had about two weeks of rationed food left to them.

Three days later, a Swedish Air Force Fokker ski plane was able to land near the red tent. Nobile had drawn up a rescue plan based on the severity of injuries, with himself listed at number four. However, the pilot insisted on taking Nobile first, as the leader of the expedition, and said he could not carry any of the other crew except for Titina, the dog. Nobile agreed to accompany him to King's Bay and that the pilot would immediately return to pick up the others. The Fokker delivered Nobile and the dog to the *Cittá di Milano* and flew back to the floe, only to crash on his attempt to land on the ice. The pilot was now stranded there with the other survivors.

Nobile, now safely back at the base ship, was furious at the lack of coordination and rescue plans. He attempted to take over the search effort. In response, the captain put him under virtual arrest. Worse, Italian newspapers reported that Nobile had abandoned his crew, demanding to be the first rescued from the crash site. Nobile's credibility was in tatters and this time, certainly, through no fault of his own.

The Soviet ice-breaker *Krassin* was working its way through the ice floes to the red tent camp. They discovered the half-starved men who had left the camp at the start of the ordeal. They had been travelling for forty days in hopes of a rescue but although they had seen seaplanes flying overhead, they were unable to gain their attention. In forty days, they had only travelled 15 nautical miles from the red tent. The two survivors were near death and the third man, the depressed meteorologist from Sweden, was missing. He had, they said, collapsed of exhaustion and guilt and had insisted that they go on without him. One of the two men was wearing the meteorologists clothes and there were rumours, after the rescue, that they might have killed and eaten the man in order to stay alive. Although there's no actual evidence of this (the two men were near starvation when they were found), the men were heavily criticised for abandoning the meteorologist and leaving him to die.

Later that day, the *Krassin* saw a pillar of black smoke in the distance: the campsite on the ice floe. The remaining crew and the pilot of the first rescue attempt were finally rescued. The Soviets recovered everything they could from the site, including the Fokker.

Another aircraft had crashed in the area during the search, leaving two survivors stranded on a nearby island. The Soviet sailors rescued them and brought everyone to safety. After maintenance and repairs, the ice breaker focused their search on the remaining six *Italia* crew who had disappeared with the airship: the chief engineer who had thrown down the supplies as the *Italia* began to climb again, the starboard and port engine mechanics, the foreman rigger, and a physicist and a journalist.

The *Italia* had last been seen drifting towards the north-east of Svalbard and then out of sight. The Red Tent survivors reported that they had seen a column of smoke in that general direction, which must have come from the six, but had no other information. The Soviets sent two more ice breakers to scour the south and east coasts of Svalbard while *Krassin* searched the west and north of the island. Meanwhile, the *Cittá di Milano* departed King's Bay, leaving the *Krassin* as the primary unit continuing the search.

One hundred and three days after the airship had disappeared, they gave up the search. No trace of the *Italia* had been seen and no further hope existed for the survival of the six who had remained on board. Almost a hundred years have passed and our understanding of the Arctic Circle is greatly increased. We now have regular flights over the arctic sea and satellite photographs and the area is littered with research centres. Still, in all that time, not a single trace of the dirigible *Italia* has been spotted—a huge craft of 115 metres (375 feet). The fabric and wood would, of course, have rotted over time but not the metal parts and certainly not the three Maybach engines. But no one has ever seen any part of the *Italia* again.

However, that's not the oddest mystery of this ill-fated expedition. The disappearance still talked about to this day is that of Roald Amundsen.

Roald Amundsen was fifty-five and retired from exploration when the *Italia* disappeared. He had released his memoirs just the year before, which made it public that he was still bitter about his expedition with Nobile. He was apparently at a public event when news of the *Italia's* distress call broke. He's said to have stood immediately, announcing that he was ready to leave at once to help.

The Norwegian government contacted the Italians to propose that Amundsen and their most experienced polar pilot (who had been the navigator on the *Norge*) travel immediately to Svalbard on two Donier flying boats. Mussolini felt that Italy's reputation would suffer if Nobile was rescued by his enemy. He rejected the proposal, insistent that the rescue mission *must* be led by Italians.

Amundsen had no faith in the Italians and he knew there was no one else with his polar experience who could do better. The Norwegian government was supportive but did not have any seaplanes which he could use for the rescue attempt. Amundsen planned a private expedition, bypassing the Italian government, even attempting to privately purchase a Dornier seaplane for the trip, but was unable to seal the deal. Eventually, he used his contacts to ask the French government for support. The French navy offered the French Latham 74 seaplane and crew for the rescue. The Latham 47 was a twin-engine flying boat designed for the French Navy for long-range, transatlantic flights. The Navy modified the Latham 47.02, the second prototype of the aircraft, for arctic conditions.

Amundsen's polar pilot had already gone to Spitsbergen to fly with the Norwegian Navy Air Force but Amundsen happily accepted the French offer along with their pilot, René Guilboud, who had planned to use the Latham for an Atlantic crossing.

On the 18th of June, Amundsen departed Tromsø for King's Bay. It's interesting to note that this was two weeks after radio contact had been made with the survivors at the red tent. Although Amundsen is frequently described as having flown to rescue Nobile, it seems much more likely that he was hoping to find the still-missing *Italia* and the six crew that had disappeared with it, as well as the three men who had left the camp, whom no one had yet heard from. Certainly, he knew the meteorologist, who had served on the *Norge*.

Amundsen and Major Guilboud planned a route to Nordaustlandet (literally, North East Land), north east of King's Bay and in the direction that the *Italia* was last seen drifting towards. There were five on board: Amundsen, Guilboud, a Norwegian pilot and three French crew.

The pilots initially sent position reports as they flew over the Barents Sea. Then at 18:45, less than three hours after their departure, they transmitted a cut-off message: "Do not leave listening . . ."

And then there was silence.

The Latham 47 never arrived at King's Bay but this did not immediately cause alarm. Amundsen could have flown directly to the red tent, as their location was already known—it was the day before the Swedish Air Force pilot dropped the supplies. Or perhaps they had diverted to start searching for the others. As more time went without word, the truth was undeniable: Amundsen and his companions on the Latham 47 were now also missing.

The Norwegian government's ship cancelled all other tasks in favour of a search and rescue mission for Amundsen. The ship sailed 10,000 nautical miles, scouring the Barents Sea. Based on the last radio position, they must have been just south of Bear Island, and yet the searchers could not find any evidence of the aircraft or its crew.

Nobile had been saved but Norway had lost its great explorer.

Three traces of the Latham 47 have been spotted since then. During the original search operation, a torn off pontoon or wing float was washed up near the coast of Tromsø. It was positively identified as coming from a Latham 47 and Amundsen's prototype was the only one which had ever flown near the area.

Then a few months later, the aircraft's fuel tank was discovered floating in the Barents Sea.

Recovered fuel tank from the Latham 47 flight that was lost in 1928 along with Roald Amundsen.

The fuel tank had been damaged, presumably in a crash, but more importantly, the damage had been crudely repaired to keep the tip from taking in water. The tank showed marks from a knife and a large hammer. Someone at least had survived the crash and had tried to repair the fuel tank, possibly closing the tip to keep the flying boat from capsizing. But who had done this and where were they?

Nothing more was found until five years later, in 1933, when a commercial fishing boat fished something large and man-made out of the Barents Sea, near the Svalbard archipelago. Some reports say they saw an engine, others just describe it as a large piece from the aircraft's wing. Whatever it was, the object slipped away into the depths of the water. The Norwegian Aviation Museum attempted to find the object or any other wreckage in the area in 1934 but were unable to conduct a thorough search of the area as a result of bad weather.

In 1964, a double sheet of plywood was found near Svalbard which was thought to possibly be a part of the aircraft but it was never verified.

With all these tempting clues, the key question for those still hoping to solve the mystery is whether modern technology could discover the Latham 47 where older searches had failed. The search area is not that large (tiny compared to many modern searches) and although most of the aircraft would have disintegrated, the twin all-metal engines would surely be intact.

Many smaller scale attempts have failed but in 2009, the Norwegian Navy initiated a serious search as a final attempt to find one of the engines.

They brought a HUGIN 1000, an autonomous underwater vehicle which creates high-resolution acoustic imagery of the seabed, which would highlight the engines or possibly other wreckage which have sunk to the depths. The search area was about 35 square nautical miles (120 square kilometres) at a depth of 1,300 feet (400 meters). For comparison, the sonar search for Malaysia Airlines flight 370 (covered in volume two) was over 20,000 square nautical miles (710,000 square kilometres) with depths reaching 15,000 feet (4,500 metres). The Navy also brought a naval minesweeper and a coast guard vessel equipped with sonar along with two additional underwater robots. All of Norway hoped to finally discover the truth of what had happened to the national hero eighty-one years before. However despite extensive searching, they were not able to recover anything that could have come from the seaplane.

And so we are left with two mysteries wrapped into one: the disappearance of the airship *Italia* followed by the loss of the man who could be credited with enabling the flight in the first place: Roald Amundsen, along with his brave companions and the prototype of the Latham 47.

This may have been the first case of an enduring mystery of a celebrity disappearing but it certainly wasn't the last. In 1937, the most famous female aviator of the time (and possibly still) disappeared and the drive to discover what happened to her is still going on to this day.

1937

Unable to Reach You by Radio

AMELIA EARHART began planning her round-the-world flight in 1936. She would not be the first to circumnavigate the globe—six male pilots had done so before her; however, if she was successful, her equatorial flight route would be in the record books as the longest: 29,000 miles (47,000 km)

She never made it. Her achievement, instead, was to become the world's most-famous missing person after she disappeared over the Pacific Ocean in 1937, with no trace of her aircraft found.

Earhart had already become a public darling after she became the first woman to cross the Atlantic in a plane in 1928—albeit as a passenger, not as pilot. By 1936 she was so well known, she was frequently recognised on the street as a celebrity. She was represented aggressively by an agent who specialised in celebrity true-life adventure stories and who set up a $10,000 deal for Earhart's story, along with lucrative lecture tours and product endorsements. Living in the public eye, she had her critics, and even one of her supporters described her as "caught up in the hero racket".

She'd promoted the round-the-world flight as a serious flight, as opposed to simply a chance to get into record books. The aircraft included a "flying laboratory" for scientific experiments, although it was unclear what, if anything, she was researching. Despite her protestations, it was clear that the primary function of the flight was publicity, specifically to promote her next book.

The aircraft was a modified Lockheed Electra 10E, which Earhart purchased with funds donated by Purdue University.

The twin-engine monoplane, launched after the US government banned single-engine aircraft from providing passenger services in 1934, had an all metal fuselage and was powered by two Pratt & Whitney R-1340 Wasp S3H1 engines with 600 horse-power each. There were only 15 of the 10-E model produced. Popular Mechanics in 1935 highlighted the "bicycle-type mudguards" placed over the wheels; the Electra was the first aircraft with retractable landing gear to include such protection. The modifications included changes to the fuselage to allow for a much larger fuel tank.

Amelia Earhart with Lockheed 10E, Miles Blaine Collection.

Earhart's team included two navigators: Captain Harry Manning, a well-qualified nautical navigator and radio operator (which at the time meant using Morse code) and Fred Noonan, who navigated the first round-the-world *China Clipper* flight from San Francisco.

Fred Noonan had a 22-year distinguished career at sea, culminating with the marine licence, "Class Master, any ocean." He then moved into aviation and was a navigation instructor for Pan Am, as well as the navigator on the first Pan Am clipper. After the first round-the world *China Clipper* flight, he became responsible for mapping the clipper routes across the Pacific Ocean.

He resigned from Pan Am, saying that he'd risen through the ranks as far as he could and that, instead, he was interested in starting a navigation school. He expected that the publicity generated from Earhart's project would help him to launch his navigation school when he returned.

On the 17th of March 1937, there were over 5,000 excited fans at the airfield at Oakland, California, where they departed for the first leg of the flight. Four were on board: Amelia Earhart, Captain Harry Manning, Fred Noonan and Paul Mantz, Earhart's technical advisor. They would be flying for three days and travelling 2,392 miles (3,850 km) to their first stop at Honolulu, Hawaii. From there, they would continue to Howland Island, in the Central Pacific.

They completed the first leg without incident. At Honolulu, they stopped for three days while the Electra was serviced: they had experienced some issues with the propeller's variable pitch mechanisms.

Finally, they were good to go. They never managed that second leg to Howland, however. They never even got off the ground.

On the take-off run, Earhart cut the left engine when the aircraft yawed slightly to the right. Unfortunately, the Electra responded by swinging left into a rapid turn on the runway (known as a ground loop). The landing gear collapsed.

From the official accident report:

> On reaching the end at the at [*sic*] Miss Earhart turned and after a brief delay opened both throttles. As the airplane gathered speed it swung slightly to the right. Miss Earhart corrected this tendency by throttling the left hand motor. The airplane then began to swing to the left with increasing speed, characteristic of a ground-loop. It tilted outward, right wing low and for 50 or 60 feet was supported on the right wheel only. The right-hand landing-gear suddenly collapsed under this excessive load followed by the left. The airplane spun sharply to the left sliding on its belly

> amid a shower of sparks from the mat and came to rest headed about 200 degrees from its initial course. The fire truck had followed along the side of the mat during the take-off and reached the scene within a few seconds as did the observers nearest the crash. There was no fire. Miss Earhart and her crew emerged unhurt. The visible damage to the airplane was as follows:- Right wing and engine nacelle severely damaged, left engine nacelle damaged on under side, right hand rudder and end of stabilizer bent. Minor damage to the underside of the fuselage. Both propellers bent. The engines were undamaged. The oil tanks ruptured. The damaged airplane was roped off under guard as promptly as possible by the Officer-of-the-Day.

The second leg was cancelled and the aircraft loaded on a ship for the journey back to Los Angeles for repairs. One interesting side effect of this unfortunate accident is that the Electra's trailing antenna was crushed in the accident and later removed. The antenna was meant for communication on 500 kHz, a low frequency with a long wavelength which was used as the international distress frequency.

Earhart also lost her access to Captain Harry Manning, who was the only one of them skilled as a radio operator. He bowed out and returned to Washington, although it is unclear whether this was because of the changes in timing or at Earhart's request or simply because he'd lost faith in Earhart's flying skills after the ground loop at Honolulu.

Earhart was able to raise additional funding and she set off again with Noonan as her navigator. This time she decided to fly east, instead of west, and on the 1st of June, she started the flight with considerably more success. A month later, they had travelled over 22,000 miles (35,000 km) to reach Lae, New Guinea.

Her next stop was once again the island of Howland. From Lae to Howland was a flight of 2,500 miles, which would require almost all of her available fuel. Noonan, her navigator, was reliant on celestial navigation and dead reckoning, in which the aircraft's position is estimated based on the heading, speed and time elapsed. This means any small error or drift can quickly lead to the navigation becoming more and more off-course, with no chance for correction without either landmarks or additional navigational help.

Itasca, a US Coast Guard patrol boat, offered exactly that help. Radio Direction Finding (RDF) is a type of navigation system which finds the direction (or bearing) to a radio source. Marine navigation uses very low frequencies to cover long distances. At the time, direction finding was common for marine navigation and (during the first world war) for locating the position of an enemy broadcaster.

Earhart's Lockheed Model 10 Electra was equipped with a circular RDF aerial which rotated mechanically. The transmitter was crystal controlled and had been modified to transmit on 500 kHz, which was the frequency for marine distress calls and radio-navigation. The receiver was also modified to receive lower frequencies, so that she could receive 500 kHz signals. A second receiver had been installed in the aircraft but was removed later to reduce the weight of the aircraft.

The *Itasca* positioned itself near Howland where it broadcast its position so that Noonan could take his bearings and correct their course accordingly.

Earhart contacted *Itasca* before her 2nd July departure from Lae to let them know the frequencies she would be using. She specified times twice an hour when she would be transmitting and when she would be listening.

Inexplicably, *Itasca* never told her that it would be almost impossible for them to take bearings on the high frequencies that she said she would be transmitting on and that her chosen frequency to home in on, 7500 kHz, was far too high a frequency for efficient direction finding. During World War II, Radio Direction Finding was improved to determine a direction of a high frequency signal in just a few seconds, specifically to locate aircraft quickly. However, this was too late for Earhart and Noonan.

The direction finding equipment onboard *Itasca* was designed to take bearings on signals in the 550 to 270 kHz range. However, the Electra had lost its trailing antenna in Hawaii. As a result, Earhart was dependent on high-frequency direction findings and never tried to transmit on 500 kHz.

At the time, radio transmissions were done by Morse code. Voice transmissions, which are now standard, were not common and *Itasca* could only transmit voice on some frequencies. In a letter to the Civil Aviation Board, the district superintendent who dealt with Earhart and Noonan at Lae commented on this as an issue.

> As the result of a talk with Mr. E. Chater and Mr. Balfour the Lae radio operator it is very apparent that the weak link in the combination was the crew's lack of expert knowledge of radio. Their morse was very slow and they preferred to use telephony as much as possible. Balfour stated that they advised him they would change the wave length at nightfall. Balfour advised them just before nightfall not to change as their signals were coming through quite strong. They apparently changed however as Balfour never heard them again.

The Electra had been equipped with two Morse code keys for transmitting messages, one for the co-pilot and one for the navigator, but both had been left behind, possibly to reduce the weight of the aircraft.

The Chater Report by the general manager at Lae Airport was equally damning.

> Miss Earhart and Captain Noonan spent a considerable time in the radio office and as previously mentioned it was learned that neither of them could read morse at any speed but could only distinguish letters made individually slowly and repeated often; in that case their direction finding apparatus would be useless or misleading unless they were taking a bearing on a station using radiophone which could give the station position on voice. We understand the "Itasca" was to do this but if the plane was unable to pick up the "Itasca" it is doubtful if the direction finder would be any use to her.

The radio operator at Lae last heard from the aircraft at dusk. Earhart had told them she would change to frequency 3104 at that time; however the operator asked her *not* to change as the signal on the current frequency was very strong and he felt they would have no trouble holding that signal. He listened for another three hours but never received a reply. She had presumably changed frequencies but he could not hear her.

The morning was overcast on the 2nd of July when *Itasca* heard a call from Earhart. Although *Itasca* received strong and clear radio transmissions from Earhart, she appeared not to receive any of the transmissions from the ship. Her first calls were at 02:45 (local time) and then again at 05:00 identifying herself. At 06:14, she transmitted to say she was within 200 miles (230 km) of the island and asked for *Itasca* to use its direction finder to provide a bearing for the aircraft. There's no sign that she was able to pick up any signals from the cutter and clearly Noonan was unable to get a bearing as she continued to ask.

The direction finder had failed two days earlier during a 30-minute air test at Lae. Earhart found that although she received the operator's signal, she was unable to get a minimum on her direction finder, i.e. she could not get a bearing. The issue here again was that the direction finding could not respond to such a high frequency. However, Earhart told the general manager at the airport that the failure was because she was too close to the station and the signal was too strong.

At 06:14, *Itasca* began laying a smoke screen stretching for ten miles to give a visual reference for the travellers who apparently could not hear them.

Meanwhile, Earhart began to whistle into the microphone, saying she was providing a constant signal for *Itasca* to home in on, in the hopes that *Itasca* could tell them their bearing.

There was no need for the whistling; the carrier wave of her transmitter should have been sufficient. Earhart simply needed to key the microphone for a minute or two. Instead, she turned the microphone off every time she ran out of breath, thus never giving the crew on *Itasca* a long enough signal to get a bearing.

Earhart called *Itasca* again at 06:45 asking for a bearing. She estimated that they were 100 miles out. At 07:42 she called again.

> We must be on you, but cannot see you—but gas is running low. Have been unable to reach you by radio. We are flying at 1,000 feet.

In other words, based on their navigation, they believed that they should be within sight of the island (and the ship) and yet still saw no sign of anyone. The direction finder should have given them the precision they needed to find *Itasca* and Howland island but it was clearly not working. Earhart and Noonan descended below the clouds in order to try to find a visual reference instead.

She called again to say that they couldn't hear the *Itasca* and asked for them to transmit so that she could try to take a radio bearing.

> We are listening but cannot hear you. Go ahead on 7500 with a long count, either now or on the scheduled time on half hour.

Itasca crew described this 07:58 transmission as the loudest, which implies that Earhart and Noonan must have been in the immediate vicinity of the cutter when she broadcast that message. However, Earhart and Noonan clearly never saw the billows of black smoke from *Itasca*, let alone the ship or the island.

The radio operator couldn't transmit a voice message ("a long count") on the 7500 frequency but he did send a prearranged signal, the letter A in Morse code, repeatedly. This was the first transmission that Earhart acknowledged, saying that she'd received a signal but was still unable to get a bearing.

Of course she couldn't. Earhart's equipment couldn't do direction finding on 7500 kHz. She may have hoped to be able to calibrate their location based on the volume, allowing her to determine the strong and weak signals. However, after hours in the aircraft, the noise of the engines and the propellers meant that she would have been too deafened to determine where the signal was weakest.

Earhart sent another message at 08:43.

> We are on the line 157/337. We will repeat this message. We will repeat this on 6210 kilocycles. Wait.

The numbers 157/337 are a reference to degrees on a compass. This is the first useful report from Earhart regarding their position. Her statement can be understood that Noonan had been trying to find the island using a single Line of Position.

A Line of Position is always at a right angle to a celestial body, in this case, the rising sun: the dawn line on the 2nd of July 1937 in the Central Pacific was 157/337.

There's a great explanation of this on the Navigation FAQ on the Amelia Earhart Search Forum.

> First of all, it's important to remember that Noonan knew that the rising sun would give them a 157/337 line. He had that information back in Lae, New Guinea as soon as he knew what day they were going to be making the flight. The only question was how far along they would be when the sun came up, and he wouldn't know that until he saw the sun and noted the time. Then he could draw his 157 337 line on his map and say, "Okay, we're somewhere on this line." All he had to do then was to draw another 157/337 line that passed through Howland Island and measure the distance between the two parallel lines. With a good idea of how fast they were going it was a simple matter to predict at what time they would reach the "advanced" LOP.
>
> Of course, knowing where they were in an east/west sense was not good enough. To find tiny Howland Island it was essential that they know if they were north of, south of, or right on, course. That's what Radio Direction Finding was supposed to do. Noonan's job was to get them close—within, say, a couple hundred miles—and it was Amelia's job to use the radio to fine tune the final approach. That's where things went haywire.

They'd been flying for eighteen hours or so by now which means that the aircraft should have still had a few hours of fuel. They knew there were other islands if they continued south-east: Baker Island, Gardner Island and Atafu. Only Howland had an airfield but finding *any* island would at least give them a land-mark for their navigation. If they could work out their position, then they could easily navigate directly to Howland. If it turned out they were too far out to make it safely, at least one of the islands would give them a location to ditch and call for help.

However, the next transmission from Earhart was the last.

> We are running on line north and south.

The Electra should not yet have been out of fuel and even if it was, Earhart should have had time to make a distress call. Her previous transmission gave vital information and made it clear that the aircraft was flying south-east on the Line of Position that Noonan had drawn at dawn, hoping to find Howland or some other island. This call, which was at Earhart's regularly scheduled transmission time, was completely unclear. The radio operator did not know what she meant and had no way of asking for clarification.

Itasca never saw any trace of the Electra and they never heard from Earhart again.

An hour after receiving the final message from Earhart, *Itasca* began searching north and west of Howland Island, following the 157/337 line of position in hopes of discovering Earhart and Noonan. The United States Navy sent all available resources to the search area to support *Itasca* in the search.

The initial search and rescue focused on the Phoenix Islands, which were 350 miles (560 km) south-east of Howland Island. If Earhart had run out of fuel, she was likely to have ditched on one of these islands if she could have. In addition, there were multiple radio transmissions which could have been Earhart or Noonan trying to make contact. If so, it meant that the radio equipment was on dry land.

Many of these transmissions were dismissed as impossible. However, the radio operator at Nauru Islands logged repeated transmissions on the correct frequency, which could possibly have come from Earhart and Noonan. The first radio call was two hours after the last confirmed transmission and he heard more transmissions about ten hours later. The United States Navy joined *Itasca* in the search, also focusing on the islands where they hoped that they might find survivors. One report on Gardner Island (now called Nikumaroro) said, "Here signs of recent habitation were clearly visible but repeated circling and zooming failed to elicit any answering wave from possible inhabitants and it was finally taken for granted that none were there." They also searched the other directions in case the Electra had safely ditched into the Pacific and was afloat. The search continued for two weeks at a cost of $4 million, the most costly air and sea search in US history at the time. The US Navy and Coast Guard, along with *Itasca* and two Japanese ships, searched 150,000 square miles (390,000 square km) but found no physical evidence and called off the search. Earhart's husband, George Putnam, funded a private search, including the Gilbert Islands and the Phoenix Islands, but again found no evidence from the Electra or the two aviators.

Rumours abounded, of course. Many believed that the Electra ran out of fuel and crashed into the sea out of sight of Howland Island, sinking to the ocean floor with both its occupants. The seafloor in that part of the Pacific is 17,000–18,000 feet (5,000–5,500 metres), far too deep for any effective search with the technology. None of these theories explains the later radio transmissions but simply dismisses them as false.

Another theory is that Earhart was captured by the Japanese. This would mean that they most likely crashed at the Mariana Islands archipelago, which was occupied by Japan at the time. A relative of Earhart's claimed that there were witnesses, including Japanese troops and natives of the island of Saipan, who saw Earhart and Noonan in Japanese custody. The Electra was said to have been cut into scrap and thrown into the ocean to hide any trace of their arrival on the island. Proponents of this theory point out that the Mitsubishi A6M Zero has many components very similar to Earhart's Lockheed Electra. Another theory is that the Electra was shot down by the Japanese, which would explain why the aircraft seemed to disappear hours before it should have run out of fuel. Another small island in the Mariana archipelago has a marked location which has been rumoured since World War II to be the burial site of Earhart and Noonan; however, an excavation at the site did not bring up any bones.

Earhart is also claimed to have disappeared on purpose to work as a spy against the Japanese for Franklin Roosevelt. Some combined two mysteries to determine that Earhart became Tokyo Rose, the radio personality in the South Pacific who broadcast Japanese propaganda in English to the Allied forces in the Pacific. Many people had been unhappy with her feminism and lack of interest in creating a home and a family, leading to a fantastical story that she had secretly returned to the US to become a housewife in New Jersey.

There's compelling evidence that Earhart and Noonan may have made it as far as Nikumaroro Island (then known as Gardner Island) where they survived only a short time as castaways.

It was three years after the search had been given up when a possible clue surfaced. Nikumaroro was initially claimed by the US in 1856 under the American Guano Islands Act, which the US used to take possession of islands with seabird excrement which was popularly harvested as fertiliser.

From the first section of Guano Islands Act:

> Whenever any citizen of the United States discovers a deposit of guano on any island, rock, or key, not within the lawful jurisdiction of any other Government, and not occupied by the citizens of any other Government, and takes peaceable possession thereof, and occupies the same, such island, rock, or key may, at the discretion of the President, be considered as appertaining to the United States.

No guano was harvested from the island and in 1892, the island was claimed by the United Kingdom, who granted a licence for coconut farming. Twenty-nine islanders were settled there but the project failed within a year during a drought and the islanders were evacuated. The island became uninhabited again other than a brief stay by the crew of the SS *Norwich City* whose steamer went aground on the reef in a storm. They were rescued a few days later and left behind a cache of provisions.

The islands then became uninhabited until they became a part of the remarkable Phoenix Islands Settlement Scheme. At the time, the Gilbert Islands were suffering from severe overpopulation. In precolonial times, island population had been held under control through abortion, disease and warfare leading to emigration. As a result of missionaries and colonisation, all three forms of population control became limited and, on the Gilbert Islands, the imbalance between people and resources became critical. The Phoenix Islands Settlement Scheme was a solution to this: move land-poor families from the overpopulated islands to the Phoenix Islands, a group of eight islands, reefs and shoals scattered over the Central Pacific Ocean (now a part of Kiribati). The islands did not have enough resources to simply move the settlers there and leave them to their own devices; the islands did not have enough natural resources to sustain the settlers. British officials were stationed on each island, who arranged for wells to be dug, houses to be constructed and coconuts to be planted. They divided the land among the settlers and organised them into functioning communities (often the settlers came from several different islands).

Nikumaroro was settled by a combination of British officials and Micronesian settlers from the Gilbert Islands, in what is now known as the last colonial expansion of the British Empire. They worked to clear the land and plant coconuts, building wide coral-gravel streets and thatched housing, including a cooperative store and a radio shack.

Gerald Gallagher arrived on the island in 1937 and in 1940 he became Officer in Charge of the Phoenix Islands Settlement Scheme. His fellow officers called him "Irish", as his father was Irish, and the Gilbertese islanders called him "Karaka". He was described as utterly committed to the scheme and the islanders trying to carve out survival on the previously unoccupied islands. In 1940, he discovered a human skeleton on Nikumaroro.

There had been various rumours about human bones discovered on the island, possibly belonging to Amelia Earhart. But it wasn't until 1991 when author Peter McQuarrie discovered official documentation: a series of telegrams between Gallagher and other British officials regarding the find. The full correspondence is reprinted on The International Group for Historic Aircraft Recovery website.

> Please obtain from Koata (Native Magistrate Gardner on way to Central Hospital) a certain bottle alleged to have been found near skull discovered on Gardner Island. Grateful you retain bottle in safe place for present and ask Koata not to talk about skull which is just possibly that of Amelia Earhardt.

Apparently, a working party on the island had found a human skull and other bones which had been scattered by coconut crabs, along with part of a shoe, a bottle and a sextant box. The shoe is identified as a woman's and the bottle as Benedictine, a French liqueur. Neither of these were common items in the Central Pacific in 1940. The shipwrecked sailors of 1929 were of course all men. Gallagher was asked to forward all the items to the High Commission in Suva, Fiji, with an agreement to keep the find strictly secret.

In the correspondence is a letter from Gallagher which appears to have accompanied the items on the Royal Colony Ship *Nimanoa* to Suva. There follows a telegram from the senior medical officer onboard, who wants to know what the story is with the human remains.

> As I am in charge of Medical and forensic investigation of such objects throughout the whole colony and have no knowledge of the matter, I presume that the package was intended to be consigned to myself?

Amelia Earhart and Fred Noonan.

The medical officer inspected the remains, despite the fact that he'd clearly been left off of the classified correspondence. He then declared that the bones were part of the skeleton of an elderly male of Polynesian race which had been scattered on the island for at least 20 years and probably longer. A further telegram from the same medical officer asked how the "wretched relics can be interesting", presumably after further enquiries into the remains. And with that, the discovery was dismissed and the "wretched relics" deemed uninteresting. American authorities were never notified.

Ric Gillespie, a former airline crash investigator, is convinced that Earhart and Noonan landed on a Pacific island where she lived as a castaway. He launched the Earhart Project in 1988 and has led numerous expeditions to search for traces of Earhart and Noonan on the island and the wreckage of the aircraft in the waters surrounding it. It is Gillespie's work which turned up small bottles on the islands which appear to be 1930s skin product containers. He successfully raised the funds for an expedition to Nikumaroro in the summer of 2017, with a specific intention to investigate an anomaly just off shore at a depth of 600 feet, at the base of a cliff on the island, which they believe could be the fuselage of the Electra. They also brought four forensic dogs which successfully identified a spot with human remains, all four targeting the same area that Gillespie had previously identified as likely. No bones were found but the soil has been collected and sent to a lab to search for DNA. Unfortunately, the remote operated vehicle which was to survey the depths was plagued with technical difficulties and eventually malfunctioned. Instead, they devised a crude camera system with which they collected 170 high definition images in the area. These photographs can't confirm whether the anomaly was the fuselage of an aircraft or not but the team hopes that with further analysis, they may be able to find some answers. Gillespie remains hopeful. "As with all previous TIGHAR expeditions to Nikumaroro, the results . . . will not be known until the data collected have been compiled, analyzed and evaluated."

If the Nikumaroro castaway story is true, we might just have a chance of resolving this mystery after all.

1938

Only an Oil Slick Remained

Pan American Airways was founded in 1927 to offer air mail services as a response to German-owned Colombian carrier SCADTA who was moving north from Colombia and lobbying hard for landing rights in the Panama Canal Zone. The US government approved Pan Am's mail delivery contract and protected it from US competitors, glad that SCADTA would have competition in bidding for routes between Latin America and the United States. Pan American Airways grew rapidly with a virtual monopoly on foreign routes.

Pam Am became well known for its rigorous training of its flight crews, including long-distance flight, over-water navigation, engine repair and even celestial navigation for night flights. Long before the advent of instrument navigation, Pan Am pilots would use dead reckoning and timed turns in bad weather. They dealt with fogged-in harbours by landing out to sea and taxiing their planes into port.

Pan Am's "Clipper Era" began in 1931. Intercontinental air travel was initially fulfilled by Clippers, flying boats with long range. The Pan Am chief called these aircraft "Clippers" to evoke the romance of the 19th century clipper ships in order to help them compete with the ocean liners which were associated with transatlantic travel at the time. Pan Am established their trans-Pacific airmail service in 1935 and began carrying passengers in October 1936.

Before World War II, airports were still uncommon and the Clippers could service any city with a sheltered harbour. Over 15 years, Pan Am placed twenty-eight Clippers into service to provide intercontinental travel, with passenger services offering first-class seats and luxury meals.

The flying boat service connected San Francisco, California to Manila Bay, Philippines, with stops at Pearl Harbor, Midway Atoll, Wake Island and Guam.

The Pan American Airways Martin M-130 *China Clipper* (civil registration NC14716) at Pearl Harbor, Hawaii, in the 1930s.

The Martin M-130 was an all-metal flying boat with four powerful piston engines, designed and developed to meet Pan Am's requirements for a trans-Pacific aircraft. There were three M-130's built, the *China Clipper*, the *Philippine Clipper*, and the *Hawaii Clipper.* A fourth flying boat, an M-156 called the *Russian Clipper,* was built for the Soviet Union. They were officially called Martin Ocean Transports but to the public they, and later all of Pan Am's large flying boats, were known as the "*China Clippers*". The weekly passenger flights across the Pacific began in October 1936 when the *Hawaii Clipper* left San Francisco for Manila, Philippines.

On the 23rd of July of 1938, the *Hawaii Clipper* was scheduled for Trip No. 229 departing from Alameda, California for its scheduled flight to Manila. The aircraft was inspected and routine service for "long airplane service" was carried out. A test flight of three hours was conducted by the flight crew the day before the scheduled departure, including an emergency landing and an "abandon ship" drill. For the "abandon ship" drill, the left raft is inflated and put overside with the crew and emergency equipment aboard. The crew set up the emergency radio and establish communication with shore stations.

The M-130 had six lower compartments: the aircraft could remain afloat so long as at least two of them remained watertight. The aircraft also held life rafts, a saltwater still, marker balloons, flares and food for 15 people for a month. The wings had orange stripes painted on top to ensure it would be visible to search and rescue.

There were six passengers and nine crew: Captain, First Officer, Second Officer, Third Officer, Fourth Officer, Engineer Officer, Assistant Engineer Officer, Radio Officer and Flight Steward. The captain was extremely experienced, with 9,200 hours flight time, of which 1,626 were "in Trans-Pacific operation" and 1,614 hours were in the aircraft. All of the crew had the required ratings for the flight and were in good physical condition with all having a thousand hours flying experience or more. The aircraft had acquired a total flying time of 4,752 hours and 55 minutes before departing Alameda.

It departed Alameda on the 23rd of July and experienced better than expected weather for the first leg; it arrived at Honolulu the following day. At Honolulu, the aircraft was inspected and "over-night airplane service" was carried out. On the 25th, the flight continued on schedule from Honolulu and arrived at Midway Atoll, an atoll equidistant between North America and Asia, on the 26th.

The clipper departed Midway Atoll on the 26th and flew a southerly route to avoid weather, arriving at its next stop, Wake Island, on the 27th. Wake Island is 3,698 km (2,298 miles) east of Guam, its next stop. Wake Island is one of the most isolated islands in the world. Both the *Hawaii Clipper* and the eastbound *Philippine Clipper* had an overnight stop on Wake Island that night. Both aircraft were inspected and had the over-night airplane service. The crew of the *Philippine Clipper* said that the entire crew of the *Hawaii Clipper* were in the best of spirits and said that their trip so far had been comfortable and normal.

The *Hawaii Clipper* continued on its westbound route and on the 28th of July 1938 the flight arrived in Guam at 05:55 UTC. The flight so far had been uneventful and the ordinary routine radio contacts were maintained throughout. Again, as per company procedure, the aircraft was inspected and the overnight airplane service was carried out. No irregularities were reported by the Flight Engineer nor detected by the chief mechanics at any of the airports with overnight stops.

The next flight was the last leg of its westbound route to Manila. The aircraft had 2,550 US gallons of gasoline on board, allowing a flight endurance of 17 hours and 30 minutes. The flight times allowed 14 hours and 50 minutes of daylight for the flight. The flight was expected to take 12 hours and 30 minutes cruising at 7,800 feet.

The *Hawaii Clipper* departed Guam at 19:38 UTC (03:39 Manila time), which involved taxiing out to sea; it took off from the water 29 minutes later. Pan Am had a radio facility at Guam who would remain on guard until the aircraft landed at Manila. Radio facilities in Panay and Manila were standing guard, which meant that someone was monitoring at all three stations at all times during the flight. In addition, other Pan American Airways radio stations were listening out. The aircraft had two independent transmitters which could communicate on assigned frequencies or on the international distress frequency of 500 kilocycles.

At 03:30 UTC the aircraft had 1,420 gallons of fuel remaining, enough for over 10 hours at normal cruise. They had plenty of fuel to reach Manila with a few hours to spare. Radio communications had been standard throughout the flight.

04:00 UTC The radio operator at Panay received a routine report.

> "Flying in rough air at 9100 feet. Temperature 13 degree centigrade. Wind 19 knots per hour[*sic*] from 247 degree. Position Latitude 12 degree 27′ N. Longitude 130 degree 40′ E dead reckoning. Ground speed made good 112 knots. Desired track 282 degree, Rain. During past hour cloud conditions have varied. 10/10ths of sky above covered by strato cumulus clouds, base 9200 feet. Clouds below, 10/10ths of sky covered by cumulus clouds whose tops were 9200 feet. 5/10ths of the hour on instruments. Last direction finder bearing from Manila 101 degree."

The radio operator acknowledged the call and offered to

transmit the weather sequence reports based on the most recent observations compiled and relayed to him by the Philippine Stations.

The response from the *Hawaii Clipper* was received as follows.

> "Stand by for one minute before sending as I am having trouble with rain static."

At 04:12 UTC, the Panay radio operator called the *Clipper* back to give them the weather sequences. The call was not acknowledged.

The Panay radio operator continued to call the *Clipper* but received no response.

04:15: The Panay radio operator sent the *Clipper*'s earlier position report to Manila.

04:35: The Pan Am Communications Superintendent, Pacific Division in Alameda, California was notified of a communications failure between the ground stations and the *Hawaii Clipper.*

04:49: Pan American Airways requested all Philippine stations to stand by on emergency frequencies. This is standard emergency procedure for any interruption of communications between shore stations and aircraft. At this stage, it was not clear whether there was cause for alarm, as interruptions to communications were not uncommon.

The *Hawaii Clipper* was due to arrive at Manila at 09:00. Up until this point, they hoped that the aircraft had suffered a communications failure but was still en route to her destination. The Naval Commandant, at the request of Pan American Airways, ordered all Navy vessels to stand by for manoeuvres. When the aircraft still hadn't arrived an hour and a half later, all Navy vessels were ordered to prepare to put to sea.

By 16:00 UTC, which was midnight local time, thirteen vessels were underway on a search and rescue mission for the missing aircraft.

The United States Army Transport *Meigs* received a report that shore stations had lost contact with the clipper. They were 103 miles west-north-west of the last known location and immediately changed course. They searched the location for three hours that day and then continued to search through the night.

It was the following day when they discovered an oil slick about 28 miles south-south-east of the aircraft's last estimated position. The oil slick was somewhere between 500 and 1,500 feet in diameter and roughly circular in shape. The *Hawaii Clipper* carried 120 gallons of engine oil so could easily have left such a marker. The current at the time was 140° at a rate of one knot. A small boat was put over the side to collect oil from the slick for testing, but night was falling and they had only collected two small samples. They stayed put that night, planning to pick up more samples from the oil slick in the morning.

They waited for daylight, expecting that the ship and the oil slick would have drifted the same distance in the night. But as the morning dawned on the 31st of July, there was no sign of the oil slick.

Meigs carefully searched the area before returning to the original location. On the third day since the disappearance, they were joined by Navy destroyers and submarines as well as Army and Navy aircraft. Together, they searched the ocean, the island shores and the interior areas of Philippine islands Luzon and Mindanao, which include large areas of tropical jungles and mountain ranges over 7,000 feet.

An inhabitant of the island of Lahuy reported that he heard a large aircraft flying above the clouds around 3 p.m. Manila time on the 29th. The weather on the island that day was overcast with a cloud ceiling of 2,500 feet.

There were no military or private aircraft reported in that vicinity on that date. An aerial search was made of the island and nearby sea.

The wind was quiet and the sea was calm. They hoped to find oil or wreckage that had floated to the surface.

They found no sign of the lost aircraft.

After a week with no further trace of the lost aircraft, the search was abandoned.

The oil collected from the slick the first evening was split into two jars. The amount collected was so small that the two samples made up less than 3 cc's each; not enough to analyse in depth. However, chemists investigated the properties of the samples and concluded that the oil recovered did not come from the engines of the *Hawaii Clipper*.

The only remaining lead was the report that the aircraft had been heard flying low over the island of Lahuy. The aerial search showed no trace but with the mountainous terrain and jungle, it could be that the wreck was hidden in the landscape. Pan American Airways Company offered a reward for any information regarding the Clipper, in hopes of encouraging land searches in the area.

The official report by the Civil Aeronautics Authority was unable to determine the probable cause.

> In conclusion, it appears that the only definite facts established up to the present time, are that between 0411 and 0412 G.C.T on July 29, 1938 was a failure of communication between the ground and the Clippers; Communication was not thereafter reestablished; and that no trace of the flying boat has since been discovered. A number of theories have been advanced as to the possible basic cause of or reason for the disappearance of the Clipper. The Board has considered each of them. Some have not been disproved, either or have been contradicted by the known facts. However, the Investigating Board feels that this report cannot properly include a discussion of conjection unsupported by developed facts. The Board, therefore, respectfully submit this report with the thought that additional evidence may yet be discovered and the investigation completed at that time.

No one ever claimed the reward offered by Pan American. No trace of the aircraft wreckage has ever been reported.

The strange disappearance caught the media's attention; it had been only a year since Amelia Earhart had disappeared in the same waters. The stories were fueled by rumours that there were three million US dollars on board, collected by the Chinese War Relief Committee, which Chinese-American restaurateur Choy Wah Sun was taking to China. The passenger manifest has a passenger of that name, but there's no information publicly available that he was transporting cash or gold.

Some people believe that the static in the last transmission is proof that the aircraft had flown into an electrical storm and was struck by lightning. In 1963, Pam Am flight 214, the Boeing 707 Stratoliner nicknamed *Clipper Tradewind* disintegrated after a lightning strike ignited the flammable fuel vapours inside the left reserve fuel tank, which led to the centre and right reserve fuel tanks exploding.

Another theory is that the aircraft was hijacked. Newspapers of the time reported the possibility that Japanese agents had slipped into the Clipper's baggage compartment on Guam. The theory goes that they took control of the aircraft mid-flight and hijacked it to an island in Japanese territory, where the crew and passengers were killed and the aircraft hidden in concrete structures. Although Japan was not yet at war with the US, they had already invaded China, so plenty of motive could be found. The four engines of the M-130 would have been quite a coup, let alone collecting three million US dollars intended for the Chinese.

Meanwhile, new research has concluded that the testing of the oil found by the United States Army Transport *Meigs* may not have been reliable. Analysis of the notes made at the time show that the oil spill may have come from the *Hawaii Clipper* after all.

The United States Army Transport *Meigs* was sunk by Japanese bombers four years later and the underwater wreck is now a popular dive site.

There's a modern twist. This 1938 disappearance has had repercussions in one of the largest mysteries of our time, the disappearance of Malaysian Airlines flight 370. Families of the victims have claimed against the airline, who had not paid out as the circumstances of the aircraft crash have not been solved. One of the case rulings cited in the case is *Choy v Pan Am World Airways* which went to court in 1941.

Wah Sun "Watson" Choy was on the aircraft, the restaurateur said to have been transporting three million US dollars. The Choy family filed the suit against Pan Am based on the Federal Death on the High Seas Act. This act created a right of action whenever death was "caused by wrongful act, neglect, or default occurring on the high seas beyond a marine league from the shore of any State" and allowed for "the personal representative of the decedent," usually the victim's family, to claim for damages. This act ensured that a passenger on a ship travelling through international waters still had some protection against wrongful death, even though the situation happened outside of US territorial waters.

In the case of Choy vs Pan Am, the argument was that the act should not only refer to ships but also to aircraft travelling *above* the sea.

The conclusion by Circuit Judge Moore was reprinted on the Ravellaw website:

> The statute certainly includes the phrase "on the high seas" but there is no reason why this should make the law operable only on a horizontal plane. The very next phrase "beyond a marine league from the shore of any State" may be said to include a vertical sense and another dimension.
>
> The Death on the High Seas Act was intended to confer a right and we recognize no reason why its language should be narrowly construed whatever doubt may now exist that a given set of facts was in the minds of any of the legislators who framed or adopted it. Laws giving a right of action for tort are never definite in their language and intentionally so. This follows from their nature for no one can imagine all the exigencies out of which causes of action arise and legislators wisely refrain from attempting to state them.
>
> We are inclined to hold, therefore, that the Death on the High Seas Act confers a right upon the plaintiff.

In other words, the means of transportation is not relevant, nor should it matter if the ship (or air ship or whatever) is literally travelling *on* the high seas rather than over or even under, as the intent is to protect the traveller, not only (or specifically) the traveller on seagoing vessels.

It is difficult to find out any hard details about this. It seems that the modern court case is claiming that the airline has a duty to settle claims of the victims' families even though the location of the crash is unknown and thus can't be proven to have taken place on the High Seas. Malaysia Airlines flight 370, like the

Martin M-130 flying boat known as the *Hawaii Clipper*, disappeared without any sign of distress or bad weather and the wreckage has never been located.

But we are jumping ahead of ourselves now before even getting started on the baffling tale of the death of Amy Johnson in 1941.

1941

DEATH OF AN AVIATRIX

THE PILOT AMY JOHNSON, aviatrix to use the term at the time, made a point of pushing her personal limits in order to become the best pilot she possibly could. She repeatedly showed her experience and skill during those dangerous flights; it appears to have been the end of a routine flight across England that was her downfall.

Amy Johnson was born in 1903 in Hull, Yorkshire, the daughter of a fish merchant. Johnson moved to London after graduating from Sheffield University. In 1928, she had her first flying lesson at the London Aeroplane Cub, where she was told that she would "never make a flier". She persevered, wanting not just to make a career in aviation but also to prove that women were as competent to fly as men.

Johnson received her aviator's certificate, No. 8662, on 28 June 1929 and her pilot's "A" Licence, No. 1979, on 6th July 1929. That same year, after she found she was unable to support herself flying, she became Britain's first qualified woman ground engineer ("C" licence) and was for some time the only female ground engineer in the world.

She swiftly set herself a challenging goal: to fly solo from London to Australia, hoping to beat Bert Hinkler's record of completing the flight in sixteen days.

Twelve days before the flight, Johnson bought an aircraft with help from her father and Lord Wakefield in support of her project. She paid £600 for the two-year-old de Havilland Gipsy Moth biplane, registration G-AAAH. It had no lights, no radio and no fuel gauge. She named it *Jason.*

She set off from the now defunct Croydon airport in South

London on the 5th of May 1930, with her father and a few friends to see her off. At the time, she had only 75 flight hours logged. She arrived at Karachi, her first stop, to much more attention. Johnson struggled with mechanical issues and bad weather. In the end, the flight took 19 days, failing to beat Hinkler's record.

On the 24th of May, she crash-landed in Darwin, having travelled 11,000 miles (18,000 kilometres) to become the first aviatrix to fly solo to Australia. The Australians rewarded her with the No. 1 civil pilot's licence in recognition of her achievement. The first licence issued in Australia was licence number 2, and licence number 1 had remained unissued until it was presented to Johnson.

Women pilots who escorted the landing of Amy Johnson in Sydney on 4 June 1930, at the end of the first England to Australia flight by a woman.

In Britain, the Daily Mail awarded her £10,000 for "a feat of daring". Johnson's celebrity status grew and she regularly encountered cheering crowds at the airports where she flew. The BBC reports that when she was driven through London in an open-topped car, the crowd lining the parade route was estimated at a million people.

In 1932 Johnson married Scottish pilot Jim Mollison, who had proposed to her during a flight only eight hours after they'd met. She then flew solo from London to Cape Town to break her husband's record for that route.

The two pilots also broke records together, including flights to India and again to Australia.

Johnson's last record-breaking flight, to regain her London to Cape Town record, was in May 1936. Public enthusiasm for her flights was waning (she may have made it look too easy) and her marriage had ended in divorce.

Her description of the long flights that she undertook is evocative:

> Hours and hours passed, with nothing to do but keep the compass on its course and the plane on a level keel. This sounds easy enough, but its very simplicity becomes a danger when your head keeps nodding with weariness and utter boredom and your eyes everlastingly try to shut out the confusing rows of figures in front of you, which will insist on getting jumbled together. Tired of trying to sort them out, you relax for a second, then your head drops and you sit up with a jerk, Where are you? What are you doing here? Oh yes, of course, you are somewhere in the middle of the North Atlantic, with hungry waves below you like vultures impatiently waiting for the end.

In 1940, Johnson joined the Air Transport Auxiliary (ATA), a British civilian organisation which recruited experienced pilots who were ineligible for RAF service. The ATA pilots freed the combat pilots for combat by taking over all of the aircraft transport requirements, ferrying aircraft from factory airstrips and maintenance units to RAF bases. Many of the ATA pilots were women and from 1943 they received equal pay to men of equal rank in the ATA, which was a first for the British Government.

The women pilots flew every type of aircraft flown by the RAF, including four-engine heavy bombers, Hurricanes and Spitfires.

Johnson was paid £6 a week, a huge salary for the time, after she rose to rank of First Officer, the equivalent of the RAF rank of Flight Lieutenant.

On the 5th of January 1941, Johnson was given the task to deliver a new Airspeed Oxford III twin-engine plane from Blackpool to RAF Kidlington near Oxford.

According to *What Did Happen To Amy Johnson*, by Roy Nesbit, after she had just delivered an Airspeed Oxford to Prestwick, she was given the option to fly back in another Oxford, delivering it to Kidlington, or return to London by train. Amy chose to fly the Oxford after staying the night at her sister's.

The British built Airspeed Oxford, nicknamed the Ox-box, is an advanced training aircraft which was popular with the RAF during World War II. A low-wing cantilever monoplane with retractable gears, it usually took a crew of three with dual controls in the front for two pilots or the second seat pushed back to the chart table for a navigator, depending on the training required.

The weather conditions were bad, with snow and freezing fog, and she's said to have been flying with a broken compass. The reason for the flight is still protected by the government although a media report says it was simply a routine flight to deliver the Ox-box to the RAF base at Kidlington.

The facts are few: Amy Johnson definitely departed Blackpool in an Airspeed Oxford shortly before noon, after reportedly dismissing concerns about the compass, which needed adjustment, and the weather forecast, which was bad.

The flight should have taken 90 minutes but there was no sign of her until four and a half hours later, when she ditched the aircraft in the Thames estuary. She was 100 miles off course and three hours late.

The HMS *Haslemere* was a converted ferry on the Thames estuary that was close enough to see Johnson's parachute, which never had a chance to properly open. The crew then saw Johnson in the water, waving frantically for help. They attempted to throw her a rope but she could not get hold of it. The waters were described as heavy sea and strong tide, and must have been incredibly cold. The commander of the *Haslemere* tied a rope around his waist and dived into the water to rescue her but failed. The cold was overwhelming and the commander died of hypothermia a few days later.

It is unknown whether Johnson got lost in the thick cloud and was blown badly off course or if she intentionally flew east, hoping for a break in the cloud. Did she bail out because she was low on fuel or because she saw the Royal Navy convoy and hoped for rescue, or had something else gone wrong?

The Air Transport Auxiliary's official explanation states that she ran out of fuel after overshooting her destination by 100 miles. However, after flying to Australia, Japan and Cape Town, it is difficult to understand how she could have failed to find Oxford or why it took her three hours to travel those 100 miles, having planned half that time for her initial flight of 120 miles.

Neither the aircraft nor her body have ever been discovered, so even the simplest questions remain unanswered. As you can imagine, rumours abound as to what, exactly, happened that day: both to the aircraft and to Johnson, including that she was attempting to fly to France with a lover who had been discovered as a spy! This seems unlikely, as it explains very little of the mystery, but may have gained popularity as there is a real question as to whether Johnson had a passenger or not.

The crew of the HMS *Haslemere* reported at the time that there were two bodies in the water, Johnson's and another, but the identity of the second body was never established and according to official reports, Johnson was flying solo for her ferry flight. One theory is that she was transporting a spy to a secret location, rather than flying to Kidlington, which explains the time lapse after leaving Blackpool and her location a hundred miles off course. One historian, however, argues that Johnson's pigskin flight bag would have been floating near her and could easily have been mistaken for a bobbing head in the rough waters and confusion.

Another popular theory has been that Johnson did not run out of fuel but was shot down by friendly fire. One version is that she was fired at by a naval convoy on the Thames Estuary at the time but the mistake was hushed up by the government who did not wish to damage morale.

There's one eyewitness report in favour of this. In 1999, a retired soldier came forward to say that he'd been ordered to shoot down an unidentified aircraft flying towards the English Channel that day, and he believes that it was Johnson. He and three other soldiers were stationed at Iwade, on the Thames Estuary. He said that after the aircraft came into sight, they radioed a request for her to cite the colour of the day, which was a signal used to identify British forces. According to the soldier, she got it wrong. He told the Guardian that he felt terrible about it but believed that the Official Secrets Act meant he couldn't tell anyone.

> The reason Amy was shot down was because she gave the wrong colour of the day over the radio. She got it wrong twice, and that's why we were ordered to shoot.
>
> Sixteen rounds of shells were fired into the sky and the plane dived into the Thames Estuary—but on the ground, we couldn't see that at the time.
>
> The next day, when we read about it in the papers, the officers told us to keep quiet and never tell anyone what happened.

When his sister died, he reread his letters to her at the time, in which he apparently was not concerned about the Official Secrets Act and had detailed the entire event. He decided that he must tell his story before he died.

The Ministry of Defence stated that they have no way of confirming the man's story. An archivist at the Royal Air Force Museum in Hendon explained that if the soldier's story was true and it was covered up, then obviously it would not have been officially recorded, either. However, he was sceptical. It was more likely, he told the Guardian, that she ran out of fuel and when she saw the barrage balloons of the navy convoy, she believed she was over land and bailed out.

Whether her Ox-box ran out of fuel or was shot down by friendly fire, the question remains of what happened to her after she bailed out.

75 years after her disappearance, a Yorkshire historian, Dr Alec Gill, claims to have solved the mystery, which he's published in a book entitled *Amy Johnson: Hessle Road Tomboy—Born and Bred, Dread and Fled.*

He is convinced that Johnson had been sucked into a boat propeller in a failed rescue attempt, which was covered up later. He was stunned to discover this after speaking to the son of a man called Harry Gould, who was a Naval reservist on board the

HMS *Haslemere.* He said that the ferry reversed to break free from a sandbank as Johnson swam towards the boat.

> I was told by Harry's son [that Harry Gould] could see what was going on so he rushed towards the bridge shouting for all his life was worth "Cut the engines, cut the engines." Someone on the bridge said "who do you think you are telling me what to do" because they couldn't see the propellers. So he kept on, I believe with the engines in reverse, and I think within those moments her body was cut to pieces and that's why her body has not been found.

Certainly if the engine was in reverse and full power, it would suck anything close to it into its propellers.

The interesting thing is that this isn't the first time this story has been told. In 2002, the BBC reported that a clerk at the RAF flight office was told that Amy Johnson had been run over. His friend was on board the HMS *Haslemere* and told him they'd spotted a parachutist coming down. The RAF clerk typed up his friend's report.

> He said that while he was on deck, a parachutist had come down in the water and had drifted near the Haslemere.
>
> She called out that she was Amy Johnson, that the water was bitterly cold, and could they get her out as soon as possible.
>
> They threw her a rope, but she couldn't get hold of it.
>
> Then someone dashed up to the bridge and reversed the ship's engines, as a result of which, she was drawn into the propellor and chopped to pieces.

Dr Gill, the historian, believes that there was a massive Royal Navy cover-up because the Royal Navy didn't dare admit that they had killed Amy Johnson. It was easier to simply claim that she had drowned.

> This ship should have gone down in history as the vessel that saved her life. Instead, historians are now beginning to conclude that the propellers of the Haslemere killed her and that's why her body was never found. That wasn't even mentioned when her parents were still alive.
>
> The Royal Navy did not want to admit to the Royal Air Force—or indeed a nation at war—that they had killed Britain's favourite female pilot.

But again, there's no way to prove or disprove this theory, as her body was never found.

Various groups, including an RAF sub-aqua association team, have been attempting to find the wreck of her aircraft in the sea off of the Kent coast. Diving is difficult in the area and the sediment means that there's little or no light. The currents are described as "tricky" and the most likely area where it is believed to have gone down is close to a shipping lane. So far, no trace of it has been discovered.

Until and unless the Ox-box is found, the reason for Johnson's bailing out can only be guessed at. It's sad to think that, even if her body is found in the Thames Estuary, we might never know what happened in those final moments. Amy Johnson was already a legend at the age of 37. As is so often the case, I can't help but wonder what she might have achieved if she had survived the war.

The war was already over by the time one of the most famous disappearances took place: five naval aircraft on a routine navigation exercise. Flight 19 is the granddaddy of mysteries that encouraged the stories of the paranormal activity in a deadly region known as the Bermuda Triangle.

1945

WHICH WAY DID WE FLY?

AS AVIATION AND maritime safety has increased, one doesn't hear much about the Bermuda Triangle any more. Known as the "Devil's Triangle", it wasn't long ago that it was considered the biggest mystery of the time. The disappearance of Flight 19, comprising five torpedo bombers and fourteen crew, along with the loss of a second aircraft that was searching for it, did much to place the area under suspicion, although it would not be referred to as the Bermuda Triangle until five years later.

The official stance was posted on the Frequently Asked Questions page at http://www.history.navy.mil/ (although it has since been removed):

> The "Bermuda Triangle" or "Devil's Triangle" is an imaginary area located off the southeastern Atlantic coast of the United States of America, which is noted for a supposedly high incidence of unexplained disappearances of ships and aircraft. The apexes of the triangle are generally believed to be Bermuda; Miami, Florida; and San Juan, Puerto Rico. The US Board of Geographic Names does not recognize the Bermuda Triangle as an official name. The US Navy does not believe the Bermuda Triangle exists.

The US Navy had already lost so many men there that it warranted a statement, although this did little to drown out the stories. There had never been an explanation as to how 306 crew vanished along with their ship, the USS *Cyclops,* in 1918. The most famous aviation disappearance, however, was the loss of fourteen crew in 1945 when Flight 19 inexplicably disappeared after a routine training exercise from Fort Lauderdale airport.

Fort Lauderdale airport started as a 9-hole golf course and became Merle Fogg Airport in 1929. The US Navy commissioned the airport at the start of the war and renamed it Naval Air Station Fort Lauderdale in 1942. It became the main training base for Naval Aviators and enlisted naval air crewmen. In 1943, Ensign George H. W. Bush arrived there for pilot training, becoming the Navy's youngest pilot and later the 41st President of the United States.

It was a few years later at Fort Lauderdale where our mystery starts.

At the end of 1945, the war was over: Hitler was dead, the Germans had surrendered, Americans had dropped an atomic bomb over Hiroshima and the Japanese Emperor Hirohito had accepted the terms to end the war: an unconditional surrender. At Naval Air Station Fort Lauderdale, however, the training for war still continued.

Flight 19 was a squadron of five TBM Avengers: a single engine aircraft manned by three crew (pilot, turret gunner and radioman/bombardier) designed by General Motors for strikes on ships, using aerial torpedoes. They were popular in World War II, when it was found that ships could evade ship-to-ship torpedoes which only travelled at about 37 miles per hour (59 km/h) underwater. In contrast, a torpedo launched from the air could travel over 1,000 miles per hour (1,600 km/h).

By the time of our story, the Avengers were mass-produced by General Motors. This is the aircraft associated with "Rosie the Riveter" after General Motors worker Rose Hicker.

Rose Hicker set a production record by drilling nine hundred holes and thirty-three hundred rivets into the tail end of an Avenger in a single six-hour shift; however she was not actually the woman shown in the famous poster. That's one mystery that was solved in 2016, when a scholar found a captioned photograph which was clearly the inspiration for the poster. The 1942 photograph showed Naomi Parker Fraley, 18, at a machine shop at a Naval Air Station. She was working at her industrial lathe, her hair tied back in a bandanna for safety, when she was photographed for a newspaper article about the war effort.

On the 5th of December in 1945, Flight 19 was booked for a

routine navigation exercise. Flight 19 consisted of five aircraft: FT-28, FT-36, FT-81, FT-3 and FT-117.

"We Can Do It!" by J. Howard Miller was made as an inspirational image to boost worker morale.

FT-28 was flown by the instructor and was an Avenger TBM-3D, the other four were all Avenger TBM-1Cs, the difference being that the 3D had increased fuel capacity and centimetric radar in the radar dome on the starboard wing leading edge.

There were 14 flight crew spread across the five bombers, all Navy or Marines, most of whom had at least 300 hours flying time in the air.

Flight leader and training pilot Lieutenant Charles C. Taylor was leading the navigation exercise with four trainee pilots. Taylor had been in the Navy for six years, with 10 months flying combat missions in the South Pacific. In January 1945 he transferred to Miami to work as a flight instructor. When he came to Fort Lauderdale, he had 2,000 flight hours logged. It was his first time flying this route.

For the rest of the crew, this was the third of a set of three navigational exercises, the last that the pilots needed before graduating. For the gunners and radiomen, it was advanced combat aircrew training. The fifteenth crew member asked to be excused, as he already had the required number of hours, which meant that one of the aircraft was short a gunner.

The training flight was booked for 13:45 local time but Taylor was late that day, apparently having asked if he could be relieved of the training flight. There were no other instructors available to take his place, so he carried on to the briefing room to speak to the crew.

Taylor briefed the trainees with the weather, described as "favorable, sea state moderate to rough" with scattered clouds and a forecast of rain. Then he briefed them on the flight: a three-hour exercise known as "Navigation Problem No. 1". This was a dead-reckoning exercise for a triangular flight plan.

A different pilot was to be the leader for each leg of the flight, with Lt Taylor flying at the rear so that he could grade the pilots on their performance. The first leg was to depart the Florida coast heading east to practise bombing runs over a shallow coral reef in the Florida Keys. Then, they were to continue on the same heading for 67 miles before turning north. On this heading, they would cross over Grand Bahama, the northernmost island of the Bahamas. From there, it was a direct flight south-west back towards Florida before crossing the coastline and heading south to return to Fort Lauderdale.

The preflight checks showed that the TBM Avengers were flight-ready: the fuel tanks were full, the survival gear was on board and the instruments were checked. Each aircraft had all the necessary equipment, except for clocks. The 24-hour clocks which had been fitted to the Avengers were easily removed and apparently they were popular as souvenirs. They were expensive and, after the war ended, the Navy stopped replacing them, with the result that none of the five avengers had accurate clocks in them. However, the pilots all had wristwatches which they could use for the dead reckoning calculations, so the missing clocks weren't seen as a big deal.

The five bombers of Flight 19 finally took off at 14:10 local time, twenty-five minutes late and not quite half an hour behind Flight 18 which was carrying out the same navigation exercise. At 14:30, they had arrived at the coral reefs and made low level passes to release bombs on the wreckage of the SS *Sapona*. We know this because the tower at Fort Lauderdale overheard a conversation from the squadron:

"I've got one more bomb."

"Go ahead and drop it."

At 15:00, the captain of a fishing boat says that he was in that general area when he looked up and saw the aircraft overhead, heading east. This is the last confirmed sighting of the squadron.

About 40 minutes later, a senior flight instructor with call sign FT-74 was taking his students out on the same navigation exercise when he heard an unidentified transmission. An unidentified man was transmitting on the same frequency and asking someone named Powers what his compass read. He repeated the question a few times and then someone, presumably Powers, responded with "I don't know where we are. We must have got lost after that last turn."

The senior flight instructor contacted Fort Lauderdale to say that either a boat or some planes were lost. Then he called out on the same frequency. "This is FT-74, plane or boat calling 'Powers' please identify yourself so someone can help you."

There was no response. But then the same voice sounded again, asking the others if they had any suggestions.

The senior flight instructor tried again and this time, the voice identified himself as FT-28, the aircraft flown by Taylor, the instructor of Flight 19. The senior flight instructor asked what the trouble was.

"Both my compasses are out and I'm trying to find Fort Lauderdale, Florida. I am over land but it's broken. I am sure I'm in the Keys but I don't know how far down and I don't know how to get to Fort Lauderdale."

The senior flight instructor knew Fort Lauderdale well. He gave Taylor clear instructions from the Keys. "Put the sun on your port wing if you are in the Keys and fly up the coast until you get to Miami. Fort Lauderdale is 20 miles further, your first port after Miami. The air station is directly on your left from the port. What's your present altitude? I will fly south and meet you."

It may have been Taylor's first time on this navigation exercise, but he'd transferred from Miami, so he should have been able to find his way back. It must have been embarrassing to have to ask for help, let alone have another aircraft lead him home. In any event, he is said to have sounded more confident when he responded. "I know where I am now. I'm at 2,300 feet. Don't come after me."

The senior flight instructor decided to head that way anyway and see if he could find the squadron.

Taylor called again. "We have just passed over a small island. We have no other land in sight." This meant that they couldn't possibly be over the Keys as he would have hit the peninsula of Florida. Taylor must have realised this. "Can you have Miami or someone turn on their radar gear and pick us up? We don't seem to be getting far. We were out on a navigation hop and on the second leg I thought they were going wrong, so I took over and was flying them back to the right position. But I'm sure, now, that neither one of my compasses is working."

"You can't expect to get here in ten minutes. You have a 30- to 35-knot head or crosswind. Turn on your emergency IFF gear."

The IFF (Identification Friend or Foe) transmitter could be used to triangulate the flight's location. Air-Sea Rescue Task Unit Four at Fort Everglades heard the interaction; however, they did not have direction-finding gear. They contacted Fort Lauderdale for help but they couldn't see FT-28 on radar although the IFF transmitter should have made the aircraft much more visible. They contacted Naval Air Station Miami to see if they had FT-28 on radar but they, too, could not see the aircraft. Word spread. Eventually, over twenty land facilities were contacted to attempt to pick up the lost flight on radar or with direction finders.

The Air-Sea Rescue Task Unit Four suggested that Taylor have another pilot in the squadron, a wingman with a good compass, take over the lead. The response from FT-28 was curt: Roger. The unit and FT-74 picked up fragments of conversation between the flight leader and the students, in which they appeared to be discussing their estimated position and headings. They did not appear to resolve the situation nor did any other aircraft take the lead.

A different aircraft in the flight, FT-117, radioed saying, "We're not sure where we are. We think we must be 225 miles east of base. It looks like we are entering white water."

Another voice said "We're completely lost."

The senior flight instructor, FT-74, was struggling to maintain contact. "Your transmissions are fading. Something is wrong. What is your altitude?" A weak transmission came back from FT-28. "I'm at 4,500 feet." That was the last message that FT-74 picked up as a relay burned out in his radio. He heard only silence on all frequencies. Frustrated, he returned back to base. In retrospect, the radio failure may have been the final nail in the coffin appearing around the aircraft of Flight 19.

After the senior flight instructor landed back at Fort Lauderdale, he told the duty officer what he'd heard and that he believed that he knew where the aircraft were.

As FT-28's transmissions were fading, Taylor believed that he must have been heading away from him, so FT-28 was flying north while FT-74 was heading south. "I believe at the time of his first transmission, he was either over the Biminis or Bahamas. I was about 40 miles south of Fort Lauderdale and couldn't hear him any longer."

The flight officer denied the senior flight instructor's request to go out and lead Flight 19 back to safety. He contacted Air Sea Rescue Task Unit 4 and told them to instruct Flight 19 to fly 270 degrees (west) and then, on the basis that there was a problem with the compasses, told him to fly towards the sun, which must have been low in the western sky by then.

Standard Navy protocol for aircraft that had lost their bearings was to head east if over land and west if over sea, so it should have been instinctive for the pilots to fly west once they no longer had any land in sight. A transmission from FT-28 appears to back this up: "One of the planes in the flight thinks if we went 270 degrees we could hit land."

The operations officer at Fort Lauderdale also wondered if the flight must be lost over the Bahama Bank. He already had a pilot ready to go but had held off, hoping for better information about where to send it. Now that he thought he knew where the Avengers were, he wanted to send the plane on an easterly course towards them. If communications improved as the aircraft continued, they could establish a relay and guide the aircraft towards land.

But Taylor disagreed. "We are heading 030 degrees for 45 minutes, then we will fly north to make sure we are not over the Gulf of Mexico." Contradicting both those trying to help him and the standard operating procedure seems crazy, but Taylor knew how far they'd gone on their navigational exercise before going wrong. He was sure that they were overflying the Gulf of Mexico, which meant that flying north-east would take them back to Florida.

Without clear information as to where Flight 19 might be and with bad weather predicted, the plane at Fort Lauderdale remained on the ground, waiting to see if the radio stations could get a fix on the IFF transmitter.

Air Sea Rescue Task Unit 4 heard Taylor transmit to the other Avengers. "All planes in this flight join up in close formation. Let's turn and fly east. We are going too far north instead of east."

Clearly not everyone was convinced. The responses were frustrated.

"If we'd just fly west, we would get home."

"Head west, dammit!"

West would have been the correct direction if the islands they had seen were part of the Bahamas rather than the Keys. Some of the crew, at least, believed that they'd overflown the Bahamas rather than ending up in the Gulf of Mexico, although it's unclear how the squadron could have ended up so confused about their position.

No further conversation was heard but presumably the argument had continued. After eight minutes of flying east, Taylor contacted Port Everglades again to say he'd decided to go west instead. "I receive you very weak," he said. "We are now flying 270 degrees. We will fly 270 until we hit the beach or run out of gas."

The transmissions were rapidly becoming weaker and garbled. Port Everglades asked Taylor to switch to 3,000 kilocycles (modern term: kilohertz). This was the search and rescue frequency, which allowed for a clearer and static free communication. His response was unexpected: he refused.

Here's an unverified version of the transcript; I could only verify the final line, which is quoted in the report and correct:

Air Sea Rescue Task Unit 4: "FT-28, If you can change to Yellow Band (3000 kilocycles), please do so and give us a call."

FT-28: "I receive you very weak. How is weather over Lauderdale?"

Air Sea Rescue Task Unit 4: "Weather over Lauderdale clear. Over Key West CAVU. Over the Bahamas cloudy rather low ceiling, poor visibility."

FT-28: "Can you hear me?"

Air Sea Rescue Task Unit 4: "Hear you strength three, modulation good. Can you shift to 3000 kcs? Over. FT-28, please change to 3000 kcs. . . . shift to 3000 kcs. Over."

FT-28: "How do you read?"

Air Sea Rescue Task Unit 4: "Very Weak. Change to 3000 kilocycles."

FT-28: "Hello, this is FT-28. I can hear you very faintly. My transmission is getting weaker."

Air Sea Rescue Task Unit 4: "Change to Yellow Band channel 1, 3000 kilocycles and give us a call."

FT-28: "My transmission is getting weaker."

Air Sea Rescue Task Unit 4: "Change to Yellow Band 3000 kilocycles and say words twice when answering."

NHA3: "FT-28, Did you receive my last transmission? Change to channel 1, 3000 kilocycles."

FT-28: "Repeat once again."

NHA3: "Change to Channel 1, 3000 kilocycles."

FT-28: "I cannot change frequency. I must keep my planes intact."

This is nonsensical. Of course Taylor could change frequency and should, especially if it meant clearer communications. His concern appeared to be that in changing frequencies, he would no longer be able to speak to the rest of the team but obviously they should *also* change frequency to the search and rescue frequency.

At Fort Lauderdale, the weather was bad and getting worse. The operations officer was worried about sending out another aircraft. He decided that as Flight 19 was now heading west, he would not send out the Lauderdale ready plane. The risk for the single-engine, single-piloted ready plane in the worsening weather was deemed not worth it when no one was sure where the missing aircraft were.

The Avengers of Flight 19 had less than two hours flight time before the aircraft exhausted their fuel supplies. Air Sea Rescue Task Unit 4 continued to monitor their transmissions and reported that the transmissions were becoming stronger. One of the pilots described an island he'd seen through a break in the clouds.

But then, Taylor was heard transmitting to the other aircraft in his command. "Holding course 270 degrees we didn't go far enough east ... we may as well just turn around and go east again." He clearly believed that they had missed landfall. Again, this made sense if they were over the Gulf rather than over the Atlantic and needed to head east rather than west. The transmissions began getting weaker again.

In the meantime, six radio stations managed to pick up FT-28's IFF transmission, which allowed them to get a fix on its position. FT-28 was within 100 miles of 29° N 79° W which meant the aircraft was north of the Bahamas and appeared to be over 200 nautical miles (230 miles, 370 km) east of the Florida coast. The senior flight instructor had been correct: they needed to fly west to find Florida.

All stations were alerted and as the dusk drew in, they all turned on their lights and beacons, hoping to give Flight 19 something to focus on in the darkness. However, no station was able to receive any communications from Flight 19 by then and for whatever reason, they didn't broadcast the information blind, although there could have been a chance of the squadron picking up the signal. So although there was now an approximate location for Flight 19, one that meant that Flight 19 needed to fly further west to reach land, no one managed to get this message to them.

Multi-engine search aircraft were dispatched from stations all along the Florida coast, hoping to determine where Flight 19 was.

Another garbled transmission came through: "All planes close up tight . . . we'll have to ditch unless landfall . . . when the first plane drops below 10 gallons, we all go down together."

By now, the sun had set. The British tanker *Empire Viscount*, was at that time passing through the area north-east of the Bahamas on its way to Fort Lauderdale. The captain reported tremendous seas and winds of high velocity in the area. In the dark, in that weather, Flight 19 had little or no chance of surviving a ditching at sea.

There is evidence that one of the Avengers broke away from the formation, defying regulations, and started flying west toward the coast. However, no trace of that aircraft or its three-man crew were ever found either.

Now everyone knew that the situation was critical: the Avengers had twenty minutes of fuel left.

They almost certainly could not make it to land. More aircraft were dispatched in hopes of finding them quickly for a rescue.

Two Martin PBM Mariner seaplanes, twin-engine patrol bomber flying boats, were dispatched from Naval Air Station Banana River (now Patrick Air Force Base) carrying radar equipment. They were instructed to fly towards the last estimated position and to conduct a radar and visual search there as well as standing by on the frequency in hopes of another broadcast. The sky was dark and overcast by now with occasional showers and high winds.

Twenty minutes after departure, one of the seaplanes radioed the tower to say that they were nearing Flight 19's last assumed position.

And here's where the Bermuda Triangle really took on the qualities of a nightmare. That was the last heard of the PBM. Crew on an oil tanker in the area reported that they saw an explosion in the air and what appeared "to be an airplane falling". An aircraft carrier in the area investigated the report and confirmed that they found an oil slick and twisted debris in the rough sea but of the three aviators and ten crew on board there was no sign.

> At present, passing through a big pool of oil. Stopped, circled area using searchlights, looking for survivors. None found.

The remains of the PBM, other than the oil slick and possible debris, was never found. The investigation focused on gas fumes and smoking regulations: the PBM was nicknamed “the flying gas tank” and there were strict regulations enforcing no smoking on board. They did not come to any fast conclusion. To this day, no one knows what happened to the PBM. The final military report explains only that the loss was caused by an explosion.

That night, one further transmission was picked up by the tower at Opa-locka airport, north of Miami, which sounded like the letters FT, the beginning of the call sign for the aircraft in Flight 19. However, they were not able to make out anything else. Assuming that this was from one of the lost pilots, it was the last transmission received.

At 20:13, the rescue boat patrolling off the coast of Miami contacted Port Everglades to say they had not been able to make contact with the missing aircraft. The fuel supply of the Avengers would have been exhausted at 20:00—if they hadn’t heard from the missing airmen by now, they were unlikely to. The search was called off for the night; the dark and stormy Atlantic was too dangerous and the chance of finding the ditched aircraft was slim.

The following morning a further search effort was launched which swiftly grew into the biggest rescue effort of peacetime. The Navy ordered 248 aircraft to take flight along with 18 surface craft to scour the area where they had triangulated the location of FT-28. Over the next five days, the search covered over 200,000 square miles (500,000 square km) of the Atlantic Ocean and Gulf of Mexico. They also combed Florida’s interior, desperate to make sense of what had happened to the squadron. The Air Force, the Coast Guard and the British Royal Air Force all joined in. For five days, they searched, hoping at least to find the wreckage, but no one ever saw another trace of the five aircraft and 14 crew.

It was this loss that fuelled the stories of the “Bermuda Triangle”, as it was impossible to make sense of the sequence of events that had led to the loss of all men. Flight 18 departed less than half an hour before on the same navigation exercise, but experienced no issues and returned safely despite the rain and rough seas. The weather did not seem to account for what had gone wrong.

The idea that a highly competent pilot with 2,000 flight hours and combat behind him could become so lost was difficult to believe. Further, his refusal to change to the search and rescue frequency to allow for a clearer transmission was nonsensical: all of the aircraft could have switched frequencies, allowing them to continue to speak to each other.

And then there were the apparent equipment failures. Multiple compasses all failing during the same short flight seems unlikely. One theory is that they must have encountered strong electromagnetic disturbances which interfered with their compasses; another, that the compasses were right but that Taylor and the other flight crew simply didn't believe what they said. Added to this, each Avenger was also equipped with a radio homing device but none of the flight crew used their receivers for guidance to the air station.

The crews' actions simply didn't make sense.

To add fuel to the fire, the board of investigation's report was not released but instead remained strictly classified for over thirty years. Some believe that was to cover-up the inefficiency of the search and rescue effort when it first became clear that Flight 19 was in trouble. Others insist that it was to hide evidence that Flight 19 had been captured or destroyed by extraterrestrials.

It's true that the initial response to the emergency was slow and there is some later evidence that the search over the following five days may not have been as thorough as it could have been.

The following quote is from Historynet's article on the subject:

> During the search, Captain J.D. Morrison, an Eastern Airlines pilot, saw red flares rising into the night sky while flying 10 miles south of Melbourne, Fla. The airline pilot knew that they were coming from a small island, of which there were hundreds in that area. Captain Morrison agreed to lead a team to the site, where he witnessed the Navy's procedure for a careful search of the area. A careful search consisted of a single

> helicopter that flew three passes over one island that was surrounded by marshy terrain. No ground units were involved in the effort, and the thick marshes could have easily prevented searchers from locating any of the airmen who might have crashed in that area—especially if they were unconscious or unable to signal for help. The board criticized the individuals who had been in charge of search operations—commentary that ultimately resulted in the demotion of several high-ranking officers, including one admiral.

However, the search didn't stop after those five days, or even that year. In the decades since the loss, there have been multiple attempts to find the wreckage of Flight 19, and areas such as this have been searched. To this day, the remains of the five aircraft have yet to be found, and certainly are unlikely to be found on any of those islands after all this time. Since the initial disappearance, a number of private searches have been instigated, none with any success.

In any event, the 500-page military report does not reveal much on either subject. The Navy Board of Investigation report concluded that Flight leader Lt Charles C. Taylor mistakenly believed that the small islands they had flown over were the Florida Keys, thus that his flight was over the Gulf of Mexico and Florida was to the north-east. The report concludes that, in fact, Taylor had passed over the Bahamas as scheduled and thus lead his squadron north-east over the Atlantic. There is no sensible explanation as to how they could have become so completely turned around or why a group of competent and experienced airmen would find a routine flight such a struggle.

In the original version of the report, Taylor was found guilty of *mental aberration*. This was later removed and the report conclusion amended to *cause unknown* after Taylor's mother argued that as the Navy had neither the five aircraft or any of the fourteen bodies as evidence, it was unreasonable to blame her son for the loss of them. Certainly, their conclusion does not appear to have been well established, as there is no argument for what type of aberration this could be or any precedent that Taylor might have suffered from mental issues at all.

In 1963, a hunter near Sebastian, Florida discovered what he believed were the remains of a naval aircraft with two bodies inside. He reported this to the Navy who recovered the wreckage and the human remains. The hunter said that, at the time, he was told that the aircraft was probably one of those from Flight 19 but this has never been confirmed by the Naval authorities. In fact, the US Navy has not released any information about the bodies or the aircraft. They also refused a Freedom of Information request submitted in 2013 by Jon Myhre, who has spent 30 years researching the strange loss.

Since then, there have been a few discoveries of aircraft wreckage in the area but none has been confirmed as Flight 19.

The oddest discovery was off the coast of Fort Lauderdale in 1991, when a research ship searching for sunken galleons and treasure discovered the wreckage of five World War II planes standing upright on the ocean floor, as if they were in loose formation. All five of the aircraft were within a mile of each other and the photographs showed that four of the aircraft cockpits were open and empty. The Navy blocked the salvage, claiming ownership of the find as the aircraft were federal property. As a part of this, they confirmed that no other group of five TBM Avengers had been lost, so it seemed clear that the treasure hunters had finally found the missing Flight 19.

The ship continued to photograph the aircraft. Unfortunately, these proved that the find was not what it seemed. The captain confirmed that the photographs showed that the registration numbers on the aircraft did not match those registrations of Flight 19. This was later confirmed through the engine serial numbers.

> “We are in the unenviable position of telling you that we`re now quite certain that the five aircraft we found are not those of Flight 19, but in fact are five other aircraft.”

So the supposed solution to the mystery only put forward a further mystery: Why were these five Avenger TBMs at the bottom of the sea and how could it be that the Navy did not know anything about them?

The official explanation is that these five aircraft were declared unfit for maintenance/repair or obsolete and, as was commonly the case in the 1940s, had simply been dumped at sea for easy disposal. A BBC documentary on the Bermuda Triangle claimed that the five aircraft head been traced with the result that they had crashed on four different days, with it being just coincidence that they ended up in the same area of the seabed and seemingly facing the same direction. There's a murky photograph in which one can just about make out FT-87 on the tail, which ditched on the water after a fuel issue, floating long enough for the crew to escape the cockpit. The other four were never identified, nor how all five managed to come together to rest in formation on the seabed.

It's somehow not surprising that the most recent update is a new mystery instead of an explanation of an old mystery. When it comes to the Bermuda Triangle, that seems only fitting. The five Avengers of Flight 19 were certainly not the last aircraft to have disappeared in this area and it was just a few years later when another mysterious case arose, with another airman acting incomprehensibly on what should have been a routine flight.

1948

The Bermuda Triangle Strikes Again

IT SEEMS ODD to reference the Bermuda Triangle a second time because, in 1948, it still wasn't known as such. The very first direct reference to the mysterious and dangerous Bermuda Triangle, which appeared to be swallowing ships and aircraft whole, was made in an article by Edward Van Winkle Jones, a Miami Associated Press Writer. *Sea's Puzzles Still Baffle Men In Pushbutton Age* was published in 1950.

> DAT OLE DEBBIL SEA has shrouded in riddles the fate of 135 persons who flew or sailed the Atlantic in recent years. Modern man with his pushbutton miracles has no clue to what happened to those who were swallowed without trace in the loss of ships and planes indicted on this map. —Associated Press

However, it was already clear at the time that something odd was happening when a passenger flight, cruising along the bottom of the as-yet-undefined triangle, disappeared; one of three DC-3s to vanish in the area.

The Douglas DC-3 was a large, fixed-wing propeller-driven airliner which revolutionized air transport with its cruise speed of over 200 miles per hour or 330 km/h and range of 1,500 miles or 2,400 kilometres—faster and further than the transport aircraft of the time.

Airborne Transport offered a scheduled passenger service between Miami, Florida and San Juan, Puerto Rico. The aircraft was considered one of the safest of the time, a Douglas DC-3, registration NC-16002, and was leased to Airborne Transport, Inc.

The DC-3 had just been through an inspection a few days earlier and the CAA Designated Aircraft Maintenance Inspector found it to be airworthy. A line inspection report on the 27th of December noted that a generator voltage regulator was changed. No other unexpected reports or maintenance issues were found.

The maintenance records weren't quite complete, in that work was reported which was never recorded. The Superintendent of Maintenance was sure that new batteries had been installed in the aircraft recently, but there was no record of this installation. A San Juan repair agency said that they'd done repair work on a malfunctioning engine in October of the same year, but there was no record of the work.

On the day of the disappearance, the 27th of December, the DC-3 flew from Miami to San Juan with three crew: Captain Robert Linquist, First Officer Ernest Hill, and one cabin-crew member, Mary Burke. As they came into San Juan, the captain reported that he was having some difficulties with the landing gear, which he said was not locked. They landed normally at 19:40 EST and as the cabin-crew member saw the passengers off the plane, the first officer went over routine checks and the captain contacted the repair facility on site. At 20:30, the captain filed an IFR flight plan for the flight back to Miami. The Captain stated at that time that the aircraft was in good working order.

The repair facility was asked to examine the aircraft batteries. They found that the batteries were discharged, with the water level low. It was simple enough to replenish the water and recharge the battery but that would take several hours, which would delay or even cancel that night's scheduled flight from San Juan to Miami. They already had to cancel the flight plan to deal with the batteries and the captain did not want to delay things further. The captain decided that he would recharge the batteries in flight and instructed the repair crew to simply add the water and return the batteries to the aircraft without charging. The landing gear issue appeared to simply be a malfunctioning light, so he simply reported it and did not wait for it to be repaired.

The decision to carry on without recharging the batteries is an odd one. After the seven-hour flight from Miami, the batteries should have been fully charged. It seems fairly obvious that as the batteries were found “in a discharged condition” when the flight arrived in San Juan, they were unlikely to begin charging again for the flight back. Despite this, there doesn’t appear to have been any attempt to look into the problem further.

Robert Linquist had flown the route before in the DC-3 but only as a co-pilot with Airborne Transport: this was his first time flying the route as captain. However, he had plenty of experience, having flown the same route for another company as well as military flying experience in the area.

In any event, at around 22:45, the twenty-nine passengers booked on that night’s flight were boarded and the aircraft began taxiing to the runway. No new flight plan was filed. The weight and balance records submitted by the flight crew showed that the aircraft had departed with 650 gallons of fuel. Based on this submission and the passenger manifest, the aircraft was 118 pounds (54 kg) overweight when it departed San Juan. It’s true that all of these things are sloppy but none of them, not even the combination of them, can explain what happened to the Airborne Transport flight.

The DC-3 taxied to the end of Runway 27. The tower did not broadcast a clearance for take-off, as they had not yet heard from the aircraft, even though the flight crew appeared to be following their instructions. After further attempts to contact the aircraft, the tower contacted the Puerto Rican Transportation Authority. The Chief of Aviation drove out to the runway to speak to the flight crew.

There, the captain told him that the aircraft’s radio receiver was functioning properly but that the weak batteries meant that the transmitter was not working: they could hear the radio calls but they could not respond. The Chief of Aviation relayed the information to the tower using his emergency car radio. He told the captain that if they stayed in the local area until they could contact the tower, he would clear them for a visual departure. They agreed that they would remain nearby until the generators produced enough power for radio transmission. Once the aircraft had power, the flight crew could file a new IFR flight plan and proceed to Miami. Both the Chief and the flight crew believed that once the aircraft was in flight, the generators would produce sufficient current to allow transmission.

The DC-3 departed San Juan at 23:03 and circled the area for about eleven minutes.

At 23:14, the flight crew attempted to contact the airport control tower, but the tower never heard the call. The transmission was picked up by CAA Communications, who responded to the aircraft. The flight crew reported that they were unable to contact the tower and so they were now proceeding to Miami on an IFR flight plan.

The flight had only been approved for local area until they were able to transmit to the tower; however the flight crew simply continued on course without further discussion.

This meant that no new flight plan was filed; the original IFR flight plan had been cancelled and with no contact to the tower, they had no means of filing a new one.

The flight crew's conversation with CAA Communications was the last two-way communications established with the flight. San Juan tower and CAA Communications attempted repeatedly to contact the aircraft but never heard another transmission from them.

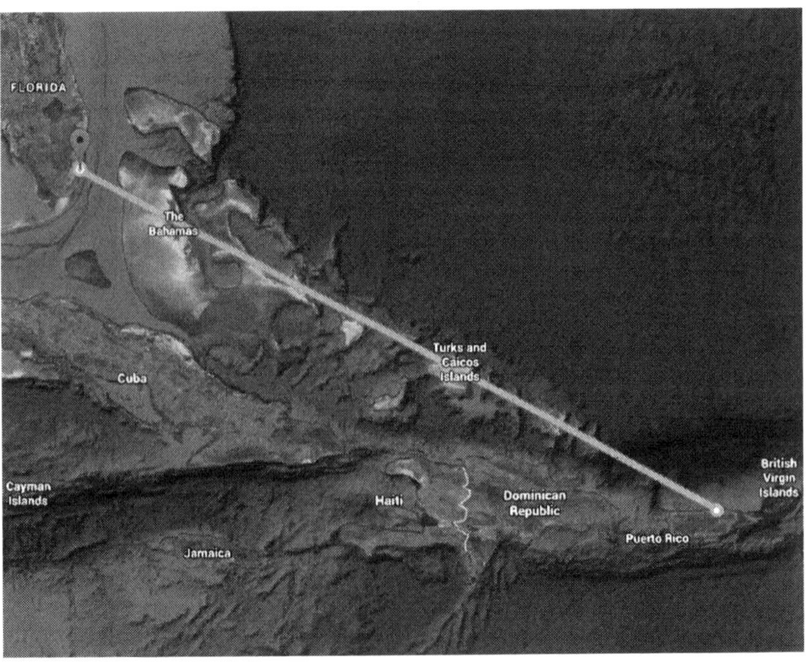

San Juan to Miami as the crow flies (shown on Google Maps).

Fifteen minutes later, the Overseas Foreign Air Route Traffic Control Center, based at Miami, Florida, heard them. They picked up a transmission from the flight crew reporting that they were flying at 8,500 feet and estimated that they would fly over South Caicos at 00:33 and arrive at Miami at 04:05.

The Airborne Transport flight were still about 700 miles (1,100 km) from Miami, so how was it that the Control Center could hear the aircraft and San Juan couldn't? This is a common refrain when it comes to the disappearances in the Bermuda Triangle, almost as if space and time work differently there.

The weather conditions that night were good: scattered clouds at 2,500 feet with visibility 12 miles. The DC-3 had planned to cruise above the clouds at 8,500 feet. Flying over South Caicos Island, the cloud cover increased and extended up and beyond 8,500 feet. However by the time the aircraft was approaching Nassau and Miami, the weather was clear and the aircraft was again cruising over scattered clouds.

When they left Puerto Rico, the wind was forecast from the north-west but during their flight, the wind direction changed to coming from the north-east. This shift was enough to cause navigational issues so Miami Traffic Control broadcast the weather details at quarter past midnight, an hour into the flight. They never received any acknowledgement from the DC-3 and it's impossible to know whether the flight crew ever heard the broadcast.

The flight continued. It was just past four in the morning when a controller at New Orleans Overseas Foreign Air Route Traffic Control Center picked up a routine position transmission from the aircraft, reporting 50 miles south of Miami. This was unexpected as New Orleans is 600 miles from Miami.

The controller relayed the information to Miami Traffic Control Center who had not received the transmission, even though the aircraft was only 50 miles away. Air Traffic Controllers in Miami and in New Orleans attempted to respond to the aircraft but they did not receive a response.

That routine transmission, from a flight crew expecting to land shortly, was the last anyone heard from the Airborne Transport flight. They'd been in the air for six hours and ten minutes and had fuel for seven and a half hours of flight. The flight crew considered that the transmitter was operating normally and that they were on course, expecting to land in about twenty minutes.

It's possible that the change in wind direction as the flight neared Miami could have blown the DC-3 off course. However that would only take them about 50 miles off course. The weather was clear and visibility was good. That drift should not have caused them to miss the Florida coast altogether.

At 08:30, four hours after they were expected in Miami, the Civil Aeronautics Board was contacted, reporting that the Airborne Transport flight from San Juan, Puerto Rico to Miami, Florida was considerably overdue. By now it was clear that they could not still be inbound, as the aircraft would have run out of fuel. If that was the case, however, then the aircraft may have glided to land or at least ditched in shallow waters. There was a good chance that there would be survivors, if they could be found quickly enough.

The United States Coast Guard was alerted and an extensive search begun. The US Navy and the Fifth Rescue Squadron of the US Air Forces joined in the search, as did many civil aircraft. The Government of Nassau, the Dominican Republic and the Cuban government also all participated in the search, covering the area from San Juan, Puerto Rico to Cape San Blas in Florida to Cape Romain, which is north of Charleston, South Carolina. The coast of Cuba, Hispaniola and the Bahama Islands were also searched. The search and rescue program lasted for six days and 1,300 flying hours in the hopes of discovering the wreck and possibly survivors from the crash. Later, they simply hoped to find pieces of the metal wreckage in the shallow water. They found nothing. Whatever happened must have happened quickly and it must have completely destroyed the aircraft or swallowed it whole. Even after half a century of wreck divers and unofficial searches, not a single trace of the missing DC-3 or its 32 occupants has ever been found.

A full investigation was of course started but six months later, when they released the final report, they had to admit they were stumped.

The investigation report was released six months later, in July 1949. As no wreckage had been found, no probable cause was determined.

Another region at the centre of an inordinate amount of mysteries has received a nickname to mark its similarity: The

Great Lakes Triangle. Two of the most enduring mysteries of all time took place in this area and, despite annual searches and dives at the lakes, they have not been solved to this day.

1950

The Great Expanse of Lake Michigan

In 1950 a Douglas DC-4 was lost over Lake Michigan. Despite searches spanning almost seventy years, the wreckage has never been recovered.

Many people still seem surprised at the reality that Malaysia Airlines flight 370 has not yet been found and in fact may never be found. I've seen a number of recent articles arguing that this must mean that the search and salvage is focusing on the wrong area, that the reconstruction of the flight must be wrong. This flight shows how confident we can be of the search area and yet still fail to find the fuselage, let alone the black box holding the recorders.

On the 23rd of June, 1950, Northwest Orient Airlines flight 2501 was carrying 55 passengers and three crew members across the United States when it disappeared into the night. It was the deadliest commercial airliner accident in American history at its time. Although continued concerted efforts have been made to find the wreckage and understand what had happened to the flight, there's never been a breakthrough.

Northwest Airlines (now Delta) was founded in 1926 to fly mail for the US Post Office. Originally based in Detroit, Michigan, the airline's initial route was delivering mail between Minneapolis and Chicago using open-cockpit biplanes. Initially Northwest only offered domestic passenger flights but by 1950, the airline had firmly established itself as the passenger airline for trans-Pacific flights, with staff based in Tokyo, Manila and Taipei. They began to advertise themselves as Northwest Orient Airlines.

The DC-4 was developed by Douglas, after United Airlines worked with them on the prototype of a four-engine long-range airliner. The DC-4E (E for experimental) was flight tested in 1939. It was three times the size of the DC-3 and could potentially fly non-stop from Chicago to San Francisco. The DC-4E never flew commercially but led the way for the smaller and simpler DC-4.

The accident aircraft was a DC-4 which had been manufactured in 1943. It was originally operated by the United States Air Force and then by a Venezuelan postal operation before being purchased by Northwest in 1947. The end of the war meant that many surplus aircraft were sold to fledgling commercial airlines. It was used for a cargo service initially but in 1950, one month before the crash, it was converted to a 55-passenger cargo-coach aircraft.

The DC-4 was in good repair and all of the maintenance records were in order. The flight crew who had flown the aircraft to LaGuardia reported it as "mechanically okay" before going off shift.

Northwest Orient Airlines flight 2501 was a scheduled transcontinental service from New York City, New York to Seattle, Washington. The captain, aged 35, qualified over the Milwaukee-New York segment in 1945 and had flown the route continuously for five years after receiving his qualification.

All times here are given as Central Standard, which was the time zone for the presumed location of the accident.

The weather wasn't good. At 15:45 that day, Northwest released a special thunderstorm forecast.

> Scattered thunderstorms along and east of the cold front, bases at 3,000 to 4,000 feet, tops 30,000 to 40,000 feet with moderate to severe turbulence at all levels in the thunderstorm and moderate turbulence below thunderstorms, advising flights below 10,000 feet to proceed with caution in the frontal zone, anticipating the activity to be at its peak between the hours of 2230 of the 23rd and 0400 of the 24th EST with possible squall line development ahead of the front during the evening.

The flight crew arrived at the Northwest Flight Control Office at about 18:00, an hour before their scheduled departure. They discussed the weather situation with the dispatcher and examined the hourly sequence reports.

The forecast was for thunderstorms in the Detroit-Minneapolis area, with moderate-to-severe turbulence above 10,000 feet and light-to-moderate turbulence at the lower levels. There was also a risk of a *squall line* developing. A squall line is a line of thunderstorms that can form along or ahead of a cold front. Typically, it contains heavy rain, hail, lightning, strong winds and possibly tornadoes. The pressures between the high pressures in the squall line and the low pressures ahead of the squall line cause high winds.

The captain and the dispatcher decided on a cruising altitude of 4,000 feet, which seems bizarrely low for a trans-continental flight by today's standards but was not unheard of in 1950. The flight route had them flying over Minneapolis, Minnesota and Spokane, Washington before continuing direct to their final destination of Seattle, Washington.

At 18:45, Northwest issued a new forecast, but the New York dispatcher didn't receive it until after the flight crew of flight 2501 had left to check the aircraft. As the 18:45 forecast predicted better weather than the 15:45 forecast, the dispatcher didn't see it as making a difference for them and so he didn't advise the flight crew of the update.

The captain requested the 4,000 altitude for the initial routing to Minneapolis but air traffic control were not able to approve it, as they had other traffic assigned to that level. Instead, the final flight plan had a cruising altitude of 6,000 feet to Minneapolis.

Flight 2501 departed LaGuardia airport at 19:31 that evening with two flight crew and one cabin-crew member. There were 55 passengers on board, including two families travelling with their children and three pregnant women. One passenger was so late, they'd already closed the cabin door . . . and then opened it again to let him on. The cabin-crew member passed out pieces of Wrigley's Doublemint chewing gum before take off.

At 21:33, the Weather Bureau issued a regional forecast for the period 22:00 to the following morning at 10:00. This forecast predicted widespread thunderstorm activity and described the development of a squall line extending from southern Wisconsin eastward into lower Michigan and moving south. The southern edge of the squall line was located west of Benton Harbor.

Passenger in a Douglas DC-4.

Regional forecasts are not routinely broadcast and the Flight Advisory Weather Service man did not ask air traffic control to warn flights about the squall line. Although the controllers had the information available, they did not think to do so either. The meteorologist at Northwest was not convinced that the squall line prediction was accurate and so no one at Northwest advised the flight crew of the forecast.

Flight 2501 flew over Cleveland, Ohio at 21:49. The flight crew again requested a cruising altitude of 4,000 feet. This time it was approved. Forty minutes later, the controller asked them to descend to 3,500 feet. An eastbound aircraft at 5,000 feet was experiencing severe turbulence over Lake Michigan and was struggling to maintain its assigned altitude. Air traffic control estimated that the two aircraft would pass each other around Battle Creek, Michigan and were concerned that 1,000 feet separation wouldn't be enough because of the turbulence.

At 22:51, flight 2501 was flying over Battle Creek at 3,500 feet. They reported that they expected to be over Milwaukee at 23:37. The controller incorrectly copied this down as 23:27.

At 23:13, the flight crew requested a cruising altitude of 2,500 feet. They did not mention any reason for this; it may have been in reaction to the turbulence. ATC were not able to approve the request, as there was other traffic.

The flight crew acknowledged that their descent was not approved and the flight continued at 3,500 feet. This was the last communication from the flight.

On the other side of Lake Michigan, Northwest Radio at Milwaukee was waiting for the DC-4 to check in. At 23:37, he began to become concerned. This was actually the correct time the aircraft was expected to overfly Milwaukee and check in. However, according to his notes, flight 2501 was expected to fly over at 23:27, ten minutes earlier, and so as far as he was concerned, the flight crew should have called him by now. He contacted both Northwest and Air Traffic Control to say that flight 2501 was ten minutes late. The mistake seemed oddly prescient; the aircraft was already lost.

Ten minutes later, Northwest Radio still had not heard from flight 2501. Hoping that this was a communications failure, the controller broadcast that the DC-4 should circle the range station at Madison, Wisconsin if its radio transmitter was inoperative. There was no response.

All CAA radio stations in the Chicago-Minneapolis area attempted to contact the flight on all frequencies.

Northwest then contacted Chicago air traffic control. At 23:58, Chicago ATC alerted the air-sea rescue facilities in the area, including the Air Force, Navy, Coast Guard as well as the state police of Illinois, Michigan, Wisconsin and Indiana.

By dawn, it was time to face facts: no word had been heard from the aircraft crew. They couldn't *still* be flying; the fuel supply would have been exhausted. flight 2501 must have come down somewhere.

As soon as the sun rose, an intensive search of foggy Lake Michigan and the surrounding area was launched.

The New York Times reported (Milwaukee, June 25, 1950):

> A Northwest Airlines DC-4 airplane with fifty-eight persons aboard, last reported over Lake Michigan early today, was still missing tonight after hundreds of planes and boats had worked to trace the craft or any survivors. All air and surface craft suspended search operations off Milwaukee at nightfall except the Coast Guard cutter Woodbine. The airplane, a four-engine "air coach" bound from New York to Minneapolis and Seattle, was last heard from at 1:13 o'clock this morning, New York Time, when it reported that it was over Lake Michigan, having crossed the eastern shore line near South Haven, Mich. The craft was due over Milwaukee at 1:27 A.M. and at Minneapolis at 3.23 A.M. If all aboard are lost, the crash will be the most disastrous in the history of American commercial aviation. The plane carried a capacity load of fifty-five passengers and a crew of three, headed by Capt. Robert Lind, 35 years old, of Hopkins, Minn. In Minneapolis, Northwest Airlines said the craft was "presumed to be down," and that they were beginning notification of relatives of passengers. In his last report, Captain Lind requested permission to descend from 3,500 to 2,500 feet because of a severe electrical storm which was lashing the lake with high velocity winds. Permission to descend was denied by the Civil Aeronautic Authority because there was too much traffic at the lower altitude.

The first day ended with no sign of flight 2501.

The following morning, the search and rescue operation was expanded to include underwater searches. They used sonar equipment from the surface and sent divers down where strong sonar contacts were made. The lake was 150 feet (45 metres) deep in these locations. But beyond that, the lake bottom was covered by a layer of silt and mud estimated to be a further 30 to 40 feet deep. Visibility was less than eight inches (20 cm). Everyone knew that the chances that they would find the aircraft this way was slight, but they continued anyway. What else could they do?

They dragged the entire area with grapnel, small anchors with hooks (like a grappling iron) to try to pull wreckage up to the surface. They found nothing.

That evening, after eleven long hours of searching, a US coast guard cutter discovered an oil slick on Lake Michigan about 18 miles north-north-west of Benton Harbor, which you might remember was the southern edge of the squall the night of the accident. Meteorological reports confirmed that a squall line was located there at the same time as experts believed that the aircraft had crashed. They finally had an approximate location.

Evidence of the crash began to appear: small floating fragments from inside of the plane. The US coast guard found the aircraft log book floating in the water.

The search continued for another day with no further results. After four days in difficult conditions, with nothing offering any further hope that the wreckage might yet be found, the Navy suspended their search. The Coast Guard and aircraft flying in that area continued to watch for any sign of the missing aircraft but the official search was over.

The only pieces of the aircraft which were recovered were fragments, debris which could float free from the main fuselage: foam rubber cushions, arm rests, clothing, blankets, pillows, pieces of luggage, a fuel tank float, cabin lining, plywood flooring and other wooden parts.

The cushions and armrests were shredded from the impact, which means that the aircraft must have struck the water at high speed.

Then the body parts began to appear. They were disintegrated and impossible to identify. The US Coast Guard officials stated that there must have been a terrible mid-air explosion to disintegrate the bodies so badly. But no sign of fire was found on any of the wreckage fragments recovered.

The popular South Beach was closed after the crash because of the large number of body parts that washed in. Years later, two unmarked grave sites were identified which are believed to hold the remains of the flight-crash victims which washed to shore. They were buried quickly and quietly as only small pieces were found, no intact bodies. One is a mass grave in a cemetery near St Joseph and the other at Lakeview Cemetery in South Haven. Both sites now have markers in the memory of the victims.

The only debris offering any information about the flight was a plywood oxygen bottle support bracket. The bracket had been installed on the forward left side of the fuselage, which meant that the impact force which ripped it off must have been forward, downward and to the left.

The Tribune quoted an unknown source from Douglas Aircraft Company speculated that perhaps the aircraft had turned onto its back. I had never heard of such a thing but the man told the newspaper that there were eight cases of this happening in high winds. He explained that usually the flight crew could recover within 6,000 feet. Flight 2501 was flying at 3,500 feet. If the aircraft was flipped by the squall, they never had a chance.

The only other source of information came from other flights which had crossed the southern Lake Michigan area shortly before and after the aircraft disappeared. They reported moderate-to-severe turbulence and frequent lightning (both cloud-to-cloud and cloud-to-ground). Several flights flew around the storm by flying to the south. Three flights turned back, refusing to carry on into the severe turbulence at the edge of the storm. One of the pilots reported that he had hoped to fly over the storm but found that it extended to over 30,000 feet.

In 1950, this was the deadliest commercial airliner accident that the United States had ever experienced. However, the investigators were not able to gain any further information as to what had happened. The small pieces of evidence showed that the aircraft struck the water with considerable force, but not how or why.

There wasn't a fire or, if there was, it was very local. It's possible that a mechanical failure occurred mid-flight, but the aircraft appeared to be in good condition and there was never any sign of a Mayday call. Normally the flight crew would have reported in if they were having problems so it seems safe to assume that whatever happened, happened very quickly.

The Civil Aeronautics Board, who was in charge of the investigation, could not determine a probable cause.

It's been sixty-six years since the DC-4 vanished and the aircraft has still not been found but, still, there is hope. Every year, the Michigan Shipwreck Research Associates conducts an organised search of Lake Michigan for the aircraft wreckage. So far, they have explored over 600 square miles of the floor of Lake Michigan and discovered nine shipwrecks. However, the 2013 expedition admitted they had exhausted the high-probability search zones; at this point it's more optimism than evidence that keeps the searches going.

The mLive news regularly covers the mystery but the chances of solving it doesn't look good.

> "I'm a bit concerned about this one," said Ralph Wilbanks, 65, an expert in sonar technology who has worked for Cussler for more than 20 years. "Most of the time when we do a search, you are getting closer to it by eliminating places it could be. But with Flight 2501, every time we search an area, we increase the potential for it to be somewhere else. I don't know if we're narrowing this one down."

Even if they find the wreckage, it may not offer any real answers. There's no data recorded, no "black box". In 1950, commercial aircraft didn't carry them. The best find would be to dredge up the four massive 14-cylinder engines to discover if they were still operational when the DC-4 crashed into the water. After all this time and all the man-hours spent searching, however, this seems unlikely to happen.

The way the DC-4 vanished was so inexplicable that some believed that the aircraft must have been kidnapped by extraterrestrials but it was the next mysterious disappearance over the Great Lakes that really received interest from the UFO communities, especially when a diving group claimed they'd found the unearthly vehicle buried in the silt.

1953

THE KINROSS INCIDENT

THE KINROSS INCIDENT is a famous aviation accident which is often cited as proof that the military has had extraterrestrial encounters. The story unfolds in late November in 1953 over the Great Lakes.

The Air Defense Command was activated in 1946 to offer air warning and air defence for the continental United States. The plan was to extend seaward the wall of powerful land-based radar with airborne early warning and control units. Within a short time the Air Defense Command grew from four fighter squadrons to 93 active Air Force fighter interceptor squadrons, 76 Air National Guard fighter interceptor squadrons, several Naval fighter squadrons, USAF and USN airborne early warning squadrons, radar squadrons, training squadrons and numerous support units.

First Lieutenant Felix Moncla Jr was a US Air Force pilot on temporary assignment at Kinross Air Force Base. He had over 1,000 hours of flight time. His last flight was an air defence intercept which was coordinated by the Air Defense Command.

On the 23rd of November, 1953, radio operators at Sault Ste. Marie, Michigan saw something unexpected at St Mary's River. St Mary's River flows between Lake Superior and Lake Huron, marking the border between Michigan, US and Ontario, Canada. Radar operators identified an unusual target in restricted airspace over the Soo Locks, the set of parallel locks on St. Mary's River which allows ships to travel between Lake Superior and the lower Great Lakes.

An F-89C Scorpion jet was scrambled from Kinross Air Force Base to investigate.

The Northrop F-89 Scorpion was an American jet-powered fighter designed for use as an all weather interceptor. The name "Scorpion" comes from the shape of the raised tail. The Scorpion has two engines, six guns (controlled by radar) and two crew: the pilot and the radar operator. The F-89A was a prototype: only eight models were ever made. F-89B entered service in June 1951; however these had considerable problems with engines and other systems and were replaced with F-89C. The problems with the engines persisted and the F-89 was grounded when structural problems with the wings were discovered. The F-89D entered service in 1954, a year after the events of the Kinross Incident.

U.S. Air Force Northrop F-89D-45-NO Scorpion interceptors.

Back to the 23rd of November: the Scorpion F-89C registration 5853 was piloted by First Lieutenant Moncla; Second Lieutenant Wilson was the Scorpion's radar operator. They departed the airfield and flew to the area as requested by the radio operator. But once they were there, Second Lieutenant Wilson reported that he was having problems tracking the bogey (the term for "unknown target" used in the Air Force) on the Scorpion's radar.

Meanwhile, the ground radar operator could see two blips on his radar screen, one for the Scorpion and another for the unknown target. The operator directed First Lieutenant Moncla towards the object, bringing them down from 25,000 feet to 8,000 feet. The Scorpion was flying at 500 miles an hour as they closed in on the unidentified blip.

The operator watched as the two blips grew closer and then appeared to merge into one over the Canadian side of Lake Superior.

The operator believed that First Lieutenant Moncla had flown either under or over the target. At the same time, the Scorpion's IFF (Identification Friend or Foe) signal disappeared. He continued to watch, expecting that the Scorpion and the object would separate again into two blips. Then he became frightened that the two objects had crashed into each other in a mid-air collision.

But neither of these possibilities appeared to be true. The single blip continued on its previous course north over Canada and then vanished.

Ground Control attempted to raise First Lieutenant Moncla on the radio but received no response. The operator contacted search and rescue. He told them that he thought there might have been a mid-air collision, even though he'd seen one of the targets fly away. He hoped that the two pilots might have bailed out before the collision. With their life jackets, they could survive for a short time in the cold water.

The US Air Force immediately initiated a search and rescue operation, asking for support from Canada. The pilot of another Scorpion joined the search and rescue and said that he heard a brief radio transmission from First Lieutenant Moncla about forty minutes after the plane had disappeared from radar. No one else heard the radio call and it could not be confirmed. There was no other trace of the Scorpion and its two-man crew.

All night, US and Canadian search planes circled over the lake. The following morning, boats joined in the search, criss-crossing the area where the aircraft was believed to have gone down.

That day, someone in the US Air Force released a statement: "The plane was followed by radar until it merged with an object 70 miles off Keweenaw Point in upper Michigan."

The Chicago Tribune published the information in the early edition but then Air Force headquarters killed the story, denying that the jet had "merged" with anything.

Neither the plane nor the flight crew was ever found.

The US Air Force official response was that the radar operators had misread the scope. They claimed that the unknown object was a Royal Canadian Air Force aircraft which had flown off course and the Scorpion was scrambled to investigate.

However, the Royal Canadian Air Force denied that they had any aircraft in the area and dismissed allegations that their aircraft was involved in an incident.

The investigators from the US Air Force took a more careful line, theorising that First Lieutenant Moncla may have experienced vertigo and crashed into the lake. They pointed to rumours that Moncla suffered from "attacks of vertigo in a little more than the normal degree" but were unable to dig up any first-hand evidence.

Certainly, the initial internal report implies that some contact had been made with the bogey based on this statement:

> The bogey was not aware of any aircraft in the area, and GCI saw no blips break off from the target. Both pilot and observer are missing and officially listed as dead.

A different explanation was given to family. One of First Lieutenant Moncla's relatives said that the Air Force told Moncla's widow that First Lieutenant Moncla had flown too low while identifying the Canadian aircraft and had crashed into the lake.

The investigative report also stated that the radar blip was a Royal Canadian Air Force aircraft:

> The unknown aircraft being intercepted was a Royal Canadian Air Force Dakota (C-47), Serial No. VC-912, flying from Winnipeg to Sudberry [*sic*], Canada. At the time of the interception it was crossing Northern Lake Superior from west to east at 7,000 feet. This flight was approximately 30 miles south of the intended flight path.

According to the report, the aircraft had been identified but was classified as a bogey because it was about 30 miles off course.

There's no reference to anyone attempting to contact the bogey before scrambling the F-89 for an interception. It could be that US Air Force Personnel were using the unexpected Royal Canadian Air Force aircraft for a mock intercept as a test of the response times.

The investigative report also says that they contacted the pilot of the Canadian aircraft and he told them that he never saw the Scorpion F-89 and did not know that he was the subject of an interception. The F-89 had crashed, the report concluded, for unknown reasons after breaking off the intercept.

Which all makes sense, except that the Royal Canadian Air Force files show no report of an incident involving any Royal Canadian Air Force aircraft in the Lake Superior area on the 23rd of November in 1953. The only aircraft nearby, a Dakota C-47 registration VC-912, was piloted by Gerald Fosberg, who denies that he was off course or ever in US airspace.

In a public letter, he wrote:

> I remember the flight reasonably well, and just checked my log books to confirm the date. It was a night flight. We were probably at 7,000 or 9,000 feet over a solid cloud deck below and absolutely clear sky above.
>
> Somewhere near Sault Ste. Marie, and north of Kinross AFB, I think a ground station (can't remember whether it was American or Canadian) asked us if we had seen another aircraft's lights in our area. I do think I recall them saying at that time that the USAF had scrambled an interceptor and they had lost contact with it. We replied that we had not seen anything. A few days later I received a phone call from somebody at Kinross who was carrying out an investigation on a missing aircraft. I could only tell them that we had seen nothing. That was the last I ever heard of the incident.

This recollection ties in with the initial statement that "the bogey was not aware of any aircraft in the area," and technically also supports the US Air Force investigation report that the pilot of the unknown craft did not know he was being intercepted and did not see the F-89. However, the pilot of the Dakota C-47 is quite clear that he was never 30 miles off course and that he was never told that the missing aircraft had been trying to intercept him.

Unfortunately, we have no record of the radio communications between First Lieutenant Felix Moncla in the F-89 and the radar controllers, so we do not know if he ever made visual contact with the C-47 or some other aircraft.

In case that wasn't all odd enough, five years later Major Donald Keyhoe wrote a book in which he exposed the cover up.

Major Keyhoe had initially been sceptical about the existence of unexplained and unidentified flying objects but, somewhere around this time, he became convinced that flying saucers were real. He wrote a book claiming that the Air Force had evidence of extraterrestrial visitations but were burying the reports in order to avoid panicking the public.

In a later book, based on interviews and official reports from the Air Force, he described the accident and said that he received a phone call on the night of the disappearance. He said that a rumour out at Selfridge Field claimed that an F-89 from Kinross was hit by a flying saucer. He followed up by phoning the Public Information Officer who told him that the unknown was a Canadian DC-3 which was over the Soo Locks by mistake.

When the book was released, the Air Force repeated that the unknown aircraft had been confirmed to be a Royal Canadian Air Force Dakota C-47. The F-89, they said, had definitely not collided with the aircraft. Instead, after breaking off the interception, something unspecified had happened which caused the interceptor to crash.

In 1968, aircraft fragments were found near the eastern shore of Lake Superior. An officer with the US Air Force confirmed that the fragments had come from a military jet aircraft and local news reports speculated that these might be from the missing Scorpion F-89. However, no further information was ever published and the Canadian government do not appear to have any record of the find.

Over fifty years later, the mystery came to the public eye again. In 2006, a well-known UFO researcher received an email which included a quoted excerpt from an Associated Press news story about the discovery of the Scorpion F-89 at the bottom of Lake

Superior. The email claimed that a group of Michigan divers had found it at the approximate location where the aircraft had disappeared from radar. The email also included a link to the website for the Great Lakes Dive Company. The website showed two fuzzy images of an almost completely intact aircraft resting on the lake bed with its nose in the silt, which they claimed was output from a side-scan sonar. The exposed wing had a tip tank and an upswept tail, characteristic of the Scorpion F-89.

The UFO researcher was intrigued, and posted the contents of the email on a UFO Updates website. The news of the discovery of the Scorpion wreckage swiftly spread. Several reporters contacted the Great Lakes Dive Company and spoke to the company spokesman who confirmed the discovery. He told reporters that the sonar images had been made with a fish finder, a sounder used by commercial fishermen to locate schools of fish underwater.

The initial response was excitement that the wreckage would finally answer the question of what happened to First Lieutenant Moncla and Second Lieutenant Wilson in 1953.

The Great Lakes Dive Company spokesman then announced that an unexplained metallic object was found near the aircraft wreckage. The metallic object was half-buried in the silt, with the exposed part approximately 8 by 15 feet. It was said to resemble the bulge often shown at the centre of a flying saucer.

Supposed sonar images were published on the website, showing a fuzzy teardrop shaped object. The Great Lakes Dive Company claimed that this was the UFO that the radar operators had seen, the blip that the Scorpion had merged with.

Journalists began to become suspicious as they delved deeper into the case. It soon became clear that the Great Lakes Dive Company didn't exist outside of these announcements. They failed to find any biographical information or background on the spokesman for the company: all that existed under his name were an email address and a cell phone. Local people involved with shipwreck hunting and maritime history in the Great Lakes had never heard of the spokesman or the company.

Then, three weeks after the discovery, the website disappeared and the spokesman no longer answered his phone or responded to emails.

The International Director of the Mutual UFO Network, the oldest and largest civilian UFO-investigative organisation in the

United States, led an investigation into the claims made by the divers. He could not find any evidence of the original news story supposedly released by the Associated Press; the original news article was a forgery. Neither could he find any records for the Great Lakes Dive Company other than the website which had existed only for a few weeks. He did make contact with the spokesman before he disappeared, but the spokesman refused to give him any information about the company or even the type of vessel they used to take the sonar images.

One would have to be very optimistic to believe that a couple of divers were insanely lucky and found the long-sought wreckage in deep water almost immediately using only primitive equipment. Anyway, the description of the equipment proved that what they claimed was impossible. The side-scan images released could not have been made with a fish finder in the 500 feet (150 m) deep waters where the wreckage supposedly had been found. The images in that water would have required a towed scanner to produce images of that quality in the deep murky water of Lake Superior. The local community and the UFO researchers agreed that the supposed discovery of the wreckage was a hoax.

Meanwhile, the F-89 jet has still not been found. Worse, no explanation has ever been made as to the conflict between the US and Canadian military reports. What really happened that night? By now it's safe to assume that we will never know.

It may seem like military flights are overly represented in this collection of missing aircraft but passenger flights were certainly not immune. It was just a few years later that a Boeing 377 Stratocruiser offering the trip of a lifetime for the rich and famous disappeared at the start of its around-the-world trip.

1957

Romance of the Skies

THIS CASE OF a disappearance over the Pacific prompted the biggest search operation since Amelia Earhart. Unlike most of our cases, the Clipper was found. Well, parts of it, anyway. Sadly, they did nothing to explain what had happened. In the end, the wreckage led to more questions than answers.

By 1957, the mysterious disappearance of the *Hawaii Clipper* in 1938 was no longer at the forefront of people's minds. Pan Am's luxury intercontinental flights continued to be a success.

The original Clippers were flying boats, with the most famous being the luxurious Boeing 314 Clipper produced by Boeing between 1938 and 1941, with which Pan Am inaugurated the first scheduled transatlantic airline service between Europe and America in 1939. Only twelve of the flying boats were built, all to fill the requirements of Pan Am. Nine were put into service and three were sold to the British Overseas Airways Corporation (BOAC). The nine were later sold to the military.

By 1949, Pan Am had put the Boeing 377 Stratocruiser into service. The Stratocruiser was based on a long-range heavy military cargo aircraft, the Boeing C-97 Stratofreighter, which had been developed from B-29 and B-50 bombers. There was no longer a need to land in harbours, as runways were now common around the world, although the nickname for the Pan Am long-range aircraft still stuck.

The big innovation that had come from the B-29 Superfortress was cabin pressurisation. The piston aircraft of World War II often flew at very high altitudes and required the crew and passengers to wear oxygen masks. The Boeing B-29 Superfortress was the first bomber to offer cabin pressurisation, but of course there were no passengers on the bombers, so this was only set up for the crew.

The Stratocruiser was not the first aircraft to offer a pressurised cabin for civilian service (that would be the Lockheed Constellation) but it was still not common. The Stratocruiser's four engines had superchargers which increased power at altitude, allowing for a higher consistent cabin pressure and air conditioning. The Boeing 117 aerofoil was the fastest wing of its time. It was considered one of the most advanced and capable of the propeller-driven transports of the time and also one of the most luxurious.

It had two passenger decks. The main deck could be fitted for up to a hundred passengers with space for an additional fourteen in the lower deck lounge. More commonly, however, the Stratocruiser offered a spacious environment, typically configured for either 63 or 84 seated passengers. For the first-class service, 28 berthed and five seated passengers shared the 6,600ft^3 (187 m^3) of interior space. To compare, the Boeing 737 has about the same cabin size and typically seats 140 passengers.

At the end of World War II, the president of the Boeing company ordered 50 Stratocruisers to be built, even though he did not yet have any customers for them. It didn't take long for them to sell.

In 1945, Pan American World Airways became the launch customer, ordering twenty aircraft in what was at the time the largest commercial aircraft order ever made. The purchase was for US $24.5 million, the equivalent of US $335.7 million by 2018 standards, less than the cost of a single Airbus A380 now.

Pan Am placed the aircraft into scheduled service flying from San Francisco to Honolulu in April 1949. By the beginning of 1950, four airlines (Pan Am, United, BOAC, and American Overseas Airline) were using the Stratocruiser for transatlantic flights and Northwest Orient Airlines (now Delta) offered domestic flights as well as a non-stop from Seattle to Honolulu. By 1956, Pan Am offered flights in the Stratocruiser from California to Sydney.

United's last Stratocruiser flight was in 1954, BOAC retired the aircraft in 1959, Northwest in 1960 and finally Pan Am, who had reduced the aircraft to a weekly Honolulu to Singapore flight in 1960, retired the aircraft in 1961. The piston airliner had been superseded by jets: The de Havilland Comet, the Boeing 707 and the Douglas DC-8.

But those days were yet to come.

In 1947, Pan Am started the first scheduled round-the-world airline flight, which was split between two aircraft. Flight 1, a DC-4, flew the first half of the route, departing San Francisco in the evening and stopping at Honolulu, Midway, Wake, Guam, Manila, Bangkok and finally Calcutta. Flight 2, a Lockheed Constellation, flew from New York to Calcutta to meet it there, where it then flew to Karachi, Istanbul, London, Shannon, Gander and then finally back in New York a week after Flight 1 had departed San Francisco.

In 1950, the company officially changed its name to Pan American World Airways and purchased American Overseas Airlines, bringing their total number of Stratocruisers up to 28.

In the mid-1950s, the Stratocruiser was still in its heyday. Described as "the ocean liner of the air", the Pan Am clippers offered Pullman-style sleeping berths, reclining seats with 60 inches of legroom (modern budget airlines offer half that) and a large cocktail lounge. Champagne and caviar were served to start off the meals, which were served on china plates.

And it was on one of these luxurious aircraft where our story begins. Disaster struck twice on the same stretch of the round-the-world trip: flying over the large expanse of the Pacific Ocean between California and Hawaii. Pan Am Flight 6 and Flight 7 circumstances were so similar that the two incidents are sometimes confused with each other. However, the outcomes were very, very different.

We'll start in 1956, with the ditching of Pan Am flight 6. For once, we'll have a happy ending.

Pan Am's flight 6 was an eastward round-the-world flight from Philadelphia, Pennsylvania to San Francisco, California, stopping in Europe, Asia and the Pacific Islands.

The final leg of Flight 6 was flown by the clipper *Sovereign of the Skies*. The clipper, registration N90943, was a Stratocruiser 10-29, one of eight which had been built for American Overseas Airlines before it merged with Pan-Am in 1950. The 10-29 was easily recognisable: it had round windows throughout the main cabin and rectangular windows in the lower cabin.

On the evening of the 15th of October in 1956, flight 6 was flying the last leg of the round-the-world flight, flying east from

Honolulu, Hawaii to San Francisco, California, a nine-hour flight. *Sovereign of the Skies* carried seven crew and twenty-four passengers (three infants) and 44 cases of live canaries (a total of 3,300 birds) as well as enough fuel for twelve hours of flight. The passengers were given a demonstration of how to use the life jacket and then provided with a folder, entitled "Just In Case," which described the ditching procedures should the Stratocruiser be forced to land on water.

Sovereign of the Skies departed normally that evening and climbed to its initial cruising altitude of 13,000 feet. At the halfway point, as per their flight plan, the flight crew asked for a further climb to 21,000 feet, which was approved. The first officer was flying the plane while the captain performed his duties at the navigator's table. As the Stratocruiser reached 21,000 feet, the first officer reduced the power for the cruise. At that moment, the number 1 engine began to overspeed, the propeller running faster than the design could handle. He reduced the power further and extended the flaps to slow the aircraft as much as possible. He attempted to feather the propeller, rotating the blades so that they were parallel to the airflow to reduce drag, but the blades didn't move. Nothing he did had any effect on the engine or the propeller.

The captain had returned to his seat by then and called to the engineer cut off the oil supply in hopes of seizing the engine. It worked. The engine RPM finally decreased, followed by the sound of a heavy thud. The propeller continued to windmill, disconnected from the engine. The Stratocruiser was now travelling at 150 knots and losing altitude at a rate of 1,000 feet per minute.

The United States Coast Guard Cutter *Pontchartrain* was a 255-foot (78 m) US Coast Guard cutter which had been built as a patrol gunboat for World War II but never saw action. In peacetime, it was used as an ocean station as well as offering law enforcement and search and rescue operations in the Pacific. At the time, it was stationed between Hawaii and California, working as a weather station at a location known as *Ocean Station November* (any ship "on station" at that location became Ocean Station November). *Pontchartrain* had 143 men on board and was there to offer weather information and radio communications and, in case of an emergency, assistance.

The captain contacted *Pontchartrain* as US Coast Guard weather station "November" to report that he might need to ditch the aircraft. He also warned the passengers and asked them to prepare for a possible water landing. (I have to admit, the change in terminology since 1956 made me smile: a water landing sounds so much nicer than a ditching, never mind that 140,000 pounds—63,000 kilos—of two-story aircraft descending quickly was never going to land gently on the rough seas of the Pacific.)

They altered their course to fly towards the cutter and applied climb power to the remaining three engines in order to stop their descent. Three engines should be enough but something else was wrong: the number 4 engine only had partial power, even at full throttle.

It was almost enough. The flight crew found that they could maintain their altitude of 5,000 feet at an airspeed of 135 knots on the three remaining engines, even though one only had partial power. They computed the fuel required to either continue to San Francisco or to return to Honolulu. Either way, it wasn't enough.

The flight crew radioed *Pontchartrain* to confirm that they were going to have to ditch the aircraft. The cutter crew responded with the best heading for ditching, informing them at the same time that the waves were five-foot (1.5 m) swells with the wind at eight knots from the northwest. It was past midnight now and dark over the sea.

Sovereign of the Skies descended to 3,000 feet while the cutter below fired mortar flares and then laid electric water lights to try to illuminate an area for the aircraft to land. Meanwhile, the passengers were fitted with life jackets and given instructions for launching the life rafts. They were moved forward, as the captain feared the tail would break off on landing, and asked to sit bent over with their arms clasped around their legs. The children were placed on the floor to be held in place by their parents' feet.

As they flew over the *Pontchartrain*, scanning the Pacific in the dark, the captain realised that the safest option would be to delay the ditching. The flight crew had plenty of fuel to circle the area, and he decided that they would remain in the air, close to the cutter, until daylight. The light would offer much better conditions and having burned the fuel, the aircraft would be easier to land at slow speeds as well as lighter and more buoyant once on the water. It also gave the crew more time to prepare the passengers. *Sovereign of the Skies* circled the cutter and waited for the sun to rise.

At 02:45, the number 4 engine backfired and lost its remaining power. The flight crew were able to feather the propeller to stop its windmilling. They lost altitude again, now circling only 2,000 feet above the rough sea. It must have been an incredibly tense time for everyone on board. As the hours passed and the fuel burned off, the flight crew were able to climb the aircraft back to 5,000 feet. When the first light glimmered in the east, they began to prepare to ditch the Stratocruiser by flying practice approaches along the heading that *Pontchartrain* had given them for landing.

At 05:40, the captain contacted *Pontchartrain* to say that they were ready. The cutter laid a trail of foam along the ditching heading as a visual marker to help the flight crew align themselves. The captain descended to 900 feet and flew a landing pattern, giving a final warning to the passengers one minute before landing. At 06:15 they touched down at a speed of 90 knots (104 mph or 167km/h). The Stratocruiser drove into the water but a moment later bobbed up to the surface and stopped. The fuselage had broken off behind the main cabin door, separating the seats that had been vacated as a part of the preparations. Passengers ahead of the fracture were hurled to the floor and two children were thrown from their mothers' arms. Amazingly, no one was seriously hurt.

Two 20-man life rafts were launched through the emergency exits over the wing and one life raft through the main cabin door. The passengers and crew followed the rafts out of the plane. One of the rafts did not inflate properly and filled with water. But *Pontchartrain* was already there and pulling the occupants off of the sinking raft and onto the rescue boat.

At 06:30, the captain and the first officer were the last to evacuate the aircraft. All passengers and crew were transferred from the rafts to the cutter only three minutes before the heavy Stratocruiser sank to the depths of the Pacific Ocean.

I said a happy ending, but not for the Stratocruiser. *Sovereign of the Skies* was gone, along with its cargo of canaries.

Without the aircraft, it was hard to prove what had caused the overspeeding engine, but it was not the only case. In at least one other accident an aircraft experienced the same symptoms. In that case, two engines developed uncontrollable overspeeds and the same inability to feather the propellers. The Civil Aeronautics Board, the aviation organisation responsible for the investigation, came to the conclusion that the propeller oil transfer bearing had failed in both aircraft.

Life rafts pull away from the *Sovereign of the Skies* just before the broken craft settles to her grave.

A redesigned propeller oil transfer bearing was designed by Pratt and Whitney, the original manufacturer of both engines. On the 25th of March, 1957, the US Civil Aviation Authority issued an Airworthiness Directive that the use of the redesigned bearing was mandatory for that engine type. Pan Am agreed that all Stratocruisers needed this work done to stabilise the propellers and avoid further dangerous incidents.

One year later, the work should have been complete, with every Stratocruiser upgraded to avoid this dangerous issue. However, the maintenance records at Pan Am are such that it isn't clear whether or not this work was consistently carried out. Were Stratocruisers still flying which had not been fixed?

The crash of Flight 6 would still have been on people's minds a year later when disaster struck a second time. The same aircraft, the same model, the same stretch of sea. Could it have been the same cause?

This time the Stratocruiser was Pan Am clipper #944 (registration N90944) named *Romance of the Skies*. It was the same model, the 10-29, as purchased by American Overseas Airlines and then added to the Pan Am fleet in 1950. Pan Am flight 7 was a westbound round-the-world flight, starting and ending in California. The first leg of this flight was the reverse of Pan Am flight 6: it would depart San Francisco in the evening for the ten-hour flight to Honolulu.

Pan Am Stratocruiser departing San Francisco.

Pan Am flight 7 carried 36 passengers and eight crew. There were four flight crew: captain, first officer, flight engineer and navigator, and four cabin crew. The pilots were experienced. The captain had worked for Pan Am for fifteen years and the first officer for twelve.

The passengers were well-to-do (one had to be to afford a ticket on a Stratocruiser) and included honeymooning couples, the vice president of Renault Auto and the general manager of Dow Chemical.

On the 8th of November 1957, *Romance of the Skies* was scheduled for a lunchtime departure, arriving in Hawaii in the early hours of the following morning.

The Stratocruiser planned to fly at a cruising altitude of 10,000 feet with an airspeed of 226 knots. Its weight at departure was the maximum allowable and they had fuel for thirteen hours. The weather forecast was good and the Stratocruiser departed San Francisco normally at 19:51 GMT (11:51 a.m. local time in California), with an expected arrival time of 05:50 GMT.

At 00:30, the captain contacted the Ocean Station November, located halfway between mainland California and Oahu, with a routine position report. Ocean Station November was again the US Coast Guard cutter *Pontchartrain*. The call was acknowledged and *Pontchartrain* fixed the Stratocruiser's position by radar as 10 miles east of the cutter. A further position report was made at 01:04. It was routine and there was no indication of anything unusual. The Stratocruiser was on course and on schedule. This was about the time that the passengers would have sat down for their seven-course gourmet dinner.

It was also the last time anyone heard from *Romance of the Skies*.

The next position report should have taken place an hour later, at 02:04. But the routine report was never received. The radio operators never heard from the aircraft again. Forty-four other flights were operating through the area, all on the same frequency, and none had heard any calls from Clipper 944.

At 01:34, radio operators noted that they'd not been contacted by the flight, which normally made an "operations normal" report at 34 minutes past the hour. When the Stratocruiser was still silent at 02:04, the next scheduled reporting point, Honolulu and San Francisco both started calling for the flight on all frequencies.

There was no response.

The last clear message received from *Romance of the Skies* was that routine radio call at 01:04 confirming their position: 1,160 miles from Honolulu and ten miles east of *Pontchartrain*.

A massive search and rescue mission kicked into gear. Coast Guard ships, Air Force aircraft and US Navy aircraft carriers with aircraft all took part as they frantically tried to find the missing Stratocruiser.

Five days later, the US Navy aircraft carrier *Philippine Sea* discovered flotsam floating in the water some 940 miles east of

Honolulu but it was far off course: 90 miles north of the aircraft's intended track. The crew pulled bodies and material onto the carrier and were quickly able to confirm that they had found the remains of the *Romance of the Skies*.

The search and rescue operation focused around the new search area north of where they'd expected to find the Stratocruiser. No further debris or evidence was found. The operation was called off the end of the following day: it was clear that there were no survivors.

Investigators from the Civil Aeronautics Board were flown out to the aircraft carrier so that they could examine the bodies and the aircraft debris as soon as possible.

The medical members of the team focused on external injuries but were soon able to confirm that there was no evidence of "foul play" on any of the bodies.

There were only limited pieces of the aircraft, mainly pieces of the fuselage interior trim except for one section of engine cowl support ring, which they found embedded in a floating pillow. They also found mailbags and items from the cabin. No part of the main airframe structure was found. The wreckage caused more questions than answers.

The Daily Mirror wrote a long article trying to make sense of the mystery.

> Unidentified civilian and military air authorities theorized that the plane might have crashed without sending a distress signal because of an explosion caused by broken fuel connection at a carburetor that sprayed gas on a manifold; an inboard engine threw a propeller through the flight engineer's position, cutting all power instantly; a time bomb exploded; an electrical fire knocked out the radio and forced the plane into the sea.

The recovered pieces of fuselage were mostly from the front of the plane, both above and below the cabin floor, with more pieces from the right side of the fuselage than the left.

Weather issues were common over that part of the Pacific but the idea was swiftly dismissed. The ships and aircraft which had been in the area were able to confirm that the weather was as forecast, with scattered to broken clouds and good visibility.

There were no reports of turbulence, icing, lightning, thunderstorm activity or precipitation of any kind.

The investigation had very little to go on. There was no way to explain the location of the crash site, 90 miles off course and flying *away* from the Ocean Station, not to mention the lack of a distress call.

Investigators had precious little to go on with evidence limited to the floating debris and the recovered bodies.

Most of the bodies were intact and fourteen out of the nineteen bodies recovered were wearing life jackets. None of the bodies showed any burns or signs of fire. The body of a senior cabin-crew member was still strapped by her safety belt to the seat, her life jacket fitted over her serving apron. The top of the cabin-crew member's thighs were bruised, as were the captain's, which showed that their seat belts were fastened at the time of the impact.

There had been enough time to react to the emergency and to prepare for a water landing.

Meanwhile, the recovered debris told a similar story. The mail was burned and some of the wreckage showed fire damage, but there was none on the recovered fuselage.

Each charred piece showed a line below which the charring did not occur. That line was a water line: the fire damage was limited to the debris and wreckage that floated on the water. None of the burned pieces showed any evidence of explosive material. This means that one thing at least was clear: the fire started *after* the aircraft impacted the water.

More importantly, the pieces of fuselage that they found showed that the impact with the sea was not violent but instead, that the aircraft had approached the water at a shallow angle.

All the evidence pointed towards an attempt to ditch the aircraft in the sea, much as Flight 6 had the year before.

But then, having decided to ditch, why on earth didn't the flight crew mirror the actions of flight 6, which they surely knew about, and fly towards *Pontchartrain* for a rescue? The Stratocruiser left its planned route and flew away from the ship, in what is a completely inexplicable decision. This turn off could only make a rescue attempt more difficult. There was no weather that could explain such an unexpected turn. There were no shipping lanes or other heavy traffic which could tempt the pilot to turn in this direction. Meanwhile, the flight crew had been in contact with *Pontchartrain* shortly before, a well-staffed ocean station equipped with radio homing, radar devices and rescue equipment. How could it not have been obvious to fly towards it?

Instead, the captain appears to have turned, flying further away from the ocean station and off course, making any rescue attempt more difficult by coming down in a completely unexpected area.

The last clear call was at 01:04 GMT, when *Romance of the Skies* made their scheduled report to Ocean Station November. *Pontchartrain* obtained two radar fixes of the Stratocruiser, which the flight navigator would have used to correct his estimate of his own position. There's no reason why they should have gone astray.

Based on their location, investigators wondered if perhaps the aircraft had sent an emergency message which never got through. The Aeronautical Radio recording tapes were analysed to see if any trace of a call could found in the time period after that last clear call. Initially, the frequency seemed quiet but after playing the section following the 01:04 position report repeatedly, a weak sound was heard on the tapes, one which could possibly have been a transmission. Over three months was spent trying to determine what the transmission sound was or what it might mean. In the end, it was a failure: no one could determine if this was a transmission from *Romance of the Skies*, an attempt to call for help, or something else entirely.

Another dead end.

Then, as now, dangerous cargo was known to be an issue. The cargo manifests were inspected, searching for any explosive or dangerous material. They discovered that a shipment of sodium sulphide was booked in the forward cargo compartment. The shipper confirmed that one pound was in a sealed glass container and ¼ pound in a second container, both padded and tucked into a wooden box. They also found that there had been a package containing radioactive medicine, which had apparently been sealed in a Babbitt metal capsule contained in a hermetically sealed can, which was then placed in a cardboard carton labelled to show that it contained radioactive material.

Neither shipment was recovered but neither was there any proof that they could have caused the loss of the aircraft. The rest of the cargo looked to be routine: passenger baggage, mail, several barrels of tranquilliser and "shipments of movie film".

Expert pathologists were called in: with so little remaining of the aircraft, the investigators could only hope for a clue from the 19 recovered bodies. They found two interesting facts.

First, some of the bodies, including the captain's, showed raised levels of carbon monoxide.

Second, ten of the victims had died from drowning, which meant that they were alive when they were thrown into the water. The conditions of the bodies did not match that of an aircraft disintegrating as it crashed into the sea. The pathologists expected extensive crash-induced mutilation. Instead, they discovered that not only was there time to plan for a ditching but that the aircraft may have almost managed it.

Further tests, including for carbon monoxide poisoning, were inconclusive as the bodies had decomposed too far for reliable results. Also, there had been a recent Navy accident where eight victims had died in a crash into warm seawater. There had not been any in-flight fire but, like flight 7, there was a post-impact fire above the surface of the water. In this case, two of the victims showed elevated carbon monoxide levels, which could mean that the initial tests on the bodies were meaningless and the increased carbon monoxide levels happened after the crash.

More useful were the wristwatches. Five of the recovered bodies had watches still on, which were examined by a "competent watch maker" to see if the time of impact could be recovered. One was still running and continued to show the correct time. Two had stopped at the same time: 27 minutes after the hour. A third stopped at 28 minutes past the hour and had water inside. The final "waterproof" watch was full of water and stopped at 35 minutes past the hour; as the watch showed no physical damage, it seems likely that the watch continued to run for a few minutes as the water seeped in. Using this information, the time of the impact into the water was concluded to have happened at 01:27 GMT, twenty-three minutes after the last radio call.

Progress was made, and yet the evidence recovered from the sea did little to answer the biggest question. Why did the plane crash? Investigators believed they'd narrowed it down to two possibilities: mechanical failure (the aircraft broke) or sabotage (someone broke the aircraft). Answering this question became the focus of the investigation.

It is clear now that the quality of maintenance at Pan Am at the time was not as well documented as it should have been.

There were rumours of cutting corners and a focus on saving costs. The case files themselves have reference to maintenance deficiencies. It's odd that the Civil Aeronautics Board report shows little of this. One source claims that the case files show that the head of the Civil Aeronautics Bureau had been unhappy with the findings in respect to Pan Am's maintenance practises. They had not, he wrote, reprimanded Pan Am for its maintenance deficiencies or done anything to ensure that the deficiencies had been corrected.

The final report itself simply says that the Stratocruiser was believed to be in good repair. The report also says that none of the on-board propellers had ever been reported as involved in an overspeeding incident with no reference at all to the fact that they could not tell whether the mandatory corrective maintenance had been carried out or not.

Instead, the report outlined a completely different maintenance issue. On the 19th of September in 1957, some six weeks before the disappearance, the crew heard a loud noise, like "dropping the navigation stool on the flight deck", while flying from Honolulu to San Francisco. The captain checked the lower nose CO2 bottles and the forward cargo compartment but found nothing amiss.

The captain asked for a tyre check before landing at San Francisco, worried that one had blown out. He extended the landing gear and flew past the tower, where air traffic control personnel confirmed that there was no damage. The flight engineer logged the incident and the tyres were checked. The company inspector wrote, "inspected aircraft and found no damage outside". When crash investigators followed up on this, concerned that the aircraft had never had an internal inspection, the company inspector was not unduly concerned about the incident. He had, he said, inspected the lower nose and forward cargo compartment along with the exterior of the aircraft and was happy that the loud sound was not a cause for concern. "Found you could duplicate loud noise by stepping hard on door between cockpit and cargo. Also loud bang could be duplicated by dropping forward toilet lid. Nothing abnormal found."

This seems to be yet another piece of evidence that the operator's inspections and maintenance were not what they should have been. Instead, the report focuses on whether or not the sound that they heard was meaningful. There were, the report says, 41 flights from the date of the report to the Stratocruisers departure from San Francisco. The pilots of these flights were all questioned and specifically asked if they had heard any unusual noises or other significant occurrences which had not been reported. Nothing of interest came up.

The last pre-flight inspection was started on the 6th of November and was finished on the date cf departure, with all items checked and signed off by maintenance personnel.

One thing to note is that at the time, a clear conflict of interest existed, as the Civil Aeronautics Bureau was a part of the Civil Aeronautics Authority, whose remit included working with the commercial carriers as well as promoting flying to the public. This was eventually resolved through the separation of the National Transportation Safety Board as an independent agency in 1967. In 1957, it could have been difficult for members of the Civil Aeronautics Bureau to point the finger at maintenance practices of a leading air carrier, both for political and public relations reasons.

So that left one other clear possibility: sabotage.

The raised carbon monoxide levels could not be dismissed. If indeed they did happen before the crash, they were hard to explain. There couldn't have been a large-scale fire in the cabin but it was possible that there was a smouldering fire which caused smoke but did not burn the fuselage. Another possibility raised by the report was the "malicious induction of pure CO into the cabin and preferably the flight deck". Without smoke, this would be odourless and could swiftly confuse or incapacitate the crew. This could explain why preparations for ditching were initiated but the aircraft flew in the wrong direction and even explain why the ditching, in good conditions, was so unsuccessful.

But who would do such a thing?

The backgrounds of all the crew, passengers and even Pan Am ground personnel at San Francisco came under intense scrutiny. Investigators found that almost a hundred different people had had access to the aircraft over the previous 48 hours after landing at San Francisco on the 6th.

As a part of this, they discovered not just one but two potential saboteurs.

The first was the purser on the flight, a 46-year-old man who was known to be unhappy with his employer at the time. His wife had died a few months before of cancer, leaving him as the guardian to his step-daughter, with whom he had a fraught relationship. He reportedly showed his father-in-law that he was in possession of blasting powder just a few days before the flight but no trace of it was found on his property after the crash. More damning, he changed his will. One source says he wrote his step-daughter out of the will completely, another says he revised it to say that she was disinherited unless she lived a moral and upright Catholic life. Certainly, he changed his will shortly before reporting for the flight, leaving it in the glove compartment of his car which was parked at San Francisco.

The second suspect was a man who had bought a one-way ticket from San Francisco to Hawaii, supposedly to recover a debt owed to him, but the amount of the debt was less than the price of the ticket. He was discovered to be an ex-Navy frogman, a demolitions expert, with some history of violent responses to confrontation. He'd purchased a $10,000 double indemnity policy just two weeks before the flight, followed by another two insurance life policies which were worth a total of $125,000 to his wife, about a million dollars in today's money. Western Life Insurance of Montana originally held off on paying out on the double indemnity policy, with the staff member in charge convinced that the victim had never been on the aircraft but instead blew it up from afar. The man's body was not one of the fourteen recovered, so it is impossible to prove that he was on the aircraft.

And with that, every trail of evidence ended. Nothing else was found which helped to shed any light on what actually happened on *Romance of the Skies* over the Pacific Ocean that night.

The official report's conclusion starts with the fact that the investigators were severely handicapped by the lack of the physical evidence. They dismissed an in-flight fire, as the evidence clearly showed that the fire damage was only on floating pieces above the waterline and thus caused by a surface fire after the aircraft had impacted the sea. Also, no sign of smoke damage on the interior pieces was found.

The condition of the bodies and recovered material meant that the aircraft must have come down at a fairly flat angle. In fact, the wreckage recovered was damaged in a way that was consistent with other Stratocruisers which had ditched successfully, including Flight 6 from the previous year.

Taking into account the condition of the recovered bodies and that the fire only ignited after they hit the water, it seems clear that the crew had time to respond to the emergency. The flight crew must have had at least some control of the Stratocruiser in order to set the aircraft up for what seems to have been *almost* a survivable ditching. The cabin crew had time to sit down and buckle in.

It's clear that the Stratocruiser broke up as it attempted to land on the sea, drowning its occupants. However, at the time, the sea conditions were favourable for a ditching. One airline captain flying in the same area at the time said that he had seldom seen sea conditions more favourable for ditching. So if the flight crew had control of the aircraft and were able to bring it down in a glide, why did the attempt fail at the last minute?

Which brings us back to, why was there no distress call? Ditching a large aircraft on the Pacific without informing anyone of your intentions and location is not much better than suicide. This is the one area where current technology could make a breakthrough. If we could analyse the Aeronautical Radio recording tapes now, we could almost certainly determine whether the sounds heard were just noise or a weak transmission from the Stratocruiser. But the tapes are gone. The University of Miami archives hold 1,500 boxes of Pan Am records, including all the details from the investigation, but no one has been able to find the tapes.

As to why the captain flew north, away from safety, that's left an open question. One theory is that damage to the aircraft could have caused violent buffeting which could in turn make it difficult if not impossible for the flight crew to steer the aircraft. If they were struggling with both directional control and altitude, it would be logical to focus on controlling the glide towards the sea and giving up on steering towards a specific direction.

For that kind of violent buffeting to happen, there must have been some great disruption to the airflow over the aircraft structure. Examples of this effect had happened before, caused by a propeller blade separating from the engine and striking the fuselage, for example.

The *Queen of the Pacific*, a DC-8, experienced exactly this just a few years earlier. An explosion wrenched the number 4 engine off and the debris struck the rudder. The December 7 1953 edition of the Chicago Tribune published the captain's description of how the vibrating aircraft went into a dive.

> We went from 10,000 to 5,500 feet very rapidly. We were completely out of control. At first we had a severe buffeting and believed that something had wrapped around the tail or damaged the tail section. We had considerable difficulty maintaining control of the airplane.

An overspeeding engine was certainly a possibility. If so, it could cause the propeller blades to separate or shatter. It could even cause the engine to explode. If *Romance of the Skies* did suffer the same fault as its sister Stratocruiser the year before, it's possible that a piece of the overspeeding propeller or engine struck the aircraft as it detached and, if so, it would also be possible the buffeting of the aircraft was such that the captain had no choice as to what direction he flew. But that's an awful lot of ifs.

The evidence shows that there was an emergency and time to respond but there are just not enough pieces to the puzzle to know what type of emergency they experienced. The fact that the aircraft was off-course is hardly proof that the captain couldn't maintain control, let alone demonstrate why. A revised will doesn't prove that a passenger on board purposely murdered the crew and passengers in order to kill himself. A set of new insurance policies by a demolitions expert doesn't show that he sabotaged the aircraft in order to fake his own death.

We could learn so much more if only we could get the wreckage. But despite finding the floating debris, which gives us a good idea where the aircraft impacted the water, the cost of trying to find the remains of the aircraft would be phenomenal. Crossing the earth's oceans remains a dangerous endeavour, even today with much increased communications and fifty years of focus on aviation safety. Like so many of these mysteries, the only chance of finding the truth remains buried under the Pacific.

It would not be the last. Another possible case of sabotage took place over the Pacific just five years later, this time with witnesses.

1962

Friendly Fire or Sabotage?

On the 16th of March, 1962, a Lockheed Super Constellation airliner disappeared over the Pacific.

It was transporting military personnel for the Flying Tiger Line, the first scheduled cargo airline in the US.

The cargo company was named after the Flying Tigers fighter unit, a World War II group of pilots from the US Army, Navy and Marine Corps whose shark-faced fighter planes became an iconic symbol of American World War II combat aircraft. They painted their fighter aircraft with sharks after seeing a Royal Air Force P-40 painted with a shark's face in the No 112 Squadron, who in turn had originally seen the shark face painted on German Messerschmitt Bf110 fighters in Crete.

The Flying Tigers had been involved in a friendly-fire incident during the war, in 1942. During the Burma campaign, the Commonwealth forces were retreating when the Flying Tiger pilots mistook them for an advancing Japanese column and more than 100 men were killed. It's not clear who or what caused the loss of the Flying Tiger airliner twenty years later but it is odd that their namesake may have suffered a similar fate.

After the war ended, ten of the former Flying Tiger pilots and some of the ground crew banded together to purchase cargo aircraft from the US Navy, war surplus that was no longer needed. The pilots and two ground crew provided half of the initial investment; oil tycoon Samuel B. Mosher funded the rest. They formed the Flying Tiger Line, offering cargo services throughout the US as well as transporting supplies across the Pacific to US Troops during the occupation of Japan.

As time went on, the fleet continued to grow. By 1961, the company was well established and became one of the first carriers in the world to offer aerial pallet shipping. Then in 1962, disaster struck.

U.S. Army Air Forces Liberator bomber crosses the shark-nosed bows of U.S. P-40 fighter planes.

Flying Tiger Line flight 739 was a charter flight operated by Flying Tiger Line on behalf of the Military Air Transport Service. The aircraft was Lockheed model 1049H registered as 6921C. The Lockheed Super Constellation transport airliner, known as the Super Connie, was a competitor to the Douglas DC-6 and was popular with the United States Navy and Air Force for transport. The Super Connie required four crew and could be configured to carry up to 106 passengers.

Flight 739 was scheduled with two flight crews (Captain, First Officer, Second Officer, two Flight Engineers and two Navigators), as well as four cabin crew and 96 passengers for a flight from Travis Air Force Base in California to Saigon in South Vietnam, with refuelling stops in Honolulu, Wake Island, Guam, and the Philippines.

Ninety-three of the passengers were jungle-trained Army Rangers, primarily highly trained electronics and communications specialists. The other three were members of the armed forces of Vietnam. The crew were all civilians. The cargo consisted of the passengers' baggage: personal articles and clothing.

The flight departed Travis Air Force Base at 05:45 GMT on the 14th of March 1962 and proceeded normally for the next twelve hours, arriving in Honolulu at 17:44 GMT. All times are given in GMT except where otherwise noted.

The Super Connie was checked and no issues of concern were found. Then the departure was delayed by half an hour after the cabin crew raised concerns about the crew rest facilities on the aircraft. The issues were resolved and the flight departed Honolulu at 20:40.

The next leg proceeded normally and flight 739 arrived at Wake Island at 03:54 on the 15th of March. Some minor maintenance was required but, again, nothing that caused any concern. The aircraft was serviced, the four cabin crew were replaced, and the flight departed for Guam at 05:15. This leg was six hours and the flight arrived in Guam at 11:14.

At Guam, the aircraft was serviced and refuelled. No maintenance was required. The next leg, to Clark Air Force Base in the Philippines, was estimated at six hours and nineteen minutes. The aircraft held enough fuel for nine hours and thirty minutes of flight.

The aircraft departed Guam at 12:57. Guam Air Route Traffic Control Centre established radar contact soon after take-off. The flight crew then contacted Guam International Flight Service Station to request that their departure message be relayed to the Flying Tiger Line offices.

At 13:25, the flight crew contacted Guam International Flight Service Station again to request a change in cruising altitude from 10,000 feet to 18,000 feet. No reason was given for the request and the flight crew were advised to contact Guam Centre. Guam Centre approved the request.

At 13:28 the flight crew reported climbing through 11,000 feet. Guam Centre advised the flight that it was 100 miles west of Guam and that radar services were being terminated.

At 13:33 the flight crew reported to Guam International Flight Service Station that they were 100 miles out and cruising at 18,000 feet.

The last transmission from the aircraft took place at 14:22. The flight crew contacted Guam International Flight Service Station and reported cruising over the clouds ("on top") at 18,000 feet, along with their position from 14:16 and their current estimated position. They expected to arrive at Clark Air Force Base at 19:16 and said that they had 8 hours and 12 minutes of fuel remaining. All of the radio calls were completely routine: there was no indication of any problem or difficulties.

A little over an hour later, Guam International Flight Service Station suffered heavy radio static while speaking to another flight en route to Okinawa. At 15:39, the operator attempted to contact flight 739 in order to receive the now-overdue 15:30 position report. He was unable to establish radio contact.

At 16:00, Guam Centre declared the flight to be in an uncertainty phase (INCERFA) in line with Oceanic Emergency Procedures. This phase level means that there is concern about the safety of an aircraft or its occupants.

An hour passed with no word from the aircraft. The status was upgraded to alert phase (ALERFA). This means there is apprehension about the safety of an aircraft and its occupants.

The distress phase (DETRESFA) was initiated at 19:33 after continuous attempts to contact the aircraft by all stations and aircraft in the area had failed.

The distress phase means that there is reasonable certainty that the aircraft and its occupants are threatened by grave and imminent danger, including lack of contact and the risk of fuel exhaustion. Search and Rescue operations were initiated from Guam and the Philippines.

At 22:27, by which the time the aircraft would have exhausted all of its fuel, Tiger Flying Lines flight 739 and all of its occupants were declared lost.

The fate of the aircraft was unknown but then a call came in from a civilian super tanker at 21:05, while the search and rescue operations were in progress. The shipboard lookouts had seen a mid-air explosion at 15:30 (1:30 a.m. local time).

The crew said that the night was moonlit and clear, with a quarter of the sky covered by small cumulus clouds, evenly distributed.

They first noticed a vapour trail or something similar overhead and slightly to the north of the tanker, moving in an east-to-west direction. At the time, the tanker was cruising on a heading of 077 degrees. The vapour trail passed behind a cloud and then followed an "intensely luminous" explosion consisting of a white nucleus surrounded by a reddish-orange periphery with radial lines of reddish-orange light. The explosion consisted of two pulses, lasting two to three seconds. The crew believed they saw two flaming objects of unequal brightness and size fall, at disparate speeds, into the sea. As they fell, a crew member noticed a small bright target on the ship's radar, bearing 270 degrees at a range of 17 miles.

The captain arrived on deck to see the fall of the slower object before it disappeared into the sea. He estimated its position in reference to a star and ordered the ship's course reversed. They aligned the heading of the vessel with the star and the captain found that the tanker's heading was now 270 degrees, the same as the bearing of the target seen on radar.

The tanker continued to the position of the radar target but found nothing there. They searched the area for 5½ hours but found no trace of wreckage or debris. The crew were unable to establish contact with the US Navy radio stations at Manila and Guam and eventually decided that the explosion must have been some kind of military or naval exercise. The tanker broke off the search and resumed her course.

The approximate location of the mid-air explosion was confirmed to coincide with the estimated position of the aircraft at that time, and no other aircraft were in the area.

The subsequent search was cited at the time as one of the most extensive ever conducted.

No trace of the aircraft or the occupants was ever found.

While writing this book, I was contacted by a member of the 1961st Air Force Communication Squadron, based at Clark Air Force Base in the Philippines. On Sunday the 19th, he and half a dozen others had taken to the skies in a DC 6 to search for the missing Lockheed Super Constellation. They flew at 500 feet for six or seven hours, flying in sixty mile increments separated by two mile turns. They never saw any trace of debris at all, only the occasional splash from schools of large fish.

Along with everyone else, he wondered what had happened to the Super Connie and the ninety-four GIs on board. It was the talk of the Air Force Base at the time ... but no one had any answers. He says that he heard no word at all about the civilian tanker which had witnessed the explosion. Some said the flight had been hijacked to China but those rumours died pretty quick. Eventually, the talk died down. Then, in May of 1966, a flight engineer with Flying Tiger told him that it was well known that the flight was accidentally shot down by a Navy Fighter and that the Navy was fighting off law suits as a result.

Certainly, no technical explanation made sense. Investigators found that although the aircraft was properly certificated and was in airworthy condition, a few weeks earlier, it had exhibited significant power loss to one of its engines after 3½ hours of flight which had not been explained, but, after minor maintenance, it appeared to be in good repair. There were no signs that day of any mechanical issues with the flight. No one had reason to believe that the Super Connie should spontaneously break apart so quickly that the experienced flight crew could not get a message out.

Unless, of course, the aircraft was deliberately sabotaged.

The investigation found that the flight line and ramp areas at Honolulu, Wake Island and Guam were not secure and anyone could enter and access non-military aircraft parked at the airfields. Specifically at Guam, the last stop, the aircraft was left unattended in a dimly lit area for some time.

If the explosion witnessed by the tanker happened, it would have been right at the point when flight 739 should have been radioing in for the next position report. This seems extremely coincidental.

There's another strong reason to believe that someone intentionally brought the flight down. That very same day, an identical craft from the same airport was destroyed. Flying Tiger Line flight 7816/14, said to have been carrying secret military cargo, departed Travis Air Force Base and encountered difficulties several hours later. The pilot reported a problem while on the instrument approach and crashed short of the runway. The main landing gear was torn off and then the aircraft caught fire; six crew members received minor injuries and one was trapped in the cockpit and died in the fire.

Flying Tiger Line stated at the time that sabotage of one or both planes or a "kidnapping" of flight 739 were possibilities but they had no evidence to back up these theories. However, with the loss of the soldiers in one aircraft and secret military cargo in another, it certainly seemed possible that their disappearance or destruction was very useful for some of those involved in the Vietnam conflict, which would rage for another 13 years.

Certainly, Flying Tiger Line's executive vice president was convinced. He later said outright that it was impossible for an explosion to occur on the Super Constellation in the course of normal operation: something violent must have happened.

The Civil Aeronautics Board concluded that the crew members of the civilian tanker most likely witnessed the explosion of the Super Connie. However, as no portion of the aircraft was ever recovered, it was impossible to determine whether mechanical/structural failure or sabotage caused the loss of the aircraft.

Whatever happened must have happened quickly, as the crew never had a chance to alert anyone of an emergency.

In 1988, The Flying Tigers were sold to Federal Express.

As no one has ever taken responsibility for sabotaging the aircraft and the wreckage is unlikely to be recovered, this is a mystery that seems will remain forever unsolved.

1968

The Spy Plane

It wasn't until July 1994 that this story could be properly understood, when a number of top-secret documents were released by the CIA. It is through those documents that we have at least a partial picture of the classified reconnaissance aircraft which were developed and operated in deep secrecy. The designers, engineers, workers, administrators and pilots all kept silent about their roles; the only leaks came from public failures of the aircraft. The disappearance of a CIA pilot in the last flight of one of these aircraft, a spy plane which could fly at three times the speed of sound for more than 3,000 miles without refuelling, has never been explained. But to understand anything at all about it, we have to go right back to the beginnings of the Cold War.

Our story starts in 1943, when the US Army Air Tactical Service Command (ATSC) met with Lockheed Aircraft Corporation. The first German jet fighters had appeared in European skies and the rest of the world was scrambling to keep up. This was four years before the Central Intelligence Agency (CIA) was formed.

The US Army met with Lockheed to discuss the need for a jet fighter to counter German aerial superiority. They needed it fast and they needed it kept quiet.

Kelly Johnson, an American aeronautical and systems engineer, created an experimental engineering department to develop the top secret jet fighter, the XP-80 Shooting Star. With Lockheed in the midst of wartime production, there was no space for his team at the Lockheed facility. Instead, they worked from a rented circus tent in Burbank, California. The project was obviously top secret and staff were warned to be careful who they spoke to and how they answered phone calls. Kelly Johnson's motto was clear: Be quick, be quiet, be on time.

The rented circus tent was next to a plastics factory which apparently stank so much that, one day, one of the team jokingly showed up to work wearing a gas mask. A popular comic strip at the time was *Li'l Abner* by Al Capp, which had a running joke about an old factory on the edge of Dogpatch called *Skonk Works*, which ground dead skunks and worn shoes into a still for some mysterious and unspecified purpose. The combination of the smell and the secrecy of the Lockheed project led Culver, the team engineer, to start referring to the facility as Skonk Works.

One day, the Navy called and ended up on his extension. Culver answered the phone saying "Skonk Works, inside man Culver speaking." His colleagues adopted the name and the secret division of Lockheed quickly became known as The Skonk Works. In the 1960s, the *L'il Abner* copyright holders complained and Lockheed officially changed the name to Skunk Works.

The secret division was a success and soon they had much better accommodation. Some of the circus life must have rubbed off, however: after the attack on Pearl Harbor, the Skunk Works plant and airport were camouflaged with netting, false buildings and fake palms.

The CIA was established in 1947 by President Truman, and tasked with gathering and analysing overseas intelligence along with the capability of "clandestine collection"; in other words, the CIA was not just coordinating intelligence that it received from other government agencies, it was funding and conducting its own intelligence operations outside of standard US Government procedures.

In 1953, US President Dwight D. Eisenhower proposed an Open Skies proposal to Soviet leader Nikita Khrushchev, to allow unfettered overflights by both nations to photograph military installations. Khrushchev refused. The United States began conducting secret reconnaissance flights using British-designed B-57 bombers. However, they only dared fly the B-57s around the border areas of the Soviet Union and even so, multiple bombers were shot down when they were caught overflying enemy territory. The US remained silent about these losses, as they didn't want to admit to the spy operations. The Soviet Union also remained silent, as they didn't want it known that they could be overflown so easily.

What the US needed was a better reconnaissance aircraft, one which could operate at higher altitudes, undetected by Soviet radar and out of the range of Soviet missiles. Having failed to negotiate with Khrushchev, Eisenhower agreed to the development, even while warning that it was likely to go wrong.

> I think our country needs this kind of information and I approve this project of reconnaissance flights. But I am warning you, one of these days one of these planes is going to be caught. When that happens we're going to have a hell of a problem on our hands.

The CIA created the specifications for an aircraft that could fly at 70,000 feet with a range of 1,750 miles and *Project Angel* began. The Skunk Works designed a single jet engine, ultra-high altitude reconnaissance aircraft which officially became known as the Lockheed U-2. US Air Force designation codes uses U for "Utility", so the U-2 fit in with the CIA cover story that the high altitude jet was being developed for innocuous weather research.

By the end of 1954, the CIA had contracted to purchase twenty of the U-2s, impressed with the development so far. Now there was a very specific problem: where could they carry out test flights for the aircraft? They clearly couldn't fly the super-secret aircraft from Burbank's airstrip; the local area was too populated and, besides, the runway wasn't long enough. They needed somewhere isolated, both on the ground and out of the way of commercial and military airways. They needed a runway of at least 5,000 feet. The site also had to be easily accessible and able to accommodate a large number of personnel and storage containers for fuel.

The search initially focused on Air Force bases which had closed or were closing but none of these offered the secrecy that the CIA wanted. The Lockheed chief test pilot and the Skunk Works foreman flew around the US in a Beechcraft Bonanza, telling their families they were on a hunting trip to Mexico, photographing and exploring hundreds of possible sites. Eventually, they decided on Groom Lake in Nevada. On the map, it was grid reference number 51 which is how the site became known as Area 51. The CIA secretly paid for the site which was set up by the Skunk Works. Kelly Johnson said he found envelopes of cash in his home, which he then used to pay for the site. But of course he didn't say anything at the time: the CIA didn't publicly acknowledge the base until 2013, almost sixty years later.

U-2 High Flight taken 20 July 2010 by Christopher Michel.

The first U-2 was loaded onto a C-124 Globemaster in 1955. The Globemaster flew towards the secret desert site not knowing what to expect. The flight crew found themselves flying in complete darkness until they were on final approach, just a few miles out from landing, when the lights suddenly came on and a runway appeared in the darkness.

The Skunk Works engineers reassembled the aircraft, ready for its first flight. The test flight was a success, the aircraft climbed to over 64,000 feet, which was the world altitude record at the time. They couldn't tell anyone.

The stealth plane was deemed ready for action in 1956. It was able to operate day and night at 70,000 feet: miraculous compared to the B-57 which could only reach 48,000 feet. US radar could only track up to 65,000 feet so the CIA felt confident that this aircraft would be invisible as it passed over Soviet airspace.

NACA (the predecessor to NASA) announced that they were using a Lockheed developed aircraft to study the weather and cosmic rays at altitudes up to 55,000 feet. The first CIA detachment of U-2s, publicly referred to as the 1st Weather Reconnaissance Squadron, Provisional, moved to Germany ready to fly over

Soviet territory. The CIA believed that the Soviets could not track the high altitude flights of the U-2. It's true that the U-2 was invisible to American radar, which was not very effective at high altitudes. Russian radar, however, was better and had improved since the Second World War. Although the Soviets could not consistently track the aircraft, it certainly wasn't invisible.

Within six months, the Soviets had already complained that USAF aircraft had flown over their territory. The US government responded that no American military planes had overflown the Soviet Union. This was true, in an extremely literal sense: the U-2 was a CIA aircraft and not a military one.

Eisenhower halted the surveillance flights over Eastern Europe, concerned over the possibilities of the secret aircraft being caught , not to mention the US public reacting badly to the US violating international law. The U-2 had barely become operational but it was already clear it was vulnerable. The CIA analysed the probabilities of the aircraft being shot down, based on the variables of the aircraft's speed, altitude and cross section. Their analysis showed that if the aircraft were able to fly at supersonic speed, it would greatly reduce the chances of detection by radar and of interception by missile. They asked Lockheed and Convair to research a new reconnaissance aircraft: one that could fly at high altitudes without being detected by radar. One that could fly fast enough to outrun a missile. Kelly Johnson wrote about the project in his diary, attempting to design an aircraft that could fly 50% faster than the top jet fighter and five miles higher than the U-2.

The first iteration of the aircraft on the Skunk Works design board was called the A-1. By the end of 1958, they'd progressed to the A-3. It was this design that got the contract from the CIA: 100 million US dollars to fund further design and to build twelve aircraft, approved by the President.

The project officially began in 1959 and the name was chosen from a random list of code-names, Project Oxcart. The design iterations were now up to the A-11 as the Skunk Works focused on anti-radar studies, aerodynamic structural tests and engineering designs. Developing a supersonic aircraft caused no end of developmental problems and, although Johnson was confident about his design, no one was really sure that the aircraft would fly when it came to it, let alone fulfil all the requirements made by the CIA.

They started recruiting pilots, a slow process as a result of the exacting physical requirements, even stricter than what is needed for consideration to become an astronaut today. Pilots needed to be qualified in high performance fighter aircraft and between 25 and 40 years old. They needed to be under 6 foot tall and less than 175 pounds, so that they could fit into the A-11 cockpit. On top of that, the CIA added numerous emotional stability and motivational requirements.

The aircraft were to be built with a titanium alloy, which had the strength and resistance to high temperatures that they needed while weighing relatively little. But titanium is a scarce resource and, at the time, most of it came from the USSR. The issues of sourcing the materials caused continuous delays.

Area 51 wasn't quite up to the task either. The existing runway needed to be extended and strengthened so that it could support the weight of the A-11. They needed 500,000 gallons of custom aircraft fuel every month, without storage facilities or transport systems in place. More accommodation was needed as the number of workers on the project increased, with over a hundred surplus Navy housing buildings transported to the base to quickly expand the living quarters.

U-2 missions were taking place over Soviet airspace again; although the US knew that the Soviets could track the aircraft using radar, they believed the aircraft were safely out of range of both fighter jets and surface-to-air missiles. The Soviets had tried to intercept the aircraft a number of times but not been successful. Initially, Eisenhower insisted that missions over the Soviet Union be flown by Royal Air Force pilots. Eisenhower was concerned that if the aircraft was captured with an American pilot, the Soviets would see this as an act of aggression and risk a war between the two countries. The initial missions were a success and Eisenhower agreed to a further two missions, these to be flown with CIA pilots, to determine the number of Soviet intercontinental ballistic missiles.

In April of 1960, a final mission was approved for a U-2C spy plane flown by CIA pilot Francis Gary Powers. After a number of delays, the mission finally took place on the 1st of May. This was a mistake. The 1st of May was an important public holiday, the *Day of the International Solidarity of Workers*, and Soviet airspace was quiet. Soviet radar began tracking the U-2 about 15 miles outside of the border. Once the U-2 flew into their territory, the Lieutenant General of the Air Force ordered his air-unit commanders "to attack the violator by all alert flights located in the area of foreign plane's course, and to ram if necessary."

One thing the CIA had right: the Soviet Air Force did not have any fighter aircraft who could reach the high altitudes of the U-2. MiG-19 fighters were pursuing the U-2 but could not reach the aircraft to intercept. The U-2 continued its reconnaissance. At four and a half hours into the flight, as the CIA plane flew over a plutonium production facility, the Soviets released three surface-to-air missiles. One of them did nothing. One missile struck one of the MiG fighter jets in hot pursuit. The MiG's IFF (Identification Friend or Foe) transponders should have identified him as *friend* to the missile, the codes updated every month. But because of the public holiday, the transponder had not been updated to the new May codes.

The third missile detonated at 70,500 feet, directly behind the Lockheed U-2. The supposedly untraceable and untargetable reconnaissance plane was hit.

Believing that the aircraft destroyed, the US stuck to their cover story. NASA announced that one of their aircraft disappeared while on a high-altitude research flight in Turkey. They then said that the weather plane's pilot had radioed in that he was experiencing oxygen difficulties. If any wreckage from the aircraft *had* been discovered, they planned to claim that the NASA aircraft had drifted across the Soviet border after the pilot was incapacitated. They then announced that all of the weather missions were halted while the aircraft underwent a mandatory inspection of their oxygen systems.

Khrushchev waited until the US was entrenched in their lies. Then he announced the unthinkable: they had both the aircraft and the pilot, who had parachuted out of the plane and landed safely. The CIA pilot carried a modified silver dollar which contained a lethal toxin-tipped needle, but he never got a chance to use it. The USSR convicted him of espionage, using the photographs of the Soviet military bases that the aircraft had collected as evidence, and sentenced him to three years imprisonment and seven years of hard labour.

The Soviets now knew all about the US's secret spy plane.

And worse, the A-11 was nowhere near ready.

A-12 #06938 on display at the USS Alabama Battleship Museum, photographed by Curt Mason.

In late 1961 the CIA, using undercover companies to work with Third World countries, had finally sourced enough titanium to build the aircraft.

Assembly line production was impossible; everything involved a learning curve and every aircraft had to be individually built. The drills, designed for working on aluminium, snapped into pieces when they attempted to drill the titanium. The Lockheed Skunk Works could not insulate the aircraft because of the weight it added, leading to the cockpit being hotter than an oven:

they had to commission a type of space suit with cooling apparatus and oxygen for the pilot. The temperature of the fuel tanks was so hot that they had to design custom fuel and oil that could operate at such high temperatures. The camera peered out of a quartz glass window which not only had to resist the high temperatures but could not suffer from any optical distortion in the heat; this window alone took three years of research and two million US dollars.

During construction, it became clear that the greatest radar visibility was coming from very specific areas: the vertical stabilisers, the engine inlet and the forward side of the engine nacelles. The Skunk Works came up with a plan to replace the tail fins and other areas with a type of laminated "plastic" material that was able to absorb the high temperatures: the details are still top secret. But it worked and the A-11 was re-designated the A-12.

The first A-12, serial number 121, was ready to be secretly transported from Burbank to Area 51, Lockheed decided to ship the aircraft by road. However, the trailer was 35 feet wide and 105 feet long and in order to make it through to Nevada, the Skunk Works had to organise clearing the sides of the highway of road signs and trees and at some point resurfacing and levelling the road completely. The initial delivery date was May 1961 but the aircraft didn't arrive at Area 51 until February 1962. The FAA expanded the restricted airspace around Area 51 with selected air traffic controllers cleared for the OXCART project, to ensure that they didn't report what they might see. NORAD (The North American Air Defense Command) established procedures to ensure that no one reported the A-12 appearing on radar-scopes. The test flights were ready to begin. By the end of the year, the A-12 had reached a speed of Mach 2.16 and an altitude of 60,000 feet.

Another U-2 was shot down in action, this one by a surface-to-air missile over Cuba, but not before confirming that the Soviets were installing missile bases and nuclear weapons on the island. The OXCART program went into high gear. The CIA needed this aircraft.

But problems still abounded. In one instance, some nuts and bolts had not been cleared away and when the A-12 engine was run up, it sucked them in, destroying the engine. The flow of air entering the air inlet system was uneven between Mach 2.4 and

Mach 2.8, but the A-12 needed to be able to reach Mach 3.0. The development and refinement continued.

In 1963 the CIA had hired the full set of Experimental Test Pilots for the project, including pilot Jack Weeks. The aircraft under development had always been referred to as *Oxcart* after the project itself. Weeks renamed it to *Cygnus*, a much more respectable name which was picked up by the rest of the pilots and ground crew.

Most of the flights were short; keeping the aircraft under wraps was a primary objective. But at full speed, the A-12's turning radius was 86 miles. They couldn't keep it close to the airfield.

The first A-12 was lost: the pilot was forced to eject when the A-12 pitched up and went out of control. The pilot was found by some civilians in a pick-up truck who offered to take him to his plane, a top-secret aircraft that they weren't supposed to know existed. The pilot told them not to go near the aircraft, that it was carrying a nuclear weapon, and asked them to take him to the local highway patrol. The CIA recovered the wreckage within 48 hours and tracked down the men from the pick-up truck so they could sign secrecy agreements. The existence of the A-12 could not be admitted and all official reports said it was a generic Air Force aircraft, a Republic F-105 Thunderchief Fighter-Bomber, which is still how the crash is listed today.

The Department of Defense was struggling to explain the funds going into the project and the secret was becoming difficult to keep.

The public still didn't know that Area 51 existed, although by now rumours of black projects had started to collect, ranging from a crashed alien aircraft to the development of time travel and teleportation technology. The Air Force buried many reports of UFOs after confirming that they correlated with U-2 and A-12 flight times.

The commander of the Area 51 base in the 1960s told the LA times recently that they were not surprised by the rumours.

> The shape of OXCART was unprecedented, with its wide, disk-like fuselage designed to carry vast quantities of fuel. Commercial pilots cruising over Nevada at dusk would look up and see the bottom of OXCART whiz by at 2,000-plus mph. The

> aircraft's titanium body, moving as fast as a bullet, would reflect the sun's rays in a way that could make anyone think, UFO.

The truth was much more interesting: the unidentified flying objects crossing the sky were certainly from a black project and they may have looked extraterrestrial; however it was our own technology making for the most innovative spy planes the world had ever seen.

In 1964, US President Lyndon B. Johnson officially announced the existence of the aircraft.

> The United States has successfully developed an advanced experimental jet aircraft, the A-11, which has been tested in sustained flight at more than 2,000 miles per hour and at altitudes in excess of 70,000 feet. The performance of the A-11 far exceeds that of any other aircraft in the world today. The development of this aircraft has been made possible by major advances in aircraft technology of great significance for both military and commercial applications. Several A-11 aircraft are now being flight tested at Edwards Air Force Base in California. The existence of this program is being disclosed today to permit the orderly exploitation of this advance technology in our military and commercial program.

The A-11 was the all-metal version of the Oxcart, so did not give away the fact that they had an aircraft which would not show up on radar. Instead, they showed off the US Air Force's Lockheed YF-12A, a twin-seat interceptor aircraft based on the Lockheed A-12 and the precursor to the SR-71 Blackbird, a two-seater version with reduced surveillance equipment.

However, the CIA wasn't ready for the president's announcement. Johnson mentioned "several A-11 aircraft at Edwards Air Force Base" so they swiftly flew two Air Force YF-12A's to Edwards to support the statement. They put them straight into the hangar for a reception, pretending they had been there all along. The heat from the aircraft activated the hangar sprinkler system, "dousing the reception team which awaited them".

A-12 on display at the US Space and Rocket Center in Huntsville, Alabama in 2014.

The A-12 was still a secret and in November 1965 the aircraft was ready to see action. Its first use was to be Project BLACK SHIELD, collecting information from Communist China. Three aircraft were selected and tested for relocation to Okinawa for the project. They reached a maximum speed of Mach 3.29 and an altitude of 90,000 feet. The A-12 was operational.

It had taken so long to become a reality, though, that support for Project OXCART had waned. The Bureau of the Budget expressed concern at the costs of the A-12 and SR-71 programmes and questioned why there was a requirement for both an Air Force and a CIA fleet. They recommended phasing out the A-12 program by 1966. Project BLACK SHIELD also had its share of detractors, as basing the aircraft in Okinawa would mean disclosing the A-12s existence to the Japanese.

In 1967, the BLACK SHIELD unit was sent to Okinawa with three CIA pilots posing as civilian pilots for Lockheed. The first aircraft, serial number 131, flew non-stop, arriving in six hours and six minutes. The aircraft serial number 127 made it in five hours and 55 minutes. Serial number 129, flown by Jack Weeks, had navigation and communication problems and was forced to land en route. He arrived on Okinawa a day late.

The Japanese on the site called the A-12 "Habu", a deadly snake that inhabits the area. Habu is still used as a nickname for the SR-71 today. Four A-12s had been lost before the aircraft had ever become operational and its first official mission didn't happen until the last day of May in 1967 successfully performing surveillance over Vietnam.

From the CIA report released in 1996:

> A typical route profile for a BLACK SHIELD mission over North Vietnam included a refueling shortly after take-off, south of Okinawa, the planned photographic pass or passes, withdrawal to a second aerial refueling in the Thailand area, and return to Kadena. So great was the OXCART'S speed that it spent only 12 1/2 minutes over North Vietnam in a typical "single pass" mission, or a total of 21 1/2 minutes on two passes. Its turning radius of 86 miles was such, however, that on some mission profiles it might be forced during its turn to intrude into Chinese airspace.

The Secretary of Defense maintained that the government could not continue to fund both the A-12 and the SR-71. In 1967, it was decided to continue with the SR-71. In 1968, Project OXCART was terminated. Lockheed were ordered to destroy all the A-12 tooling and Air Force SR-71s were flown to Okinawa to replace the A-12s.

There were only three missions flown in 1968. The first, by pilot Jack Weeks in serial number 129, was the first flight over

North Korea but, at the time, the top-secret flight was marked as an abort. Only in 2007 was Jack Week's flight log released showing the mission was successfully completed. But the State Department were nervous of diplomatic repercussions if the aircraft came down in hostile territory and the last operational mission flown by the A-12 was on the 8th of May in 1968.

The BLACK SHIELD unit prepared to go home, with flights of the A-12 limited to those essential for maintaining flight safety. The A-12s were to return to the US on the 8th of June and be placed in storage.

Four days before their return to the US, the aircraft serial number 129 underwent repairs, leading to a replacement of the right engine. A Functional Checkout Flight (FCF) was required to ensure that the aircraft was operating correctly after the maintenance.

Pilot Jack Weeks took serial number 129 up for the simple check flight using the call sign "Dutch 29". Twenty minutes after take-off, he refuelled, taking on 34,000 pounds of fuel. When the refuelling was complete, he disconnected from the tanker and the tanker crew watched the A-12 climb away. They were the last to see the aircraft.

A routine flight check would involve flying towards the Philippines and then a long shallow 190° turn back towards Okinawa. A standard communication was received at the start of the southern turn of the standard route.

The A-12 included a flight monitoring system called Birdwatcher. If Birdwatcher sensed vital aircraft systems or equipment going outside of their normal ranges, it would send a coded signal using the High Frequency transmitter. The signal included the item which triggered the Birdwatcher and the flight data for all of the monitored items and the aircraft identity. That means that the operator would know which aircraft system or equipment triggered the Birdwatcher to send the message and the status of all the other items.

A Birdwatcher transmission was received 19 minutes after the refuelling, showing that the right engine exhaust gas temperature was over 860°C. Then the Birdwatcher transmitted that the right engine fuel flow was low.

Eight seconds later, a further transmission was made that the A-12 had descended below 68,500 feet (still higher than any other aircraft except the U-2). Birdwatcher's control panel would also be visible in the cockpit, so Weeks had as much notification as the controllers and the time to react to the issue, whatever it may have been.

Operations attempted to contact the pilot using High Frequency Single Sideband (HF SSB) mobile radio and UHF, and through Birdwatcher, but received no reply. An SR-71 departed to look for the aircraft. Jack Weeks never reported in, nor did he respond to any of the attempts to contact him.

No further transmissions were received from Birdwatcher.

The aircraft, deliberately undetectable by radar, had vanished, somewhere around 500 nautical miles east of the Philippines and 600 nautical miles south of Okinawa. All channels were monitored until the aircraft, if in flight, would have run out of fuel. An intense search and rescue operation was initiated. They searched for weeks but they found nothing. No cause for the accident could be ascertained.

There were rumours, of course, especially when more information was released in the 1990s. Some believed that Weeks had defected, maybe to China, maybe to Korea. Others wondered about a recurring fault in the A-12, based on issues on the flight to Okinawa and the "aborted" flight over Korea at the beginning of the year.

The most secret spy plane in the history of the Cold War had simply disappeared.

Not that the public knew. The official news release identified the lost aircraft as an SR-71, maintaining the secrecy around the A-12 for one last time.

The OXCART project was finished.

The SR-71 Blackbird continued to fly with the US Air Force until its retirement in 1998.

And the U-2 is still in service and has served the US Air Force for over 50 years—the current U-2 began service in 1980—credited with its ability to change targets on short notice, which surveillance satellites can't do. Lockheed says the aircraft can easily remain viable until 2050.

Conclusion

THESE INCIDENTS all have one thing in common: despite a concerted effort to discover what happened, the mystery remains. It's easy to believe that we have the answers, if only we look; that without an answer, there must be a cover-up. It's frustrating not to know. But, as these cases show us, it's nothing new.

It may be tempting to believe that this is something that happened long ago, that with modern technology it is no longer possible for planes to simply disappear. Fabric rots away; the aircraft are lying at the bottom of a lake, covered with decades of silt and sand; there just isn't enough detail to work out where the aircraft went down, let alone what happened. Now we have radio and radar, sonography and satellite photography. And yet, mysteries that boggle the mind still occur.

The year 2017 was a milestone: the safest year on record for commercial air travel. It marks the first year since aviation became a viable means of public travel that not a single passenger fatality occurred in a commercial accident. It would be tempting to believe that these tragedies and mysteries are a thing of the past, if it weren't for the incredible story of Malaysia Airlines flight 370 looming large in our minds. As I write this, a new search for MH370 is underway: another attempt to discover the truth.

The loss of that aircraft with 239 souls on board four years ago does not stand alone. It is not even the most recent. The second volume of *Without a Trace* continues the collection of inexplicable disappearances starting in 1970, when a military pilot chases an unidentified object in the sky glowing with a golden light. The mysteries continue until 2016, with the sudden disappearance of an Antonov An-32 on a routine courier flight, while the aircraft ahead and behind saw nothing.

Where did the stolen Boeing go? How did India manage to misplace five fighter jets? Did the young pilot chasing an inexplicable aircraft over the Australian coast really get abducted by aliens? These questions and more are explored in volume 2 of *Without a Trace*.

SPECIFICATIONS

The Disappearance of Aeronaut Walter Powell

The Saladin

Fabric: Calico
Empty weight: 492 pounds (223.16 kilograms)
Instrument and kits: 82 pounds (37.19 kilograms)
Three occupants: 494 pounds (224 kilograms)
Ballast: 632 pounds (286 kilograms)
Total: 1,700 pounds (771.1 kilograms)
Capacity: 38,600 cubic feet of coal gas (1,093 cubic meters)
Max height reached of 6,000 feet (1,829 meters) during final flight

The Last Known Whereabouts of the White Bird

L'Oiseau Blanc

Manufacturer: Pierre Levasseur Company
Construction: Single bay wood and fabric covered biplane. Reinforced plywood fuselage
Crew: Two
Length: 9.75 metres (31 ft 11 in)
Height: 3.89 metres (12 ft 9 in)
Wingspan: 15 metres (49 ft)
Wing area: 61.0 m^2 (656 sq ft)
Empty weight: 1,905 kg (4,200 lb)
Gross weight: 5,000 kg (11,000 lb)
Powerplant: 1 × Lorraine-Dietrich W-12ED, 340 kW (460 hp)
Maximum speed: 193 km/h (120 mph)

Cruising speed: 165 km/h (102 mph)
Range: 7,000 km (4,350 miles)
Flight Endurance: 40 hours
Service ceiling: 7,000 m (22,965 feet)

The Golden and Deadly Age of Arctic Exploration

Italia

Designer: Umberto Nobile
Form: Semi-rigid airship
Length: 105.4 metres (345 ft 9 in)
Diameter: 19.4 metres (63 ft 7 in)
Capacity: 18,500 cubic metres (654,000 cubic feet) of gas
Performance: 112.3 km/h (70 mph)
Payload: 9,405 kg (20,900 lb)
Power plant: Three Maybach 560 kW (750 hp) engines

Unable to Reach You by Radio

Lockheed Model 10 Electra

Manufacturer: Lockheed Aircraft Corporation
Construction: Twin-engine all-aluminium aircraft with retractable landing gear, twin tail fins and rudders
Crew: Two (pilot and navigator)
Length: 38 ft 7 in (11.7 metres)
Height: 10 ft 1 in (3 metres)
Empty Weight: 6,454 lbs (2,927 kg)
Powerplant: 600 horsepower Pratt & Whitney R-1340 Wasp SH31 engine
Cruise speed: 190–194 mph (305–312 km/h)
Maximum Speed: 202 mph (325 km/h)
Range: 619 nm (1,146 kilometres)
Service Ceiling: 19,400 feet (5,913 metres)
Earhart made a number of modifications to her aircraft: Six fuel tanks were added to the wings and fuselage to accommodate for longer trip leg, allowing a total capacity of 1,150 US gallons (4,363 litres) of fuel,

extending her range to over 220 hours of flight time at a normal cruise.

Only an Oil Slick Remained

Martin M-130 "Hawaii Clipper"

Manufacturer: Glenn L. Martin Company

Construction: All metal "flying boat" with streamlined aerodynamics

Crew: Six to nine (Captain, First Officer, Junior Flight Officer, Engineering Officer, Assistant Engineering Officer, Radio Operator, Navigation Officer, plus cabin stewards)

Passenger Capacity: 36 seated or 18 sleeping berths

Length: 90 ft 10½ in (27.7 metres)

Height: 24 ft 7 in (7.5 metres)

Wingspan: 130 feet (39.7 metres)

Max. takeoff weight: 52,252 pounds (23,701 kg)

Powerplant: 4 × Pratt & Whitney R-1830-S2A5G Twin Wasp 14-cylinder radial engines, 830 hp (620 kW)

Maximum speed: 180 mph (290 km/h)

Cruise speed: 130 mph (209 km/h)

Range: 3,200 miles (5,150 km)

Service ceiling: 10,000 feet (3,000 metres)

Death of an Aviatrix

De Havilland DH.60 Gipsy Moth "Jason"

Manufacturer: De Havilland Aircraft Company

Construction: Wooden construction biplane with plywood covered fuselage and fabric covered surfaces

Crew: one

Passenger capacity: One (or navigator or student)

Length: 23 ft 11 in (7.29 metres)

Height: 8 ft 9½ in (2.68 metres)

Wingspan: 30 feet (9.14 metres)

Wing area: 243 sq ft (22.6 m²)

Empty weight: 920 pounds (417 kg)

Loaded weight: 1,650 pounds (750 kg)
Powerplant: 1 × de Havilland Gipsy I, 4 cylinder, upright, in-line piston engine, 100 hp (75 kW)
Maximum speed: 102 mph (89 knots, 164 km/h)
Cruise speed: 85 mph (74 knots, 137 km/h)
Range: 320 miles (278 nm, 515 km)
Rate of climb: 500 ft/min (2.5 m/s)
Service ceiling: 14,500 feet (4,500 metres)

Which Way Did We Fly?

TBM-1C Avenger (x4), TBM-3 Avenger (x1)
Manufacturer: Grumman General Motors
Crew: Three
Length: 40 ft 11.5 in (12.48 metres)
Height: 15 ft 5 in (4.70 metres)
Wingspan: 54 ft 2 in (16.51 metres)
Wing area: 490.02 sq ft (45.52 m^2)
Wing loading: 36.5 psf (178 kg/m^2)
Empty weight: 10,545 pounds (4,783 kg)
Loaded weight: 17,893 pounds (8,115 kg)
Powerplant: 1 × Wright R-2600-20 Twin Cyclone radial engine, 1,900 hp (1,420 kW)
Maximum speed: 275 mph (442 km/h)
Range: 1,000 mi (1,610 km)
Rate of climb: 2,060 ft/min (10.5 m/s)
Service ceiling: 30,100 feet (9,170 metres)

The Bermuda Triangle Strikes Again

Douglas DC-3
Manufacturer: Douglas Aircraft Company
Construction: twin-engine metal monoplane
Crew: Two
Capacity: 32 passengers
Length: 64 ft 8 in (19.7 metres)
Height: 16 ft 11 in (5.16 metres)
Wingspan: 95 ft 2 in (29 metres)
Wing area: 987 sq ft (91.7 m^2)

Wing loading: 25.5 psf (125 kg/m²)
Aspect ratio: 9.17
Airfoil: NACA2215 / NACA2206
Empty weight: 16,865 pounds (7,650 kg)
Gross weight: 25,199 pounds (11,430 kg)
Fuel capacity: 822 gallons (3,111 litres)
Powerplant: 2 × Wright 1820-G102A engines, 1,100 hp (820 kW) each
Propellers: 3-bladed Hamilton Standard 23E50 series, 11 ft 6 in (3.51 metres) diameter
Maximum speed: 200 knots (370 km/h, 230 mph) at 8,500 feet (2,590 metres)
Cruise speed: 180 knots (333 km/h, 207 mph)
Stall speed: 58.2 knots (67 mph, 108 km/h)
Rate of climb: 1,130 ft/min (5.7 m/s)
Service ceiling: 23,200 feet (7,100 metres)

The Great Expanse of Lake Michigan

Douglas DC-4

Manufacturer: Douglas Aircraft Company
Construction: Four engine, propeller driven airliner, metal construction
Crew: Four
Capacity: 40 to 80 passengers
Length: 93 ft 10 in (28.6 metres)
Height: 27 ft 6 in (8.4 metres)
Wingspan: 117 ft 6 in (35.8 metres)
Wing area: 1,460 sq ft (135.6 m²)
Wing loading: 43.5 psf (212.4 kg/m²)
Empty weight: 43,300 pounds (19,640 kg)
Loaded weight: 63,500 pounds (28,800 kg)
Max. takeoff weight: 73,000 pounds (33,100 kg)
Powerplant: 4 × Pratt & Whitney R-2000 radial engine, 1,450 hp (1,081 kW) each
Maximum speed: 280 mph (243 knots, 450 km/h)
Cruise speed: 227 mph (197 knots, 365 km/h)
Range: 4,250 miles (3,793 nm, 6,839 km)
Service ceiling: 22,300 feet (6,800 metres)

The Kinross Incident

F-89C Scorpion

Manufacturer: Northrop Corporation
Crew: Two
Length: 53 ft½ 9 in (16.4 metres)
Height: 17 ft 6 in (5.33 metres)
Wingspan: 59 ft 8½ in (18.2 metres)
Wing area: 606 sq ft (56.3 m^2)
Empty weight: 25,194 pounds (11,428 kg)
Loaded weight: 37,190 pounds (16,869 kg)
Max. takeoff weight: 42,241 pounds (19,161 kg)
Powerplant: 2 × Allison J35-A-35 after-burning turbojets
Dry thrust: 5,440 lbf (24.26 kN) each
Thrust with afterburner: 7,200 lbf (32.11 kN) each
Maximum speed: 635 mph (552 knots, 1,022 km/h) at 10,600 feet (3,200 metres)
Range: 1,366 miles (1,188 nm, 2,200 km)
Rate of climb: 7,440 ft/min (37.8 m/s)
Service ceiling: 49,200 feet (15,000 metres)

Romance of the Skies

Boeing 377 Stratocruiser

Manufacturer: Boeing Commercial Airplanes
Construction: Double bubble fuselage
Capacity: Up to 100 passengers on main deck plus 14 in lower deck lounge; typical seating for 63 or 84 passengers or 28 berthed and five seated passengers
Length: 110 ft 4 in (33.6 metres)
Height: 38 ft 3 in (11.7 metres)
Wingspan: 141 ft 3 in (43 metres)
Wing area: 1769 sq ft (164.3 m^2)
Empty weight: 83,500 pounds (37,876 kg)
Max. takeoff weight: 148,000 pounds (67,133 kg)
Powerplant: 4 × Pratt & Whitney R-4360-B6 Wasp Major 28-cylinder radial engines four-bladed propellers, 3,500 hp (2,610 kW) each

Maximum speed: 375 mph (603 km/h, 326 knots)
Cruise speed: 301 mph (483 km/h, 262 knots)
Max cruise: 340 mph (295 knots, 547 km/h)
Range: 4,200 miles (3,650 nm, 6,760 km)
Service ceiling: 32,000 feet (9,800 metres)

Friendly Fire or Sabotage

Lockheed Super Constellation

Manufacturer: Lockheed Corporation
Crew: Four
Capacity: 47–106 Passengers
Length: 113 ft 7 in (34.6 metres)
Height: 24 ft 9 in (7.5 metres)
Wingspan: 123 ft (37.5 metres)
Wing area: 1,650 sq ft (153.29 m^2)
Empty weight: 69,000 pounds (31,300 kg)
Max. takeoff weight: 120,000 pounds (54,431 kg)
Powerplant: 4 × Wright R-3350 972-TC-18DA-1 radial, 3,250 hp (2,245 kW) each
Maximum speed: 330 mph (287 knots, 531 km/h)
Cruise speed: 304 mph (264 knots, 489 km/h)
Range: 5,150 miles (447 nm, 8,288 km)
Service ceiling: 25,700 feet (7,833 metres)

The Spy Plane

Lockheed U-2

Manufacturer: Lockheed Skunk Works
Construction: High aspect ratio wings (imparts glider-like characteristics)
Crew: One
Length: 63 feet (19.2 metres)
Height: 16 feet (4.88 metres)
Wingspan: 103 feet (31.4 metres)
Wing area: 1,000 sq ft (92.9 m^2)
Aspect ratio: 10.6
Empty weight: 14,300 pounds (6,486 kg)
Max takeoff weight: 40,000 pounds (18,144 kg)

Powerplant: 1 × General Electric F118-101 turbofan, 17,000 lbf (84.5 kN)
Maximum speed: 434 knots (Mach 0.67, 500 mph, 805 km/h)
Cruise speed: 373 knots (Mach 0.56, 429 mph, 690 km/h)
Range: 5,566 nm (6,405 miles, 10,308 km)
Service ceiling: 70,000+ feet (21,300+ metres)
Maximum lift-to-drag: 23:1
Flight endurance: 12 hours

Lockheed A-12
Manufacturer: Lockheed Skunk Works
Construction: Titanium Monococque and super-high-temperature plastics
Crew: One
Length: 98 ft 8 in (30 metres)
Height: 18 ft 6 in (5.6 metres)
Wingspan: 55 ft 7 inches (16.9 metres)
Wing Area: 1,795 sq ft (166.7 m^2)
Empty Weight: 60,000 pounds (27,200 kg)
Max takeoff weight: 120,000 pounds (54,400 kg)
Landing Weight: 52,000 pounds (23,586.8 kg)
Powerplant: 2 x Pratt & Whitney JT11D-20A (J58) with 32,500 pounds of thrust
Maximum Speed: Mach 3.3 (2,200 knots, 2,530 mph, 4075 km/h)
Service Ceiling: 95,000+ feet (29,000+ metres, 18 miles)
Maximum Unfueled Range: 2,500 miles (2,170 nm, 4,000 km)

IMAGE CREDITS

IN ORDER OF APPEARANCE

The Disappearance of Aeronaut Walter Powell

"Two men are inside the basket of a hot-air balloon. Coloured wood engraving."

Credit: Wellcome Collection (CC BY 4.0)

The Last Known Whereabouts of the White Bird

Postcard of Charles Nungesser and François Coli and their biplane *L'Oiseau Blanc.*

Source: Carte postale 1927

The Golden and Deadly Age of Artic Exploration

The Airship *Norge* at Ny-Ålesund, Norway.

Repository: The Norwegian Polar Institute Photo Library

Airship *Italia* overflies Stockholm.

Credit: Tekniska museets arkiv

Recovered fuel tank from the Latham 47 flight that was lost in 1928 along with Roald Amundsen. Currently in the Polarmuseet in Tromsø, Norway.

Photographer: Ealdgyth (Wikimedia user)

Unable to Reach you by Radio

Amelia Earhart with Lockheed 10E.

Collection: Miles Blaine Collection
Repository: San Diego Air and Space Museum Archive

Amelia Earhart and Fred Noonan in 1932.

Repository: San Diego Air and Space Museum Archive

Only an Oil Slick Remained

Pan American Airways Martin M-130 China Clipper (civil registration NC14716) at Pearl Harbor, Hawaii, in the 1930s.

Collection: U.S. National Park Service Gallery

Death of an Aviatrix

Women pilots 1930.

Repository: National Library of Australia (gifted by Miss Meg Skelton)

Which Way Did We Fly?

"We Can Do It!" by J. Howard Miller was made as an inspirational image to boost worker morale.

Current location: National Museum of American History, Smithsonian Institution

The Bermuda Triangle Strikes Again

San Juan to Miami as the crow flies.

Imagery (C)2081 Data SIO, NOAA, U.S. Navy, GEBCO, Landsat / Copernicus, Map data (C)2018 Google, INEGI

The Great Expanse of Lake Michigan

Passenger in a DC-4 Scandinavian Airlines System (SAS) Douglas DC-4 Dan Viking OY-DFI en route from Oslo Airport, Fornebu to Bodø Airport.

Photographer: Leif Ørnelund
Repository: Oslo Museum

The Kinross Incident

U.S. Air Force Northrop F-89D-45-NO Scorpion interceptors of the 59th Fighter Interceptor Squadrons, Goose Bay, AB in the 1950s

Source: USAF Museum
Photographer: USAF

Romance of the Skies

Life rafts pull away from the "Sovereign of the Skies" just before the broken craft settles to her grave in the Pacific Ocean on Oct. 16, 1956.

Photographer: William Simpson, US Coast Guard
Source: US Coast Guard
Collection: Pan Am Historical Foundation

Pan Am Stratocruiser departing San Francisco

Repository: San Diego Air and Space Museum

The Spy Plane

U-2 High Flight 20 July 2010.

Photographer: Christopher Michel
Source:
https://www.flickr.com/photos/cmichel67/156281
38499/

A-12 on display at the US Space and Rocket Center in Huntsville, Alabama in 2014.

Photographer: Curt Mason
Source: http://projecthabu.com/post/87159455509
/during-1967-and-1968-06930-flew-over

A-12 #06938 on display at the USS Alabama Battleship Museum.

Photographer: Curt Mason
Source: http://projecthabu.com/post/82748660355
/a-12-06938-on-display-at-the-uss-alabama

References

The Disappearance of Aeronaut Walter Powell

Mike Dash (26 April 2010) "Walter Powell, the Saladin, and some very early cases of lights in the sky (1881-1902)", Fortean Times. Available at http://blogs.forteana.org/node/117 (Accessed 17 Dec 2017)

(17 December 1881) "Mr. Walter Powell, M.P. for Malmesbury, has, we fear, long ago paid the penalty", The Spectator. Available at http://archive.spectator.co.uk/article/17th-december-1881/3/mr-walter-powell-mp-for-malmesbury-has-we-fear-lon (Accessed 17 Dec 2017)

David Forward (undated) "Walter Powell—Malmesbury Memories". Available at http://davidforward.com/contents/local-history/walter-powel (Accessed 17 Dec 2017)

Portia Hobbs (1985) "Walter Powell MP: Balloonist"

Charles Hoy Fort (6 April 1905) "New Lands", Boni & Liveright. Available at http://www.resologist.net/landsei.htm (Accessed 12 Jan 2018)

The Last Known Whereabouts of the White Bird

(undated) "Project Midnight Ghost", TIGHAR. Available at https://tighar.org/Projects/PMG/PMG.html (Accessed 23 Jan 2018)

Clément-Pascal Meunier, translation coordinated by Patricia R. Thrasher (1 March 1990) “Nungesser & Coli Disappear Aboard the White Bird”, TIGHAR. Available at https://tighar.org/Projects/PMG/FrenchReport.htm (Accessed 23 Jan 2018)

Sebastian Moffett (6 September 2011) “Charles Lindbergh Won the Prize, but Did His Rival Get There First?”, The Wall Street Journal. Available at https://www.wsj.com/articles/SB10001424053111904480904576498061491234304 (Accessed 23 Jan 2018)

(9 May 2006) “The Secret of the White Bird: The Everest of Aviation Mysteries Still Stands”, Aero News Network. Available at http://www.aero-news.net/index.cfm?do=main.textpost&id=c22b14fc-5c71-4b9b-ac77-a08f5528439f (Accessed 23 Jan 2018)

Victoria Woollaston (10 May 2013) “What happened to the White Bird?”, Mail Online. Available at http://www.dailymail.co.uk/sciencetech/article-2322392/Fresh-search-begins-remains-White-Bird-plane-mysteriously-vanished-86-years-ago-killing-pilots.html (Accessed 23 Jan 2018)

The Golden and Deadly Age of Arctic Exploration

(1 July 2017) “The Disastrous Latham-47 Polar Rescue, From Caudebec-En-Caux”, Normandy Then and Now. Available at http://www.normandythenandnow.com/the-disastrous-latham-47-polar-rescue-from-caudebec-en-caux/ (Accessed 17 Dec 2017)

(24 August 2009) “Hunt on for explorer’s lost plane”, BBC News. Available at http://news.bbc.co.uk/2/hi/science/nature/8214237.stm (Accessed 17 Dec 2017)

Garth Cameron (2017) “Umberto Nobile And the Arctic Search for the Airship Italia”, Fonthill Media (Accessed 17 Dec 2017)

Harvey M Solomon and Philip Cala-Lazar (21 February 2008) "The role of radio in rescuing the survivors of the airship Italia". Available at http://onlinelibrary.wiley.com/doi/10.1111/j.1751-8369.2008.00047.x/full (Accessed 17 Dec 2017)

Lee Krystek (undated) "The Flight of the Norge on the Museum of UnNatural Mystery". Available at http://www.unmuseum.org/norge_1.htm (Accessed 17 Dec 2017)

(undated) "The 1928 Crash of the Airship Italia", 90° North. Available at http://90north.tripod.com/italiacrash1.htm (Accessed 17 Dec 2017)

Eva Holland (18 August 2017) "Flying to the North Pole in an Airship Was Easy", Smithsonian Magazine. Available at https://www.smithsonianmag.com/history/flying-north-pole-airship-was-easy-returning-wouldnt-be-so-easy-180964560/ (Accessed 17 Dec 2017)

Jeremy Scott (2011) "Show Me a Hero", Biteback Publishing

Christoph Seidler (25 February 2009) "Dive Robot to Aid in Search for Legendary Polar Explorer", Spiegel Online. Available at http://www.spiegel.de/international/zeitgeist/the-search-for-amundsen-dive-robot-to-aid-in-search-for-legendary-polar-explorer-a-609863.html (Accessed 17 Dec 2017)

Roald Amundsen (1927) "My Life As An Explorer", Doubleday, Page & Company

Unable to Reach You by Radio

(22 March 1937) "The Luke Field Crash Report: Proceedings". Available at https://tighar.org/Projects/Earhart/Archives/Documents/Luke_Field_Crash_Report/LukeFieldProceedings.htm (Accessed 31 Jan 2018)

Eric H. Chater (25 July 1937) "The Chater Report". Available at https://tighar.org/Projects/Earhart/Archives/Documents/Chater_Report.html (Accessed 31 Jan 2018)

(undated) "Significance of Earhart's statement 'We are on the line 157/337' ", The Amelia Earhart Search Forum. Available at https://tighar.org/Projects/Earhart/Archives/Forum/FAQs/navigation.html (Accessed 31 Jan 2018)

(23 September 1940) "Discovery of Human Remains on Gardner Island". Available at https://tighar.org/Publications/Ttracks/13_1/tarawa.html (Accessed 31 Jan 2018)

Judith Thurman (14 September 2009) "Missing Woman", The New Yorker. Available at https://www.newyorker.com/magazine/2009/09/14/missing-woman (Accessed 31 Jan 2018)

(undated) "Records Relating to Amelia Earhart", National Archives. Available at https://www.archives.gov/news/topics/earhart (Accessed 31 Jan 2018)

(undated) "Itasca, 1930", US Coast Guard. Available at http://collection.europarchive.org/nli/20110225063908/http://www.uscg.mil/history/webcutters/Itasca_1930.pdf (Accessed 31 Jan 2018)

Only an Oil Slick Remained

Jon F. Myhre (undated) "The Hawaii Clipper- A Revised Estimate". Available at http://www.discoveryofflight19.com/hawaiiclipperestimate_2-16-13.pdf (Accessed 25 Jun 2015)

(undated) "Hawaii Clipper", Check-Six. Available at http://www.check-six.com/lib/Famous_Missing/Hawaii_Clipper.htm (Accessed 5 Feb 2018)

Madeleine Noa (11 January 2010) "The Hawaii Clipper Disappearance", Historic Mysteries. Available at https://www

.historicmysteries.com/hawaii-clipper-disappearance/ (Accessed 5 Feb 2018)

Gregg Herken with Ken Fortenberry (1 September 2004) "The Mystery of the Lost Clipper", Air & Space Smithsonian. Available at https://www.airspacemag.com/history-of-flight/the-mystery-of-the-lost-clipper-5467157/?no-ist (Accessed 5 Feb 2018)

Guy Noffsinger (undated) "The Lost Clipper". Available at https://lostclipper.com/ (Accessed 5 Feb 2018)

(undated) "Preliminary Report of Investigation of the Disappearance of an Aircraft of Pin [*sic*] American Airways, Incorporated, in the Vicinity of Latitude 12 Degree 27' North, Longitude 130 Degree 40' East, on July 29, 1938", United States Civil Aeronautics Board. Available at http://dotlibrary.specialcollection.net/Home (Accessed 5 Feb 2018)

Circuit Judge Moore (2 October 1958) "D'Aleman v. Pan American World Airways, Inc.—D'aleman v. Pan American World Airways, Inc., 259 F.2d 493 (2nd Cir. 1958)", Ravel. Available at https://www.ravellaw.com/opinions/ea29dbd151e1d8d7c2ce40f2caac5cb8 (Accessed 11 Feb 2018)

Death of an Aviatrix

Sarah Hall (6 February 1999) "I shot down Amy Johnson's plane", The Guardian. Available at https://www.theguardian.com/uk/1999/feb/06/6 (Accessed 31 Jan 2018)

(21 October 2002) "Inside Out: Amy Johnson", BBC News. Available at http://www.bbc.co.uk/insideout/yorkslincs/series1/amy-johnson.shtml (Accessed 31 Jan 2018)

(13 May 1941) "Whitehall SW1 15th May 1941", The London Gazette. Available at http://www.london-gazette.co.uk/issues/35164/supplements/2804/page.pdf (Accessed 11 Feb 2018)

(undated), Kent History Forum. Available at http://www.kenthistoryforum.co.uk/index.php (Accessed 11 Feb 2018)

Roy Nesbit (19 August 2010) "Missing, Believed Killed", Pen and Sword Aviation (Accessed 11 Feb 2018)

Sophie Jameson, Patrick Foster (6 January 2016) "Flying pioneer Amy Johnson 'chopped to pieces by Royal Navy'", The Telegraph. Available at http://www.telegraph.co.uk/news/uknews/12085305/Flying-pioneer-Amy-Johnson-chopped-to-pieces-by-Royal-Navy-ships-propeller-historian-says.html (Accessed 11 Feb 2018)

(undated) "Amy Johnson: Pioneer Airwoman 1903-1941", Ninety-Nines. Available at https://www.ninety-nines.org/amy-johnson.htm (Accessed 11 Feb 2018)

(undated) "Archives biographies: Amy Johnson 1903-1941", The Insitute of Engineering and Technology. Available at https://www.theiet.org/resources/library/archives/biographies/amy-johnson-biography.cfm (Accessed 11 Feb 2018)

Which Way Did We Fly?

(undated) "The Mystery of Flight 19", Naval Air Station Fort Lauderdale Museum. Available at https://www.nasflmuseum.com/flight-19.html (Accessed 25 Dec 2017)

Don Van Natta Jr (Knight-Ridder News Service) (5 June 1991) "Experts say planes off Fla. aren't the Lost Squadron", The Baltimore Sun. Available at http://articles.baltimoresun.com/1991-06-05/news/1991156054_1_flight-19-lost-squadron-avengers (Accessed 25 Dec 2017)

Michael McDonell (1 June 1973) "Lost Patrol", Naval Aviation News. Available at http://www.aviatorsdatabase.com/wp-content/uploads/2013/07/Lost-Patrol.pdf

Operational Archives Branch, Naval Historical Center (7 August 2006) "The Loss of Flight 19", Naval Historical Center. Available at https://web.archive.org/web/20090413074152/http://www.history.navy.mil/faqs/faq15-1.htm (Accessed 25 Dec 2017)

(6 December 2006) "Five TBM Avender Bombers Lost in the Bermuda Triangle", HistoryNet. Available at http://www.historynet.com/five-tbm-avenger-bombers-lost-in-the-bermuda-triangle.htm (Accessed 11 Feb 2018)

Charlotte Crouch (24 November 2014) "Flight 19: The Lost Squadron", Man Myth Magic. Available at http://manmythmagic.blogspot.com.ee/2014/11/flight-19-lost-squadron-part-one.html (Accessed 11 Feb 2018)

(11 April 2007) "The Bermuda Triangle", Naval Historical Center. Available at https://web.archive.org/web/20090413054319/http://www.history.navy.mil/faqs/faq8-1.htm (Accessed 11 Feb 2018)

The Bermuda Triangle Strikes Again

(15 July 1949) "Airborne Transport, Inc—Miami, Florida, December 28, 1948", United States Civil Aeronautics Board. Available at http://dotlibrary.specialcollection.net/Home (Accessed 27 Dec 2017)

Edward Van Winkle Jones (1950) "Sea's Puzzles Still Baffle Men In Pushbutton Age", Miami Associated Press

(undated) "Into the Blue: The Disappearance of NC16002", The Quester Files. Available at http://www.thequesterfiles.com/dc-3-_nc16002_airborne_transpo.html (Accessed 27 Dec 2017)

The Great Expanse of Lake Michigan

Ursula Zerilli (6 June 2013) "Unsolved mystery: Location of Flight 2501 that disappeared over Lake Michigan eludes searchers 63 years later", Mlive. Available at http://www.mlive.com/news/kalamazoo/index.ssf/2013/06/west_michigan_author_claims_to.html (Accessed 27 Dec 2017)

(18 January 1951) "NORTHWEST AIRLINES, INC.—BENTON HARBOR, MICH., JUNE 23, 1950", United States Civil Aeronautics Board. Available at http://dotlibrary.specialcollection.net/Home (Accessed 27 Dec 2017)

Carla Friedman (undated) "Northwest Orient Airlines Flight 2501 Disappears", World History Project. Available at https://worldhistoryproject.org/1950/6/23/northwest-orient-airlines-flight-2501-disappears (Accessed 2 Jan 2017)

V.O. van Heest (1 June 2013) "Fatal Crossing: The Mysterious Disappearance of NWA Flight 2501 and the Quest for Answers", In-Depth Editions, LLC

(25 June 1950) "DC-4 Last Reported Over Lake Michigan; Oil Slick Located", New York Times. Available at https://www.clickondetroit.com/features/the-unexplained-disappearance-of-northwest-flight-2501-over-lake-michigan# (Accessed 31 Jan 2018)

(undated) "Northwest Airlines Flight 2501 (DC4)", Michigan Ship Wrecks Association. Available at http://michiganshipwrecks.org/shipwrecks-2/shipwreck-categories/airplane-losses-lost-and-found/northwest-airlines-flight-2501-dc4 (Accessed 31 Jan 2018)

Brent Ashcroft (23 November 2015) "New mass grave found for victims of NWA Flight 2501", WZZM13. Available at http://www.wzzm13.com/news/new-mass-grave-found-for-victims-of-nwa-flight-2501_20160405082754180/120783474 (Accessed 31 Jan 2018)

The Kinross Incident

(undated) "The Kinross Incident", National Investigations Committee on Aerial Phenomena. Available at http://www.nicap.org/reports/kinross2.htm (Accessed 2 Jan 2017)

Gord Heath (undated) "What Happened to F-89", UFO*BC. Available at http://www.ufobc.ca/kinross/openingQuestions/whatHappenedToF89.html (Accessed 2 Jan 2017)

Dirk Vander Ploeg (6 August 2006) "New Evidence: The Kinross UFO Incident", UFO Digest. Available at http://www.ufodigest.com/news/0806/kinross.html (Accessed 2 Jan 2017)

(18 October 2006) "Truth or Hoax...Disappearence of F89", Express. Available at https://www.northernexpress.com/news/feature/article-2162-truth-or-hoaxdisappearence-of-f89/ (Accessed 31 Jan 2018)

Brendon Baillod (2003) "Brendon Baillod's Great Lakes Shipwreck Research". Available at http://www.ship-wreck.com/shipwreck/projects.jsp (Accessed 13 Feb 2018)

Romance of the Skies

(9-21 November 1957) "Plane Lost in Pacific: 44 Persons on Board", The Daily Mirror. Available at http://latimesblogs.latimes.com/thedailymirror/2007/11/plane-crash-kil.html (Accessed 13 Feb 2018)

Gregg Herken with Ken Fortenberry (1 September 2004) "The Mystery of the Lost Clipper", Air & Space Smithsonian. Available at https://www.airspacemag.com/history-of-flight/the-mystery-of-the-lost-clipper-5467157/ (Accessed 13 Feb 2018)

Kevin Fagan (4 November 2007) "Romance of the Skies plane crash haunts pair 50 years later", SFGate. Available at https://www.sfgate.com/news/article/Romance-of-the-Skies-plane-crash-haunts-pair-50-3236600.php (Accessed 13 Feb 2018)

(9 November 1957) "Fear Plane, 44 Aboard Lost At Sea", New York Times. Available at http://www.rarenewspapers.com/view/579887 (Accessed 13 Feb 2018)

Dave O'Malley (undated) "This is it: Captain Richard Ogg and the Mid-Pacific End of Pan Am Flight 6", Vintage Wings of Canada. Available at http://www.vintagewings.ca/VintageNews/Stories/tabid/116/articleType/ArticleView/articleId/563/This-is-it.aspx (Accessed 13 Feb 2018)

Christine Negroni (8 November 2017) "1956 Version of Landing an Airplane on Water", New York Times. Available at https://www.nytimes.com/2017/11/08/nyregion/a-miracle-on-the-pacific-53-years-before-sully-landed-on-the-hudson.html (Accessed 13 Feb 2018)

(20 January 1959) "Pan American World Airways, Inc, Boeing 377, N90944", United States Civil Aeronautics Board. Available at http://dotlibrary.specialcollection.net/Home (Accessed 13 Feb 2018)

Friendly Fire or Sabotage?

(10 April 1963) "The Flying Tiger Line Inc., Lckheed Super Constellation 1049H N6921CD Between Guam and the Philippine Islands", Civil Aeronautics Board. Available at https://www.stripes.com/polopoly_fs/1.231964.1374684946!/menu/standard/file/1962%20CAB%20Report.pdf (Accessed 2 Jan 2018)

(10 April 1963) "The Flying Tiger Line Inc., Lookheed Super Constellation 1049H N6921C", Civil Aeronautics Board. Available at https://www.stripes.com/polopoly_fs/1.231964.1374684946!/menu/standard/file/1962%20CAB%20Report.pdf (Accessed 13 Feb 2018)

(undated) "Flying Tiger Line History", Flying Tiger Line Pilots Association. Available at https://www.flyingtigerline.org/ (Accessed 13 Feb 2018)

(16 March 1962) "U.S. Plane Lost with 107, Pacific Search Launched", Milwaukee Sentinel. Available at https://news.google.com/newspapers?id=F60VAAAAIBAJ&sjid=1BAEAAAAIBAJ&dq=flying-tiger&pg=5346 %2C2638051 (Accessed 13 Feb 2018)

The Spy Plane

Annie Jacobsen (16 September 2014) "The Road to Area 51", Los Angeles Times. Available at http://www.latimes.com/entertainment/la-mag-april052009-backstory-story.html (Accessed 24 Jan 2014)

Thomas P. McIninch (2 July 1996) "The Oxcart Story", Central Intelligence Agency [US]. Available at https://www.cia.gov/library/center-for-the-study-of-intelligence/kent-csi/vol15no1/html/v15i1a01p_0001.htm (Accessed 22 Jan 2018)

TD Barnes (undated) "Secret Heros". Available at http://www.area51specialprojects.com/ (Accessed 22 Jan 2018)

Stephen Dowling (2 July 2013) "SR-71 Blackbird: The Cold War's ultimate spy plane", BBC Futures. Available at http://www.bbc.com/future/story/20130701-tales-from-the-blackbird-cockpit (Accessed 22 Jan 2018)

Don Hildebrant (24 June 1905) "Time Line of the SR-71", Roadrunners Internationale. Available at http://roadrunnersinternationale.com/sr-71timeline.pdf (Accessed 5 Feb 2018)

(undated) "Secret Heroes". Available at http://www.area51specialprojects.com/ (Accessed 5 Feb 2018) (undated) “The Blackbird Archive”. Available at https:// www.sr-71.org/blackbird/ (Accessed 5 Feb 2018)

(undated) “Speed Regimes: High Supersonic”, NASA. Available at https://www.grc.nasa.gov/WWW/K-12/airplane/hisup.html (Accessed 5 Feb 2018)

Without a Trace

1970–2016

CONTENTS FOR

WITHOUT A TRACE VOL. II 1970–2016

2019

Introduction

THIS SECOND VOLUME of *Without a Trace* is focused on true mysteries in modern times. My definition of "modern" is somewhat arbitrary, where I counted any case that is younger than I am. I've also been slightly more creative in this volume, in that I've not limited myself to vanishing aircraft. I couldn't resist the story of Dan Cooper, the passenger who disappeared mid-flight with $200,000 in his backpack, and the mystery Boeing 727 which appeared rather than disappearing . . . to this day no one knows where it came from.

The past half-century has had its fair share of unsolved puzzles, but they are overshadowed by Malaysian Airlines 370, which I would call the greatest aviation mystery of our time. However, I hope you will find the rest of the chapters interesting and intriguing as I offer you a wide variety of locations and aircraft types, all of which remain shrouded in mystery to this day.

As always, there are more people to thank than I could possibly list. Special mention goes to Anatoly Belilovsky, Brenta Blevins, CL Holland, Debra Jess, Dan Koboldt, Jim Noble, Mark Nolan, Laura Pearlman, Cliff Stanford, Jon Wickenden and Connor Wrigley for sparing endless time for discussion and research and read-throughs. My editor, Rick Fisher, has nit-picked every line to polish my writing till it shines (and to politely point out when I've confused left and right) and done a sterling job of formatting complicated text so that it looks perfect in every ebook format. Any remaining errors are mine alone.

1970

The Mysterious Truth Behind Foxtrot 94

The 1970s are said to have been the deadliest decade in aviation history, with 16,766 deaths. This is double the 8,318 deaths in the 2000s, the least deadly so far. The second decade in this millennium is looking less rosy—our excitement over 2017 being the first year with no commercial airline fatalities has been tempered by a rash of fatal accidents in 2018 and the loss of two Boeing 737 MAX passenger aircraft in recent months.

Foxtrot 94 is one of my favourite aviation mysteries, in which a military pilot chases after an unidentified object in the sky before disappearing completely. His aircraft was found undamaged at the bottom of the North Sea, with the canopy shut and no trace of the pilot. A favourite of UFO aficionados, here's the whole story.

RAF Binbrook is a former Royal Air Force station in north-east Lincolnshire, England. RAF Binbrook was originally a Bomber Command station during World War II. The Royal Air Force No. 12 Squadron was stationed there until 1942, when they moved to RAF Wickenby. After the war, RAF Binbrook hosted the start of the RAF's transition to jet bombers.

RAF Binbrook also served as the base for the last two RAF squadrons who used the English Electric Lightning, a fantastic aircraft. The Lightning is an all-British Mach 2 fighter aircraft, developed and manufactured by English Electric. It was the RAF's primary interceptor for over twenty years and pilots described flying it as "being saddled to a skyrocket." The aircraft was retired in the late 1980s.

RAF Binbrook closed in the 1990s and was sold off for development, with the control tower demolished in 1995. As of now, most of the accommodation blocks have been demolished except for the married quarters, which form private housing in the new village of Brookenby. The old hangars are now an industrial estate used by private businesses.

In 1970, however, things looked very different. The US and its allies had been at odds with the Soviet Union and its satellite states since the end of the second world war: two superpowers in a political and ideological struggle that showed no sign of resolution.

Soviet aircraft were regularly flying into the North Atlantic to test the reaction from NATO fighters. A little-known radar station called Saxa Vord was a vital part of Britain's air defence, a "front-line" unit offering early warnings of Soviet bombers entering UK airspace. RAF Saxa Vord was the most northern military base, situated on the island of Unst in the Shetland Isles. The island of Unst is farther north than Leningrad and on the same latitude as Anchorage, Alaska.

RAF Saxa Vord gets its name from the hill where the station is located: at 935 feet (285 metres) it is the highest hill on the island of Unst. Saxa Vord's modern claim to fame is that it holds the unofficial British record for highest wind speed: in 1992 the wind was recorded at 197 mph (317 km/h) just before the measuring equipment blew away. The site had been used for highly classified operations since the 1950s, including top-secret radar installations and trials of anti-submarine equipment.

Until recently, the primary source of information about the tragic accident was a series of investigative articles by journalist Pat Otter, who had covered the original search and rescue for local news. This was followed by *Alien Investigator,* a detailed book by a retired Yorkshire police sergeant who confirmed Pat Otter's information and used military contacts to further investigate the mysterious disappearance of the pilot from the aircraft discovered in the North Sea.

The sequence of events started in the evening of the 8th of September in 1970. At 20:17, a radar operator at Saxa Vord spotted an unidentified blip flying over the North Sea, between the Shetlands and Norway. This required a response from the RAF station on Quick Reaction Alert.

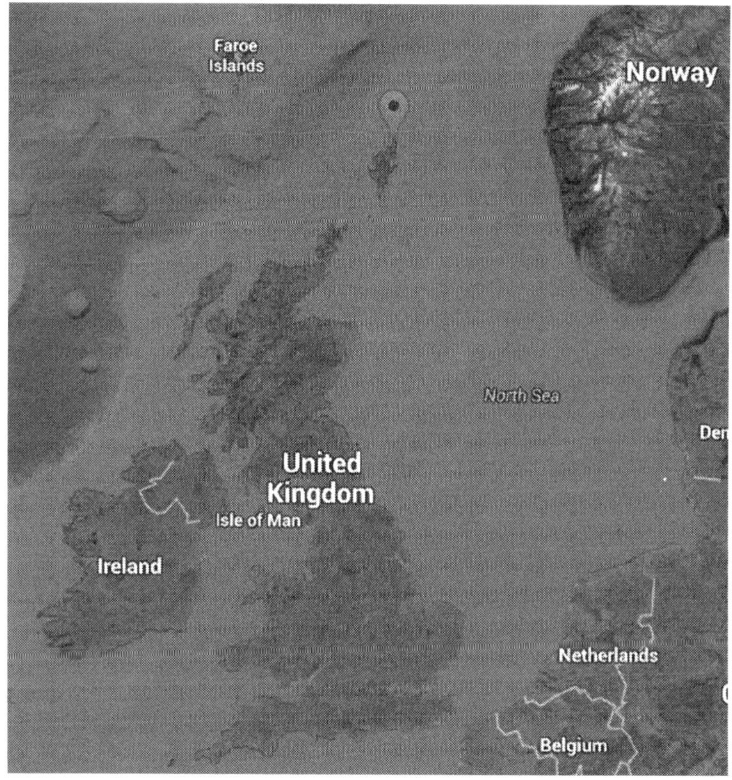

Google Maps screenshot. Map data: Geobasis-DE/BKG, Google, Inst. Geogr. Nacional. Imagery: Data SIO, NOAA, US Navy, NGA, GEBCO, Landsat

Quick Reaction Alert is the 24-hour Royal Air Force air defence maintained by NATO. A Quick Reaction Alert response is to scramble fighter aircraft to investigate an airspace infringement. RAF stations on Quick Reaction Alert have pilots on duty who are fully dressed and waiting in the Aircrew Ready Room, which is always situated next to the hangars housing interceptor aircraft. The duty shift is about twenty hours. Each pilot is on shift once or twice a month. There are currently two Quick Reaction Alert RAF stations: RAF Coningsby and RAF Lossiemouth with two Eurofighter Typhoons loaded and ready to go.

At the time, the Quick Action Alert stations were RAF Coningsby and RAF Binbrook. A 28-year-old American pilot named William Schaffner was on duty at RAF Binbrook.

Captain William Schaffner was a pilot in the United States Air Force stationed in England as an American exchange pilot, flying Lightnings with 5 Squadron out of RAF Binbrook. The Lightning was XS894 and in some references the aircraft was referred to as call sign Foxtrot 94.

The radar operator at Saxa Vord reported the unidentified target, and RAF Leuchars, on the east coast of Scotland, immediately scrambled two English Electric Lightnings. Three radar stations tracked the target: RAF Fylingdales in the North York Moors in England, the US Air Force radar station at Thule Air Base in Greenland and the Cheyenne Mountain Complex in Colorado Springs, Colorado in the US.

The two Lightnings returned to base at the same time as two American F4 Phantoms with more sophisticated radar equipment were scrambled from Keflavik in Iceland to patrol the area. However, the target had been lost. Tensions were high as US and UK military waited.

It was an hour later, at 21:30, when radar operators picked up another unidentified target, almost certainly the same target again, this time heading south-west over the north end of Denmark. Again, two Lightning interceptors were scrambled from RAF Leuchars to patrol north-east of Aberdeen. Another two Lightnings were scrambled from RAF Coltishall.

RAF Staxton Wold in North Yorkshire picked up the unidentified target, which was now flying east of Whitby, parallel to the English coast.

Captain Schaffner was pacing in the Aircrew Ready Room, waiting for his orders to intercept. The Lightning was armed with two Red Top air-to-air missiles.

Finally, the call came. Schaffner boarded the aircraft while they were still filling the fuel tanks. At 22:06, he took off from RAF Binbrook in Lightning XS894. By now, the radar target had held military attention for over four hours.

In 1992, an unofficial transcript of Captain Schaffner speaking to the radar station at RAF Staxton Wold in North Yorkshire was published by the Grimsby Evening Telegraph, which claimed to have got it from a retired investigator from the crash investigation team. In the transcript, Schaffner tells the radar operator that he had made visual contact with the target.

"Can you identify the aircraft type?"

"Negative, nothing recognisable, no clear outlines. There is bluish light. Hell, that's bright . . . very bright."

Schaffner pulled up closer to the unidentified object and described it as a conical shape, so bright that it hurt his eyes to look at it.

The radar operator had two blips on his radar screen, one representing the Lightning and the other representing the unidentified aircraft. "How close are you now?"

"About 400 feet. He's still in my three o'clock. Hey wait, there's something else. It's like a large soccer ball . . . It's like made of glass."

The unidentified aircraft went into a gentle descent and Schaffner continued to follow. He confirmed that the ball object was still with it. "It's not actually connected . . . maybe magnetic attraction to the conical shape. There's a haze of light yellow . . . it's within that haze. Wait a second, it's turning. Coming straight for me. I'm taking evasive action . . . a few . . . I can hardly. . . ."

The radar operator saw the two blips merge into one. The single blip slowed, coming to a halt around 140 miles from the coast, and then disappeared.

And that was the last anyone knew.

The transcript, never confirmed by official sources, was chilling.

Records show an official inquiry into the crash but the results weren't made public. When Captain Schaffner's sons asked for further information, desperate to know how their father had disappeared, they were told that all the reports on the crash had been shredded.

The lack of official information along with the supposed transcript published in the news combined into a perfect storm. Many concluded that the secrecy was a question of international security. Captain Schaffner had been chasing an unknown entity from another world, which had then abducted him when he got too close, dropping his empty aircraft into the North Sea. The story became the best-documented British example of interactions with an unknown extraterrestrial object and probable alien abduction.

It wasn't until 2002, over thirty years after the incident, that the Ministry of Defence succumbed to pressure from the British Broadcasting Corporation to release the classified documents relating to the accident. This included a copy of the inquiry report, the *actual* transcript of the Captain's final conversation with ground controllers and photographs showing the Lightning's empty cockpit.

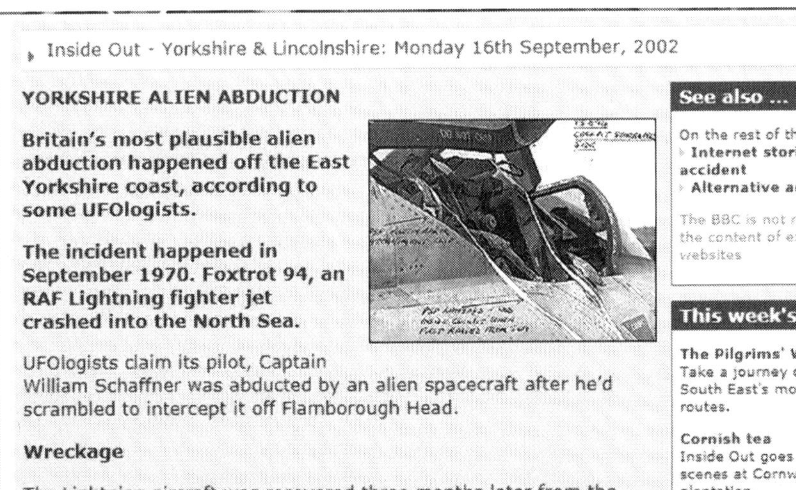

Inside Out - Yorkshire & Lincolnshire: Monday 16th September, 2002

YORKSHIRE ALIEN ABDUCTION

Britain's most plausible alien abduction happened off the East Yorkshire coast, according to some UFOlogists.

The incident happened in September 1970. Foxtrot 94, an RAF Lightning fighter jet crashed into the North Sea.

UFOlogists claim its pilot, Captain William Schaffner was abducted by an alien spacecraft after he'd scrambled to intercept it off Flamborough Head.

Wreckage

The Lightning aircraft was recovered three months later from the seabed. Remarkably, it was virtually undamaged.

See also ...

On the rest of th
Internet stori accident
Alternative a

The BBC is not r the content of e websites

This week's

The Pilgrims' W
Take a journey o South East's mo routes.

Cornish tea
Inside Out goes scenes at Cornw plantation.

Storm chasers

BBC News features Yorkshire's famous UFO story

The first revelation from the Ministry of Defence report is that the radar target wasn't unknown at all. It was British. The radar operators were tracking a slow-moving Shackleton, a long-range maritime patrol and reconnaissance aircraft used by the Royal Air Force. According to the Ministry of Defence, there was never an incursion of British airspace. Instead, it was an exercise to practice shadowing low-flying targets at night.

In that case, why the secrecy? Why not publish the details on the spot instead of letting rumours gather traction? The answer is disturbing: the Ministry of Defence may have wanted the incident to remain secret to hide the results of the inquiry, which showed that Captain Schaffner had not been properly trained to carry out the exercise he'd been asked to undertake.

The RAF's Board of Enquiry report from June 1972 stated that a Tactical Evaluation exercise (TACEVAL) was taking place that night, with RAF Shackletons simulating defecting Soviet aircraft that intended to land in the UK. The point of the exercise was to test the responses of front-line pilots, who only knew that their object was to locate and intercept an unknown radar target.

At the time, Captain Schaffner had flown a total of 121 hours on the Lightning, of which only 18 were at night. He was declared *Limited Combat Ready* after only eight weeks with 5 Squadron, an unusually short time. He had not yet completed his training. Specifically, he was weak on shadowing and shepherding and only considered safe to do so if he had visual contact with the target.

His squadron commander who authorised Captain Schaffner to take part had believed that the exercise that night would *not* include shadowing or shepherding at all, which is why he was happy that the pilot was competent to take part. It was planned as a locate-and-intercept exercise; however at some point that night it was changed and the pilots were asked to shadow and shepherd the slow low-flying targets.

The Shackletons were flying 160 knots (185 mph or 300 km/h, fast for a car but slow for a fighter jet) at just 1,500 feet over the sea.

The man on duty in the Flying Clothing section issued Captain Schaffner with his helmet and oxygen mask on that night and recalled that Captain Schaffner did not want to take his anti-g suit, used to stop the pilot from blacking out during the high-g turns. He was impatient to get going.

Schaffner spent an hour in the crew room in a state of "cockpit readiness" before finally receiving his orders to scramble. As he was taxiing the Lightning, the scramble was cancelled. He returned, asking for fuel only and no turnaround servicing, but the engineering officer overruled him and ordered a full turn-around. During the delay, Captain Schaffner heard that he would be scrambled again as soon as he was ready. He started his engines and taxied before the servicing was complete and was airborne at 20:30.

He climbed to Flight Level 100 (10,000 feet) where he was told to join another Lightning which was shadowing an unknown target, one of the Shackletons. At 28 nautical miles from the target, he was asked to accelerate to Mach .95 (612 knots or 705 mph or 1,135 km/h—fast by anyone's standards) so that he could take over from the other Lightning. A moment later, at 2,000 feet above the water, he reported in a strained voice that he was visual with the lights of the target but needed to manoeuvre to slow down. There's no mention of a bluish light in the transcript released by the RAF, just the description of a "set of lights".

The controller tells him to keep a sharp lookout.

The Other Lightning: Target still at 1,500 feet heading 255.

Captain Schaffner: I'm slowing down I'll be weaving and then I've got 2 one white and one red flashing.

Controller: I'm beginning to lose you on the R/T [radio] now say again.

Schaffner reported contact with two aircraft, which the controller confirmed was the target (the Shackleton) and the other Lightning shadowing it. Schaffner said that as soon as he got the speed burned off, the other Lightning was clear to depart.

The other pilot said that he saw Schaffner at about 2,000 yards astern and about 500 to 1,000 feet above the Shackleton, turning to the left. The Shackleton crew then saw Schaffner and said that the Lightning was flying very low.

Too low.

Schaffner, completely focused on losing speed so he could shadow the slow-moving target, lost sight of his altitude. Following procedures for a shadowing manoeuvre whilst flying low and slow with two targets to track, with radio communication issues too boot, was simply too many different things happening at once for a low-hours pilot who had just been declared *Limited Combat Ready*. With only eighteen hours of night flight, the confusion of the false scramble and interrupted turnaround combined with his lack of training created a level of pressure which was bound to end up in a mistake. This was exactly why he would normally not have been invited to participate in a shadowing exercise at night.

The controller told Schaffner that the target's estimated range from the coast was five miles and if the target came within three miles of the coast, it was to be intercepted to RAF Binbrook. This added time pressure to the already stressful situation. Schaffner acknowledged the instruction. The controller then called again with a new instruction: if the target aircraft approached to within three miles of the UK coastline, it was to be directed to land at Waddington rather than RAF Binbrook.

This time, Captain Schaffner did not respond. The controller continued to call, as did the other flight crew active in the area at the time, but they never heard another word from Schaffner.

The Shackleton broke off the exercise to search the area. At first light, aircraft and ship joined in the search and rescue operation but they found no sign of the aircraft or the pilot.

One of the controllers working that night was willing to share his recollections. I have altered his text slightly, expanding the acronyms and shortenings.

> I well remember this one. I was aht Patrington on my first tour, and was on position beside the guy controlling the Lightning in question. It was a lousy night, stormy, driving rain, low cloud and high winds. We had all been called in because of the Tactical Evaluation. My Flight Commander [controller] was controlling the Lightning that crashed. The Shackleton target came in low, heading due West . . . The Lightning was under him because the A123B radar gave a better picture looking up. At that height, on look down, all it would have seen was sea returns. Both aircraft disappeared into the overhead (about 30 mile radius of clutter) and the Lightning was called, but no reply. We got the Shackleton to double back and start a search, but nothing was found. The Shackleton stayed for several hours, if I remember correctly.
>
> No idea why he wasn't found, but he didn't have his dingy pack, so he couldn't inflate his Mae West.* He wouldn't have survived for long in that sea. Sad day for us all, and made such an impression on me that I remember it vividly after 36 odd years. My old Flight Commander is still around, and I see him from time to time. He was a damn good controller.

---

* This was a popular nickname for an inflatable personal flotation device, because someone wearing the inflated life jacket appeared to be as well-endowed as the voluptuous American actress Mae West.

Some of the details remain hard to explain. For example, the military inquiry confirmed that divers located the aircraft wreckage. The Lightning was resting at the bottom of the seabed, undamaged, with the canopy shut and no sign of Captain Schaffner. The ejection seat handle had been pulled to the full extent but the ejector seat was still in place.

Once the details were made public, the UK Royal Air Force Flight Safety Magazine published a summary of the military inquiry's results.

> It was concluded that the difficult task, carried out in rushed circumstances, combined with a lack of training in this profile, led to the pilot failing to monitor his height while slowing down. He had inadvertently flown into the sea but had attempted to recover the situation by selecting reheat; this was ineffective with the tail skimming the water. He attempted to eject, but this was unsuccessful due to the canopy failing to jettison. He then manually abandoned the aircraft, but was never found. He was, therefore, presumed to have drowned during or after his escape.

Thus, the investigators concluded that as Schaffner slowed down to shadow the low-flying target from underneath, he realised he had dropped too low. When he tried to bail out, the ejector seat failed. The aircraft struck the sea at low speed and skidded along the surface, allowing Schaffner a chance to pull himself out of the aircraft. Then, as the aircraft sank to the bottom of the sea, the canopy drifted shut.

Michael Schaffner, the youngest son of Captain William Schaffner, is happy with the inquiry's results.

> For many, this has become a complicated question of conspiracy theories, allegations, deceptions and the like. However, I think that this is a situation that best illustrates Ockham's Razor: the simplest answer is usually the best. It is an unusual stretch of the imagination to believe that UFOs and government cover-ups are responsible for the tragic death of my father. This is especially true

> having read the Summary Report of the RAF concerning this accident. Contrary to the assertions made by UFO "enthusiasts", it is far simpler, and more logical, to understand these events in their factual context.
>
> My father simply did not notice that he had lost altitude while trying to decelerate to the proper intercept vector. Given the inclement weather, poor instructions, improper training, and overall stress of flying at high speed and high G, it is no stretch of the imagination to believe that he simply made a mistake. I am completely satisfied that my father died because of a chain of unfortunate events, none of which had anything to do with someone's subjective need to believe in UFO's.

Only a few questions remain; however it is still a fascinating story, which in my opinion doesn't suffer in the least for not likely being a case of alien abduction, after all.

Another story involving a missing man is the intriguing tale of Dan Cooper, who disappeared mid-flight during a hijack just one year later.

1971

WHO WAS THE REAL DAN COOPER?

IT WAS A COLD and overcast day in Portland, Oregon on the 24th of November in 1971. Northwest Airlines flight 305 was a scheduled 45-minute flight to Seattle, Washington, the last flight of the day. The aircraft, a Boeing 727-100, was configured for 94 passengers, 66 in coach and 28 in first class. But on that day, the day after Thanksgiving, just 37 passengers were on board, along with six crew members: the captain, the first officer, the flight engineer and three cabin crew. Among those passengers was one who had an entirely different plan of how the flight would end.

A man who identified himself as Dan Cooper bought a one-way ticket to Seattle, paying cash. The ticket agent wrote D. Cooper on the passenger manifest and gave him a boarding card for the aisle seat 18C. The agent remembers the man as white with a swarthy complexion. He wore a business suit with a black tie and carried a briefcase and a small brown paper bag. He paid for the flight with a twenty-dollar bill.

The flight was running late, scheduled to depart at 14:35 local time. After he boarded the aircraft, he drank a bourbon and soda while waiting for take-off. The aircraft finally departed at 15:07.

A few minutes after takeoff, the passenger calling himself Dan Cooper handed a note to a cabin crew member. She was young and pretty, and businessmen often passed her their phone numbers. She stuck the note in her pocket without reading it.

As she walked past him again, he gestured for her attention. "You better read that," he told her. "I have a bomb."

She looked at the briefcase on his lap and pulled the piece of paper back out of her pocket.

The note told her that he had a bomb in his briefcase and that she should sit down next to him. He moved to the window seat and when she sat down, he opened the briefcase. Inside was a mess of wires and a battery and red sticks. This, he told her, was a bomb. Then he dictated a note for her to deliver to the cockpit.

She showed it to another cabin crew member and they both rushed to the cockpit to give the note to the captain.

The actual note is lost but we can work out what it said based on the captain's TTY message to Northwest, rephrased here for easy reading.

> Stewardess has been handed note requesting two hundred thousand and a knapsack by 5 pm Seattle this afternoon. Wants two backpack parachutes, wants money in negotiable American currency, denomination of bills not important. Has bomb in briefcase and will use it if anything is done to block his request. En route to SEA.

Cooper told the cabin crew member that the aircraft should keep flying until they had the money and the parachutes ready for them to pick up. The captain announced over the PA system that they had a technical issue and, as a result, their landing at Seattle would be delayed.

Meanwhile, ATC called the Seattle police to tell them about the situation. The Seattle police contacted the FBI. The FBI contacted Northwest Orient's president, asking him whether he wanted to pay the ransom.

The president didn't hesitate: he quickly agreed that they would pay the $200,000; if the hijacker was serious and blew up the plane, the financial impact to the airline would be much worse than that. But Northwest employees say that he wasn't concerned about the publicity so much as the well-being of the people on board, the crew and the passengers. In any event, he decided immediately that they needed to comply completely with the hijacker's demands.

The FBI created a hijacking crisis crew, consisting of the Seattle police, the FBI, Northwest representatives and the FAA.

They contacted Seafirst Bank, now part of Bank of America, to explain what the hijacker wanted. Seafirst Bank already had cash set aside which had been photographed and the serial numbers recorded, presumably for use in bank robberies. The money had been separated into bundles secured with rubber bands, each one with a different amount, so that it looked like the money had been quickly gathered on the spot.

A police officer picked up the cash and drove it to the airport to hand to Northwest Airlines officials, who put it into a canvas bag for delivery to the aircraft. At the same time, flight operations purchased parachutes from Seattle Sky Sports and Pacific Aviation, who put them into a taxi to the airport.

Northwest flight operations contacted the flight crew to tell them that everything the hijacker had asked for was ready. Ten minutes later, they landed in Seattle. Once the money and the parachutes were on board, Dan Cooper allowed the 36 passengers to disembark. He told the flight crew and one cabin crew member to stay on board.

The request for two full sets of chutes was odd. The FAA's chief psychiatrist thought that the second set might be for the cabin crew member that he had told to stay on board, so that she could jump with him to safety if he blew up the aircraft. As they didn't know who would use the second set—possibly a crew member or a passenger kept as a hostage, they didn't dare sabotage either set. In retrospect, this was undoubtedly Cooper's intention. As it happens, one of the parachutes was actually a training chute and sewn shut, but this was not intentional and the mix up wasn't discovered until it was too late, when the shop realized they no longer had the training chute that they'd sewn up.

Dan Cooper then asked for the aft stairs to be lowered. The Boeing 727 has built in stairs: a rear (ventral) airstair that is built clamshell-style into the aircraft. This means that passengers can board and disembark without needing the airport to provide a mobile stairway or a Jetway. The Boeing 727 airstair also allows the aircraft to be serviced from the rear while the passengers exit from the front. The request was interesting because it meant that Cooper had aviation knowledge; his plan required an aircraft with airstairs that could be released. This meant that he didn't choose a random flight to hijack; he effectively needed a Boeing 727 or a McDonnell Douglas DC-9.

The flight crew explained that the Boeing 727 couldn't take off unless the aft stairs were stowed and Cooper agreed that they could take off with the airstairs up and then lower them after take-off. The truth was that neither the flight crew nor Northwest Airline flight ops knew what would happen if the aft stairs were extended in flight, but they were able to confirm with Boeing experts that it was possible.

Northwest flight operations advised the flight crew that there was no chance the hijacker could successfully parachute out of a 727. They did not pass this information to Cooper.

The truth was that the CIA had already proven that it was possible in 1968 during the Vietnam War. Supposedly, the Boeing 727 was used for cargo airdrops and jumpers in border regions where US troops were not supposed to be. But this wasn't known outside of the CIA and their contractors until years later.

Cooper gave the flight crew instructions to fly towards Mexico City at no higher than 10,000 feet, with the wheels lowered, the flaps set to 15° and all the lights turned off. This meant that they would be flying low enough not to require pressurisation and at a slow and stable speed, while the lights off would make it more difficult to track the aircraft in the cloudy dark night.

The flight crew couldn't follow the instructions to the letter, though. Configured for low and slow flight, their fuel burn would be tremendous: they would never make it to the Mexican border without refuelling on the way. Cooper took this complication in his stride and agreed to a refuelling stop at Reno, Nevada.

Whether Cooper expected and planned for the stop hinges on how much aviation knowledge he had. It's possible that he knew the 727 wouldn't make it to Mexico and was willing to agree to refuel because he knew the aircraft would pass over the area where he wanted to jump: Reno is pretty much due south of Seattle. Or it's possible that he didn't have a plan and simply accepted that he was going to have to jump earlier than he'd anticipated. Certainly, he must have known he needed to be off the plane before they landed in Reno.

Either way, the details were agreed and the Boeing 727 departed Seattle at 19:34; just over five hours had elapsed since the man had first boarded the plane. He still had half a glass of bourbon.

As they climbed away to their cruising height of 10,000 feet, the cabin crew member showed Cooper how to operate the airstairs. He then sent her forward, telling her to close the curtains between first class and coach, where he was sitting, and to wait with the others in the cockpit.

As she closed the curtains, she saw him tying the canvas bag of money around his waist.

A few minutes later, the flight crew saw a light in the cockpit—the indicator showing that the aft door was open had illuminated. Then a warning light illuminated in the cockpit to show that the aft stair was extending. The aircraft's tail pitched up suddenly at quarter past eight, when the aircraft was over Clark County, Washington, but other than that, the Boeing flew normally. No one was sure what was happening in the back.

The captain called Cooper over the intercom system but there was no response. They continued towards Reno, calling again intermittently to see if the hijacker would respond. Nothing.

The flight to Reno was three hours at their speed and altitude. Sparks flew as they touched down as the aft stairs scraped along the runway. The captain tried one more time to speak to Cooper using the intercom as they taxied and parked away from the main apron, in case there was still some sort of bomb on board. When there was no response, they opened the cockpit door. The cabin was empty.

Snap on black tie and tie clip, found on the seat after Cooper disappeared.

The police and the FBI were waiting. As soon as the captain gave the all clear, they boarded the aircraft and began to search for evidence. The money and the hijacker were gone but, if he'd left evidence behind, they could discover who he was and hopefully where he had gone. Searching the cabin, they recovered eight cigarette butts, filter-tipped Raleigh cigarettes, and the plastic cup of bourbon that he'd ordered from the cabin crew. Slung over a seatback near his assigned seat was a narrow black clip-on tie with a tie clip still attached. One full set of parachutes had been abandoned; Cooper had put one set on while the cabin crew member was still watching and had taken the training chute as a reserve. All of the notes to the cockpit were gone.

In 1971, they didn't have access to the kind of DNA testing that we would use now but they did a thorough search for fingerprints, stating at the time that they had recovered a total of sixty-six prints which did not match the crew or any of the passengers released at Seattle.

However, a lot of people pass through a commuter aircraft on any given day, from passengers to crew to maintenance staff and cleaners; narrowing down a suspect seemed an impossible challenge. The FBI called their investigation NORJAK, short for Northwest Hijacking. They interviewed hundreds of people and tracked leads across the nation, but found only dead ends.

Local law enforcement and military personnel conducted massive ground searches over the possible drop zone over many months. By the end of 1972, the searches had been discontinued; they'd found no sign of the man, the parachute or the money. The investigation focused on discovering the identity of the man who had bought the ticket under the name of Dan Cooper. Despite media portrayals, the hijacker never used the initials DB. This was a name created by a journalist, which was picked up by newspapers at the time. Although many Northwest staff had interacted with the man, their descriptions varied wildly and it was difficult to get a real sense of who he was: white with a medium complexion, probably around 40, with a height of about 5′10″ (179cm) and brown hair and brown eyes. A final unexpected lead came from a French comic book series which had never been published in the US. The comic featured a Royal Canadian Air Force test pilot named Dan Cooper. In one issue, published in 1971, Cooper is shown on the cover, falling through the sky as his parachute opens. If this was the source of the name that the hijacker gave when he purchased his ticket, then it's particularly interesting because the series was never released in English, only in French. The FBI wondered if it was proof that the hijacker spent time overseas, perhaps stationed in Europe with the Air Force. This would also explain the aviation and parachuting experience.

These leads didn't offer much in the way of narrowing down the search. Clearly Cooper had either civilian or military parachuting experience, although it seemed crazy to jump into the dark on a rainy night without protective clothing. Many suspected he'd died in the fall; but then, where was the parachute?

Meanwhile, a new problem had arisen: airlines were hit by a spate of copycat crimes in the months after the Cooper case hit the news. In 1973, Boeing added a simple outside wedge to the Boeing 727-100s, which disabled the airstairs during flight but allowed the stairway to be lowered once the airflow decreased. This mechanical device, still used on 727s and DC-9s, is known as a Cooper Vane. The same year, the FAA began requiring that passengers and carry-on luggage be screened before boarding US aircraft.

It took seven years for the first piece of physical evidence to be found. A hunter was with a friend in a heavily forested area north of Ariel, Washington when he found a thin piece of plastic. Thinking it was litter, he picked it up to throw away but when he took a closer look, he realised that it was a placard with instructions for opening the aft stairs of a Boeing 727. He handed it in and the FBI were able to confirm that the placard had come from the Northwest flight overflying the area. This find, along with the wind and weather information and the speed that the aircraft was flying, helped tremendously to reduce the possible drop zone.

Then in 1980, a young boy was digging a fire pit on the shore of the Columbia River when he struck a lump in the sand. He dug it out and he discovered a rotting package of twenty-dollar bills still wrapped in rubber bands, totalling $5,800. The serial numbers on the dollar bills matched the serial numbers recorded by the bank almost a decade before: the boy had found key evidence for the case. No one knew how the money got to that location: it might have floated down the river and become embedded in the shore or someone might have stashed it there, burying it on the beach. The problem is that this location doesn't tie in with the likely drop zone, which means that either one of the eyewitnesses has the timings wrong or the money was moved. Also, the lump that the boy found was above a clay layer which had been caused by dredging . . . dredging which had happened *after* the hijacking in 1971. Finally, the rubber bands were in awfully good shape for having sat in sand and mud for ten years. Thus, it seemed unlikely that the bundle had been in that location since the hijacking. But it also couldn't be taken as evidence that the hijacker survived the jump: the bundle could have been dislodged from a more protected spot at any time over the last few years or found by an unrelated searcher. Law enforcement officials and treasure hunters scoured the area hoping to find more of the missing money but to no avail. The package that the boy had found was the only cash recovered from the $200,000 delivered to the hijacker.

One of the most intriguing things about the mystery hijack of Northwest Airlines flight 305 is the number of people who have claimed to be or have been turned in as Dan or DB Cooper. The FBI received some ten thousand calls pointing the finger at the "real" hijacker, of which over a thousand were seriously investigated. Although many suspects could have been Dan Cooper, or at least could not be excluded, the FBI needed more than that. They needed some piece of evidence linking their suspect to the crime and that's what they never had. This was particularly difficult because there was a clear lack of evidence collected at the scene. In the end, they had only one partial fingerprint, taken from a cigarette butt, which could be said to be unquestionably from the hijacker. By the time identification techniques had been refined, the cigarette butts had been lost. The tie and tie clip were still in evidence and were tested; however the FBI only recovered a partial DNA sample and there's no way to be sure that the tie and clip were definitely from the hijacker or that he was the only one to handle them.

Meanwhile, there have been a number of deathbed confessions, and amateur sleuths continued to announce that they have solved the mystery, with the most recent solution published in late 2018. Many led the most fantastic lives even if they weren't the hijackers of flight 305. I have put together a short description of each of the most interesting suspects, which you can find in the Appendix.

However, one can safely draw only one clear conclusion from the parade of suspicions and confessions: most of them are wrong. Also, all of the main suspects are based on the assumption that Dan Cooper got away with his crime, but many believe that the hijacker did not survive the jump. It's possible or even probable that the hijacker died in the attempt, especially as most of the cash was never found in circulation. Certainly, this is the conclusion that the FBI reached. On the other hand, four further jumps occurred from hijacked Boeing 727s in 1972, during the spate of copycat crimes. All four of those hijackers survived.

The FBI agent in charge of the case in 2009 said, "He came from somewhere and from someone. And that is what we want to know." The agent admitted that the FBI was no longer committing substantial resources to the case but he encouraged the public and those whom he calls "citizen sleuths" to continue to search for clues.

Then in 2016, the FBI closed the case completely.

> The FBI continues to receive tips from members of the public, but none to date have resulted in a definitive identification of the hijacker. The tips have conveyed plausible theories, descriptive information about individuals potentially matching the hijacker, and anecdotes. Unfortunately, none of the tips provided or applications of new investigative technology have yielded the necessary proof of culpability beyond a reasonable doubt.
>
> Consequently, in July of 2016, we redirected resources allocated to the D.B. Cooper case in order to focus on other investigative priorities, following one of the longest and most exhaustive investigations in FBI history. It would be inappropriate to comment on any specific tips provided to us in this case, however our continued posture is to review any physical items provided [directly related to the hijacker's parachute or ransom money] and pursue follow-up actions, as appropriate.

The FBI conceded that although there were many plausible theories, they needed real evidence linking the suspect to the crime, something none of those stepping forward to confess or to finger a family member were able to provide.

Also, the profile changed. Although initially they had said that the hijacker was an accomplished skydiver, later investigators concluded that he probably only had minimal skydiving experience, claiming that he'd left two better parachutes on the aircraft; one of the two that he took was a training parachute that wouldn't open, which had been included accidentally. In addition, they concluded that an experienced skydiver would be unlikely to jump into the rainy dark night without protective clothing.

It's difficult to say. Cooper requested "front and back parachutes" which sounds like a novice but he also turned down instructions as to how to use it and put it on competently, which sounds like an expert. He specified that he wanted a military chute, which was not steerable but, on the other hand, would better withstand the conditions of his jump. His reserve chute was a training parachute which was sewn closed, which is certainly a rookie mistake, but under the circumstances easy to miss: certainly those who packed the parachutes for him didn't realise, as this was not supplied on purpose. Did Cooper have civilian or military parachuting experience? It's very difficult to find a clear answer.

In any event, no further suspects will be considered unless there is new physical evidence, specifically the remains of the parachute or the missing money. Too many resources had been used following up too many false leads, with over 10,000 names being put forward as possible suspects for the case. A retired FBI agent put it clearly:

> Every so often one would come along, and I'd get the rush of adrenaline. There's a guy in a bar with a bunch of $20 bills, he's limping on one leg and someone asks where he got the roll, and he says he might have hijacked an airplane. You track those things down and they just burn out.

There's still the chance that some of the missing money or the remains of the parachute might be found but until that happens, Dan Cooper's heist is a cold case.

It was just a few years after the hijacking, in 1975, when a businessman took off on a similar dark and rainy night, this time on the sleepy Scottish island of Mull. He and his aircraft disappeared and authorities concluded that the aircraft had crashed into the sea. But then six months later the corpse of the pilot was found, alone on top of a hill near the airfield, with only minor damage and no sign of the plane that he'd been flying.

1975

GREAT MULL AIR MYSTERY

I HAVE FLOWN TO the beautiful Isle of Mull in the Scottish Hebrides a number of times and enjoyed beautiful holidays there, so you can bet that when I learned of a forty-year-old mystery there, I started finding out everything I could, like a modern Miss Marple.

The Isle of Mull is the second largest island of the Inner Hebrides, just a short flight (or ferry trip) from Oban on the west coast of Scotland. It has an area of around 875 square kilometres (340 square miles) and a population of around 2,500 people. It's a popular holiday destination in the summer and extremely quiet in the winter. Everyone knows each other. No one locks their door. It's not easy to keep a secret on a place like Mull.

In 1965, the Corps of Royal Engineers of the British Army set up Glenforsa to act as a fixed-wing air ambulance evacuation facility. Glenforsa airfield is a grass runway with no margin for error: hills on one side and the Sound of Mull on the other. The chart for inbound air traffic gives all the technical details and a request to phone before flying in, so they can clear the sheep from the strip.

There's never been an accident on the strip, although there have been altercations. People still speak fondly of the time when Sir Hugh Fraser of Harrods turned up unannounced by helicopter. He and his companions jumped out and the helicopter flew straight back to the mainland. When Old "Fa" Howitt demanded the landing fee, Sir Hugh argued that as the helicopter had never touched down, no money was owed to the airfield. He settled his bill eventually by buying a round of doubles for everyone in the bar.

But that story pales in comparison to the strange events on Christmas Eve in 1975 known locally as the *Great Mull Air Mystery*.

It starts with a Scottish pilot who purchased a Cessna 150, a lovely little single engine plane, in September of that year. He kept it at North Connel airport, near Oban, just ten minutes flight from Glenforsa airfield on the island.

Meanwhile, Peter Gibbs, a 55-year-old London businessman, had arrived on Mull with his girlfriend. They came to explore the Hebrides, he said, looking for opportunities for investment. When he heard there was a small plane for hire nearby, he got on the phone to hire it. He and his girlfriend took the ferry back to the mainland to pick up the aircraft on the 23rd of December.

Gibbs was an experienced pilot with over 2,000 flying hours. He learned to fly Spitfires in the Royal Air Force during World War Two and owned his own aircraft, a Tiger Moth, until 1959 when the aircraft was destroyed in a crash. He didn't purchase another aircraft but continued to fly. An acquaintance from an orchestra he played with described him as passionate about flying but not circumspect.

> He remained passionately devoted to flying and would often take his plane to engagements. He rarely bothered with a map, but would dive down to read the road signs; in fact he showed a lofty disregard for the laws of aviation, at times flying under bridges, etc.

When he chartered the Cessna 150, it seems no one asked to check his paperwork. His private pilot's licence had lapsed over a year earlier and his medical certificate had expired, details that neither his girlfriend nor the owner of the Cessna were aware of.

The couple flew to Glenforsa airfield, planning to use Glenforsa hotel and the airstrip as his base while visiting the rest of the islands.

On the 24th of December, the couple left Glenforsa at dawn to spend the day on the Isle of Skye. They flew back, arriving back at the Glenforsa hotel just in time for Christmas Eve dinner. One report says that they had a bottle of wine with dinner, another claims that Gibbs finished off the meal with a glass of whisky.

After the meal, Peter Gibbs said that he thought it would be possible to do night landings at Glenforsa. If so, this would be very beneficial to him as an investor: night flights to the airfield would increase the opportunities for travel, which would be good for the hotel and other businesses in the area. As someone looking to invest locally, easy access to the island would be a critical issue.

Glenforsa Airfield taken by Keith Boardman in 2005

However, although Glenforsa is a perfectly pleasant airfield, it's hard to imagine a night landing there. The grass strip is 780 metres (2,500 feet) long and there's not much room for expansion. It seems likely that Peter Gibbs might have encountered some argument or even laughter at the thought. For that matter, it seems odd that Gibbs, a very experienced pilot, would have taken the idea seriously.

Whatever the response, Gibbs was adamant that the small airstrip with no lighting was totally suitable for night flights. He stood up and announced to the hotel guests and staff that he was going to prove it. He would do a night circuit, that is, depart the airfield and follow a standard pattern to bring him back around for landing. At Mull, the circuit is always to the north at

800 feet, because of the hills near the coast. So whichever direction you took off on the runway, for a standard circuit you would turn 90° towards the water for your crosswind leg, then 90° again for downwind, flying parallel to the runway you just departed from. Once you have passed the runway, you fly another 90° turn for the base leg before turning 90° for a final approach, leading you straight onto the runway. At Glenforsa, if coming in to runway 08, you need to fly a slightly curved approach for final to avoid the high ground, but the concept is the same. In a Cessna 150, flying carefully, I'd expect a single low-level circuit to take about five minutes, certainly less than ten.

So Gibbs announced he could do a night circuit and land in the dark. The owner of the hotel tried to stop him. It was clearly a foolhardy plan and Gibbs had been drinking. But he received a terse response from the man: "I am not asking permission, I just thought it was courtesy to let you know."

A storm was forecast to arrive that night but when Gibbs and his girlfriend walked out of the hotel, the sky was clear and moonless. They took with them two powerful torches (flashlights) to use as makeshift landing lights. They agreed that she would stay on the ground and use the lights to guide him in while he flew.

The manager listened in on the radio, ready to call an emergency. The other guests at the hotel came out to the field to watch. The girlfriend taxied with Gibbs to the far end of the runway, where she got out and placed the two torches to mark the runway in front of him. These "landing lights" would show Gibbs where the runway threshold was so that he could return to it after his circuit.

Some claimed they saw two sets of lights out on the coast, moving independently, which would suggest someone else was out there. However, Gibbs' girlfriend denied this. She insisted that she was the only one on the runway and there were no other lights other than those on the aircraft.

According to one eyewitness, the Cessna paused for a few minutes with the engine running, an excessively long time. Then the engine revved and the aircraft accelerated down the runway before it took off into the darkness. The guests watched the navigation lights as the Cessna turned out over the Sound of Mull and then turned again, parallel to the runway, before it disappeared from view. One of the guests was a pilot and described it as a perfect take-off. They retreated back to the warmth of the hotel.

Half an hour later, the girlfriend came back into the hotel, alone. She said she hadn't seen or heard any sign of the aircraft, now definitely overdue. The weather had turned bad: rain and sleet battered the field. The others came out. When there was still no sign of the pilot and his aircraft, they called the police.

The police and local volunteers searched the area that night in the face of the storm, following the expected flight path as far as they could. It seemed likely that he had misjudged his location or his height and crashed into the hills near the airfield. They did not find any sign of a crash and gave up until the next morning.

At daybreak, the searchers continued. Word got out and more came to help, hoping there might yet be time for a rescue. Hundreds of volunteers combed the countryside and local fishermen went out in their boats to search the Sound of Mull for floating debris. A Police Mountain Rescue unit searched the hills. The RAF and the Naval Air Service joined the search, bringing helicopters and sonar equipment. A group of people in Oban, on the mainland, said they heard a light aircraft in the darkness overhead the night previous and the search area was extended. It was a massive search effort but it did no good; after a fortnight, the search was called off. The pilot and the Cessna 150 had disappeared without a trace. It was as if he had never been there.

Theories were plentiful. Some thought that he had purposefully disappeared to escape business debts, deliberately setting off in circumstances that would lead to the conclusion that he'd crashed. Others claimed he was an MI5 agent, with secret business in Northern Ireland and he was unable to return in the bad weather. Or perhaps it was a mission gone wrong and he'd been kidnapped or even murdered. He might have gone off course and crashed into the water out of sight, too far from the coast for any flotsam to be found the following morning. One thing they were sure of: he hadn't crashed on the island or else they would have found him.

It was a sad and confusing accident but in the spring of 1976, it became even odder. Four months had passed since the businessman had vanished when a local shepherd discovered a body lying on a hill less than a mile from the airfield. The manager of the hotel and airfield rushed to the scene and confirmed that he recognised the clothes and flying boots: It was Peter Gibbs, still wearing the same clothes as he'd had on that night.

This unexpected discovery raised more questions than it answered. The body was in plain sight, so it made no sense that it hadn't been discovered as a part of the massive search effort. Literally hundreds of people had searched the small island, especially the area near the airfield where he'd been found. How could they possibly have missed him?

The body was taken for forensic tests. There were no signs of injury other than a scraped leg. There were no signs of impact, which would be unmistakable if he'd crashed in the missing aircraft or if he'd jumped (or fallen) out. The cause of death was exposure. There was no trace of drugs or alcohol, even though the other guests at the hotel said they had seen him drinking that night.

How did the body get there? And where the hell was the Cessna?

I could not find any details of the investigation which must have taken place at the time but the conclusion is described in contemporary reports. The authorities decided that it was most likely that Gibbs had ditched the Cessna in the Sound of Mull and then swum to the shore. Cold and disoriented, he crossed the road and collapsed on the hill, where he died. However, further searching for the wreckage in the sound turned up nothing and there were still many unanswered questions. If the aircraft could be found it could help to confirm or deny this sequence of events, which seemed more optimistic than realistic.

Another ten years passed before anyone reported any trace of the Cessna 150. A local diver (some reports say a pair of divers) discovered the wreckage of a red-and-white aircraft in 100 feet of water, about a mile to east of the direct approach to the runway. He said that the aircraft was in pieces: the engine was lying some distance away, one of the wheels was torn off the front Perspex windscreen was shattered and both wings were missing. The diver said that he had read the aircraft's registration and that it was definitely G-AVTN. The doors were locked. Inside the cockpit, he said, was only a large lobster.

Now, it wouldn't be surprising if the pilot lost sight of the airfield and flew into the sea. Taking off in the dark on a whim, after a pleasant evening in the Hotel Glenforsa—quite frankly, it would have been more surprising if he hadn't crashed. But none of this explains how the pilot and his aircraft became separated.

The red-and-white aircraft was found close enough to the coast that he could have swum to shore, which fit in with the investigation theory that he crawled out of the wreckage after landing on or in the water. The divers said that the windscreen of the cockpit was reported as shattered, which could have given him an escape route out of the plane.

Though the forensic tests on his clothes didn't show any sign of salt water or marine life, medical personnel said that it might have been washed away by the rain and snow of the previous four months.

And still, it seems hard to believe this version of events. The damage to the aircraft means that it must have crashed into the water with violent force, rather than the slow ditching that the investigators put forward, and yet the pilot was uninjured. Having climbed through the broken windshield, would he really leave his clothes and boots on as he struggled to swim to shore through the freezing water? By the time he made it to shore, he must have been close to exhaustion. Then, to end up where he was found, he needed to clamber up a steep wall (described in some accounts as a cliff) and then cross a road and then hike up the hill, where he finally collapsed.

Why would he do that? And more importantly, why would he? To get to the hill where his body was found, he needed to cross the road which led to the Glenforsa Hotel. Even if he wasn't sure where the road went, even if he was disoriented, surely it would make more sense to follow the road in hopes of finding people. Or simply collapse upon it, rather than using his last remaining strength to cross it and clamber up the hill in the dark.

These discrepancies led some locals to wonder if he managed to escape the aircraft *before* it crashed into the sea. This is also unlikely, simply because it is pretty difficult to pull yourself out of a crashing aircraft. It wouldn't be simple to escape the cockpit of a flying Cessna 150 let alone while the aircraft is racing towards the sea. If he could get the Cessna stable enough that he could climb out of it, then surely he would have had no need to jump. If he had lost sight of the runway (which seems likely), it would make more sense to search for the lights of Oban and fly there rather than attempt to jump from the aircraft into the black below. Nor could he have somehow accidentally fallen out of the moving 150 unless perhaps while wing-walking. And again, he had no impact injuries, nothing consistent with falling a few hundred feet from a moving aeroplane and smacking into a hill.

The mystery was far from solved. Worse, no one other than the diver had actually seen the wreckage. The photographs taken were so unclear that it was impossible to tell that it was definitely an aircraft, let alone see any details of the Cessna 150, so none of his descriptions could be corroborated. One report claims that the registration number was not painted on the part of the aircraft where the diver had said that he'd seen it. The diver himself returned to the area many times but was never able to find the sunken aircraft again. Other divers also explored the area but found nothing. It was impossible to confirm that he had indeed found Gibbs' aircraft.

Finally, after two more decades, it seemed there was a breakthrough. In 2004, three Royal Navy minesweepers were in the Sound of Mull, testing equipment for detecting mines. They discovered signs of a "mystery aircraft" in the seabed near where the diver had said he'd seen the aircraft. Underwater divers attempted to take video footage but the visibility was too poor. The British Air Accident Investigation Branch reopened the case, hopeful that the discovery would shed new light on the case.

Photographs taken with an underwater camera seemed to show a modern civilian aircraft and the area seemed correct for the missing Cessna, except that one of the wings was still attached. However, with the wreckage apparently just past the maximum depth that the Royal Navy divers could safely reach, it took some time to explore the site. It still isn't clear whether the remains were the same as the diver had discovered and then lost again in the 1980s. One thing was certain: it wasn't a Cessna 150. The wreckage was eventually identified as a Royal Air Force flying boat which had been lost in 1945 in a training exercise.

It's hard to feel confident about the diver's initial find. He may have seen the Cessna 150 and lost it again, or he may have misidentified the 1945 flying boat. Worse, there's at least one other red-and-white aircraft known to have crashed in the sound of Mull which could also be what he saw in the murky water. Although he said he checked the registration, there's never been any evidence to back this up and he may simply have been overcome with the excitement of his apparent find. As a local, he certainly would have known the strange story.

So now we just don't know: is G-AVTN submerged in the waters there or not?

If we presume that the wreck was misidentified and the Cessna 150 has *not* been found in the depths of the sound, then there are other possibilities. Some on the island still believe that the pilot was never involved in a plane crash at all. They believe that someone must have dumped his body on the hillside that spring, some time after the search had been abandoned. If Gibbs had arranged to meet someone, it would explain why he insisted on going out in the dark. Also, a second person on the airfield would explain why some of the guests at the hotel believed they saw more lights on the runway than just the two torches, before the Cessna took off. The theory is that he was attacked and overcome by unknown strangers who then dumped his body there later. But why leave the body on the hill? It seems useless as a warning as no one knew what had happened. The action simply awakened more interest in the mystery and confirmed that Gibbs was definitely dead rather than simply disappeared in the aircraft.

Another explanation recently put forward is that Gibbs was not even flying the plane. As Gibbs' girlfriend set up the torch lights, she could not see in the cockpit. Gibbs could have left the aircraft, trading places with some unknown person who was hiding nearby, who took Gibbs' place in the cockpit. The unknown stranger, then, executed that flawless take off while Gibbs disappeared into the darkness, as a part of a plan to fake his death, but then somehow became disoriented in the wild hills of Mull. But then, what do we make of the poor fool who agreed to fly the aircraft away in order to aid Gibbs' disappearance? Where did he take the Cessna, that no record of it has ever come up again? And also, if a man were to plan to disappear, surely there must be easier ways, without an accomplice, that would not have involved drawing the attention of the entire small island. And finally, it does nothing to explain why he would have stayed behind to hide on the wintry island rather than continue with the aircraft and its supposed other pilot, who have never been found.

The fact is, none of the theories sensibly answers all of the questions raised by this bizarre case. Sadly, they are likely to be all we will get unless somewhere, somehow, G-AVTN or its wreckage is recovered. As it stands, the facts as they are known offer nothing more than a fascinating conversation when warm and dry in a cosy island pub.

It was three years later when another Cessna disappeared under bizarre circumstances, this one a Cessna 182 on the other side of the world. The story of its disappearance is still cited as one of the most persuasive cases of alien abduction in this century.

1978

A UFO Hunter Finds What He's Looking For

Frederick Valentich was 20 years old when he disappeared. His father believed that one day, the aliens would bring him back. Australia's most famous case of alien abduction, Valentich's lost flight is how the Bass Strait Triangle got its nickname.

In 1978, Valentich was a pretty average Australian kid. His dream was to become a professional pilot: he applied to the Royal Australian Air Force twice and then settled for the Air Training Corps. He was studying part-time to become a commercial pilot but struggled with the examinations and failed them twice. He had a private pilot's licence with about 150 total hours flying time and had completed his night rating.

The young man was enthralled with UFOs and the idea of an alien invasion. Shortly before his mysterious flight, Valentich told others that he had seen a flying saucer, moving away very fast. His father said that his son was very worried about what would happen if the extraterrestrials attacked.

It was a sunny evening on the 21st of October in 1978 when Valentich went to Moorabbin Airport, near Melbourne, for a training flight. Moorabbin Airport is a popular general aviation airport and one of the largest aviation education facilities in the world, with 15 flight schools and over 650 instructors. In 2011, Moorabbin was the second busiest airport in Australia.

Valentich was well known there and had no problem booking a rental aircraft for the 21st of October. He received VH-DSJ, a Cessna 182 four-seater single engine light plane.

The weather forecast was good. He filed a flight plan for a trip to King Island, one of the islands of Tasmania, across the Bass Strait.

The Bass Strait is a sea channel which separates Tasmania from the Australian mainland. Pilots always try to reduce the amount of time flying over water, so rather than fly straight across the strait from Melbourne, the standard route is to fly southwest along the coast to Cape Otway, to the western entrance to the Bass Strait. From there, it is only 85 kilometres (50 miles) to fly across the narrow passage between Cape Otway and King Island. Navigating ships through this western approach to the Bass Strait was known as "threading the eye of the needle", as at least 18 ships were wrecked there.

It's about a ninety-minute flight following this route from Moorabbin Airport to King Island Airport.

The first mystery is why Valentich wanted to go to King Island. Originally, he told his family and his girlfriend that he was going there to pick up some crayfish. Once he arrived at Moorabbin airport, he said that he was going to bring some friends back and he took four life jackets with him for the return flight. He planned to depart at 6 pm and told his girlfriend that he'd be back by 7:30 pm, which should have been his estimated time of arrival at King Island.

Another odd detail was that he didn't phone King Island airport to tell them that he was inbound to them, which was important for a night flight. The small airfield on the island is uncontrolled, which means it doesn't have a tower or a controller. Pilots flying there need to know the airspace and the airport layout and follow set procedures, announcing their actions on the radio so that any other aircraft in the area are aware of their movements. They can't rely on anyone being on the ground to offer support or guidance.

Sunset was at 18:43 that evening, which means that the airport would be dark. Unless he phoned in advance and asked someone to turn on the runway lights, he had no chance of landing there.

He had enough fuel to fly to King Island and back to Moorabbin airport without stopping: the round trip journey is about 235 kilometres (145 miles) and would take about three hours in the Cessna, well within its range. So the fact that he hadn't phoned ahead wasn't dangerous, he could circle the island and fly back home without issue. But if King Island was his planned destination, then he was at the very least embarking on a pointless journey.

The lack of that phone call, which he certainly knew was needed, combined with his conflicting explanations as to why he was going to the island, was distinctly odd. Was he picking up crayfish or people? How could he hope to be home by 7:30 pm? Did he actually mean to go to King Island at all that evening?

He might have been up to something nefarious, smuggling along the coast. Maybe he wanted to be alone in the dark looking for UFOs and didn't want to admit it on a flight plan. Or it could have been a simple oversight, one he would have been embarrassed about when he drew near the airport and realised no one was there. All we know for sure is that he never made that phone call.

Shortly past six, he filled the Cessna's tanks, which meant he had five hours flight time. About ten minutes later, he left Moorabbin Airport and flew southwest, as per his flight plan.

The sun set at 18:43. Valentich was flying in the dusky light over the coastline. Pilots get specific training for flying at night because it can be very disorienting. In Australia, night flying requires a separate rating for visual flights. Flying at night over water can be especially dangerous, because the lack of light and terrain features means that you can't judge where the ground is or use it to know if you are straight and level.

As the sunlight faded, Valentich would have seen a sky full of stars above and darkness below.

He contacted Melbourne Air Traffic Control and gave his location as over Cape Otway on the south coast of Victoria. Cape Otway has a lighthouse, which makes it an easy visual reference point. He confirmed that he was proceeding to King Island. His flight plan showed that he would remain below 5,000 feet and that he had estimated it would take him 41 minutes to fly to Cape Otway and then a further 28 minutes from Cape Otway to King Island. He was right on schedule.

A few minutes later, now flying over the gap between the mainland and King Island, he called Melbourne again.

Valentich: Is there any known traffic below five thousand?

Melbourne Flight Service Unit: No known traffic.

Valentich: I am . . . seems to be a large aircraft below five thousand.

By this he means that the aircraft is below five thousand feet and he is wondering if air traffic control know about the aircraft or have it on radar. They don't.

Melbourne Flight Service Unit: What type of aircraft is it?

Valentich: I cannot affirm. It is four bright . . . it seems to me like landing lights.

An obvious question is: Did Valentich really see anything out there in the dark? At the time, there were rumours that the whole thing was simply a hoax and Valentich was having a laugh before purposefully disappearing. But Valentich had no reason to disappear and his actions before the flight don't seem to be that of someone planning to leave. He was close to his father and to his girlfriend, both of whom are sure that he had no intention of going away. Valentich also truly believed in extraterrestrial beings, so it would be very odd for him to pretend to see something that wasn't there as a joke.

Certainly, the air traffic controller who spoke to Valentich has said that he is convinced that it wasn't a joke. He is sure that Valentich saw *something*.

Valentich: Melbourne, the aircraft has just passed over me at least a thousand feet above.

Melbourne: Roger. And is it a large aircraft? Confirm.

Valentich: Er, unknown, due to the speed it's travelling. Is there any air force aircraft in the vicinity?

Melbourne: No known aircraft in the vicinity.

It's possible that the lights were another light aircraft with no transponder and small enough not to show up on Melbourne's radar. From what Valentich is saying, it is travelling too fast for that, unless it was a military jet. There were no reports of military aircraft in the area.

What makes this case particularly eerie is that there were a number of reports of UFOs that night. Mt Stromlo Observatory advised that the night of the 21st was the peak of a meteor storm and they recorded 10–15 meteor sightings per hour. The uptick in UFO sightings was expected: studies show that 29% of UFO reports are the result of bright stars and planets, and a further 9% are explained by meteors. The UFO sightings that night were almost certainly reactions to the meteor storm. A meteor might also explain a fast moving craft in the sky. However, the meteor storm doesn't explain the four clear lights ("like landing lights") that Valentich reported over him.

Valentich: Melbourne, it's approaching now from due east, towards me.

Melbourne acknowledged the call and then there was the hiss of an open microphone for two seconds. Valentich had pressed to transmit but did not speak immediately. When his voice finally came, it sounded stressed.

Valentich: It seems to me that he's playing some sort of game. He's flying over me two, three times at a time, at speeds I could not identify.

Melbourne: Roger. What is your actual level?

Valentich: My level is four and a half thousand. Four Five Zero Zero.

Melbourne: And confirm you cannot identify the aircraft.

Valentich: Affirmative.

Melbourne: Roger, standby.

Valentich: Melbourne, it's not an aircraft, it is . . . [open microphone for five seconds]

Melbourne: Can you describe the, er, aircraft?

Valentich: As it's flying past it's a long shape. [open microphone for three seconds] Cannot identify more than that it has such speed. [open microphone for three seconds] Before me right now, Melbourne.

Some of what he saw could be explained by fast-moving meteors out of the corner of his eye. However, that doesn't account for a hovering aircraft directly above him.

One of the Department of Transport officials stated that Valentich might have become so confused that he had turned over in the dark. "Valentich became disorientated and saw his own lights reflected in the water, or lights from a nearby island, while flying upside down."

It's possible that it was just the stars and an optical illusion, as they say, but he was very clear that he had seen the other "aircraft" moving.

Melbourne: Roger. And how large would the, er, object be?

Valentich: It seems like it's a stationary. What I'm doing right now is orbiting and the thing is just orbiting on top of me. Also it's got a green light and sort of metallic-like. It's all shiny on the outside.

The mention of the green light doesn't fit with the theory of the planets and stars but neither does this description give us any real hint as to how clearly he could see the object.

It's not clear what Valentich might have meant when he said that he was orbiting, possibly that he was flying in a holding pattern in order to get a better look at the "thing" which he said was orbiting on top of him. What's absolutely clear is that his entire attention is taken by the unidentified flying object.

The sound of an open microphone filled the frequency for another five seconds and then Valentich spoke. "It's just vanished."

Valentich: Melbourne, would you know what kind of aircraft I've got? Is it a military aircraft?

Valentich seems terribly distracted from what he should be focused on: flying the plane. But his curiosity was piqued.

Melbourne: Confirm that the, er, aircraft just vanished?

Valentich: Say again?

Melbourne: Is the aircraft still with you?

Valentich: It's ah no. . . . [open microphone for two seconds] Now approaching from the south west.

A dangerous configuration that has killed many pilots, especially visual pilots who have not been trained to fly by instruments, is known as the *graveyard spiral* or *suicide spiral* and is common in poor weather conditions . . . and at night. As with all illusions, it can be difficult to explain without direct experience in the cockpit.

The pilot becomes disoriented and loses the ability to judge the orientation of the plane. He believes he is flying straight, with the wings level; but, in fact, he is pulling the yoke slightly, leading the aircraft into a bank. The aircraft starts to fly a large circle and, if the pilot does not recognise the situation, the plane will begin a gentle spiral towards the ground.The *graveyard spiral* is the most common of the vestibular illusions caused by the middle ear's balance organ. As you are turning, the fluid inside your ear canal starts moving but, after about 20 seconds, the friction causes the fluid to catch up with the walls of the canal. When this happens, the hairs inside the canal return to their straight-up position, which tells your brain that the turn has stopped even though you are still turning. When you have other senses giving you correct information, it results in a feeling of dizziness. When you don't, it results in the spiral.

Your brain tells you that you are still straight and level, even though you are still in the right turn. If you level out the wings, your brain will believe you are turning and banking to the left, although now you are actually straight and level. Even if you know, it is disconcerting how strong the temptation is to correct for the bank. The compelling belief that you are now turning left leads you to go back into the right turn, correcting the turn that you are certain that you are in. Now that slight bank feels like straight and level: if you correct the bank to straighten the plane, it feels like you are turning. The plane will very slowly and gently continue to fly in circles that get increasingly tighter as the aircraft decends.

Pilots are trained to understand this; however, the illusion cannot be stopped, it can only be ignored. Instrument training teaches you to disbelieve everything you think you know and to trust the instruments. Unfortunately, the certainty that you are turning when you shouldn't be is hard to ignore.

Valentich said that he was orbiting and "the thing" was just orbiting on top of him, so he was probably in a low, slow turn. He did not have much experience with night flights and only had the most basic instrument training. It was dark and he was flying over water, with no horizon to help him to orient himself. He initially saw four white lights but then mentions a green light. His right wing tip has a green light on it, a navigation light.

Could it be that the Cessna was spiralling down and what he saw was his own wing tip, above him?

His next call to Melbourne fits in with this.

Valentich: The engine is, is rough idling. I've got it set at twenty three/twenty four and the thing is coughing.

Melbourne: Roger. What are your intentions?

Melbourne wants to know if he is declaring an emergency and where he plans to go: with engine trouble, the best thing you can do is to land as soon as possible.

Valentich: My intentions are ... to go to King Island. Ah, Melbourne, that strange aircraft is hovering on top of me again. [two seconds open microphone] It's hovering and it's not an aircraft.

His engine was running rough but instead of wondering why, he was still staring out the window at the UFO. Even when asked directly what his intentions are, he didn't consider breaking off the water crossing as a result of his engine trouble.

The rough engine coughing sounds like a fuel issue. If he's flying in a tightening spiral or even upside down, that will decrease the fuel flow, leading to exactly those symptoms.

However, the air traffic controller who spoke to him doesn't believe that this explains what happened. He told the media that he heard nothing that night that made him think that Valentich had become disoriented or lost his bearings.

It doesn't much matter whether the lights were from another aircraft or extraterrestrials or his own wingtip. What Valentich needed to do at that moment was to stop watching his UFO and fly the plane.

Valentich called Melbourne again, and again holds his finger down, pressing the transmit button without speaking. This time, there's 17 seconds of open microphone and then silence.

There were no further transmissions.

Melbourne declared a Search and Rescue alert immediately and at 19:33, when Valentich did not arrive at King Island, an intensive air, sea and land search started. An oil slick was found eighteen miles north of King Island but they established that it could not have come from the Cessna.

They scoured the area for four days but were unable to find any trace of the aircraft. The Department of Transport admitted they had no idea where the young man might be, reporting that "it seems likely that the aircraft did not crash in the sea between Cape Otway and King Island."

COMMONWEALTH OF AUSTRALIA DEPARTMENT OF TRANSPORT

AIRCRAFT ACCIDENT INVESTIGATION SUMMARY REPORT

Reference No. V116/783/1047

1. LOCATION OF OCCURRENCE

	Height a.m.s.l.	Date	Time (Local)	Zone
Not known	-	21.10.78	Not known	EST

2. THE AIRCRAFT

Make and Model	Registration	Certificate of Airworthiness
Cessna 182L	VH-DSJ	Valid from 14 February 1968

Certificate of Registration issued to	Operator	Degree of damage to aircraft
Cephus Day, 33 Reserve Road, Beaumauris, Victoria	SAS Southern Air Services, Northern Avenue, Moorabbin Airport, Victoria	Not known
		Other property damaged: -

Defects discovered: -

3. THE FLIGHT

Last or intended departure point	Time of departure	Next point of intended landing	Purpose of flight	Class of operation
Moorabbin	1819 hours	King Island	Travel	Private

4. THE CREW

Name	Status	Age	Class of licence	Hours on type	Total hours	Degree of injury
Frederick VALENTICH	Pilot	20	Private	Not known	150 (Approx.)	Presumed Fatal

Department of Transport Aircraft Accident Investigation Summary Report V116/783/104

The Bureau of Air Safety Investigation took four years to complete their investigation but they found nothing, concluding that: "the reason for the disappearance of the aircraft has not been determined." The coronial inquiry (a public hearing held to examine the cause and circumstances surrounding an unusual or unnatural death) listed Valentich as missing, presumed dead.

The investigation documents refer to one piece of recovered wreckage, an engine cowl flap washed ashore on Flinders Island (east of King Island) five years after the aircraft had disappeared. But the document could only identify the flap as coming from a Cessna 182 manufactured as a part of the same batch as the rental aircraft that Valentich was flying. It is not at all clear that it came from the same aircraft. Then the flap itself disappeared or was mislaid.

No other trace of the Cessna or Valentich was ever found.

Frederick Valentich's father joined the Victoria UFO Research Centre and continued to hope that his son was alive and abducted by aliens. He waited for his son's return until his death in 2000.

The mystery remains unsolved and the questions with no answers are many. Was Valentich actually planning to go to King Island that night or was he out there searching for signs of extraterrestrial activity? We don't have any hard evidence as to where, exactly, he was. He was not visible on radar and eyewitness reports are confused. Melbourne police received a report of a light aircraft landing near Cape Otway but no evidence of this was found. Another witness said he saw "an erratically moving green light in the sky" which could have been the same lights as Valentich saw or could have been Valentich himself or could be completely unrelated.

Presuming that Valentich did in fact see anything out there, what did he see? The Committee for Skeptical Inquiry have dismissed the idea that it could have been a flying object, convinced that the inexperienced pilot misinterpreted stars in the night as he stared out looking for signs of life. If they're right, then the tragic accident might never have occurred but for the young pilot's fascination with UFOs.

Whether or not UFO hunting was actually the reason for his flight that evening, the fascination of the unknown could easily have ended in a tragic crash. In that case, however, presuming he was where he said he was, why did they not find the wreckage in that narrow gap between the mainland and the island? Where was he really?

And then there's the odd fact that many UFO sightings were reported in Australia that year, including multiple reports of "cigar-shaped objects" from King Island. This is one of the reasons why many still believe that Valentich saw an extraterrestrial flying object. The air traffic controller is one of them. "If he suffered disorientation and crashed into the water you think they would have found a lot of debris. Surely there would have been something found during the intense searches, oil or something."

In 2013, thirty-five years after the disappearance, an astronomer and retired US Air Force pilot put forward a different explanation for the four landing lights. He co-wrote an article for the Committee for Skeptical Inquiry entitled *The Valentich Disappearance: Another UFO Cold Case Solved.*

As it happens, a computer search of the sky for the day, time, and place of Valentich's flight reveals that the four points of bright light he would almost certainly have seen were the following: Venus (which was at its very brightest), Mars, Mercury, and the bright star Antares. These four lights would have represented a diamond shape, given the well-known tendency of viewers to "connect the dots," and so could well have been perceived as an aircraft or UFO. In fact, the striking conjunction was shaped as a vertically elongated diamond, thus explaining Valentich's saying of the UFO that "it's a long shape."

This combined with the "graveyard spiral" leading Valentich to his own green navigation light (or the reflection of it) as above him could explain the disappearance of the aircraft and pilot in a fatal crash . . . but not the lack of any evidence from the crash.

Meanwhile, in 2014 the New Zealand *Herald Sun* reported that UFOlogists believed they were close to a breakthrough in regards the mystery. They have uncovered an amateur photo taken at Cape Otway just twenty minutes after the last transmission from Valentich. The photograph, taken facing Bass Strait, shows . . . well, they describe it as a "dark unidentifiable shape in the sky" which is a pretty accurate description. It's pretty much just a blob in the distance, to be honest. But the Victorian UFO Action group believe that it corroborates the story of a farmer near Adelaide who saw a 30-metre (100-foot) object hovering over his property the morning after Valentich had gone missing. He said that the large object had a light aircraft stuck to the side of it, with the registration clearly visible. He scratched the registration number onto his tractor: it was the same as the Cessna 182 which had disappeared. When the farmer told his friends, they ridiculed him, and so he did not come forward with the information after he heard about Valentich's disappearance. The lead investigator for the Victorian UFO Action group conceded that they did not have any solid proof that the photograph and the sighting were related to Valentich's disappearance but said it was the best new lead for the case.

> It's easy for some to dismiss, but there are corroborating stories confirming that there was a UFO near Adelaide at the time . . . This was an experienced pilot who should have been able to identify another aircraft but was clearly unable to.

There are many UFO stories and sightings in Australia but the disappearance of Frederick Valentich remains one of the most intriguing and inexplicable mysteries.

Just a few years later, Australia was again the site of aircraft that disappeared without a trace, this one in the forests of New South Wales.

1981

THE 38-YEAR SEARCH OF BARRINGTON TOPS

ON THE 9TH OF AUGUST in 1981, a businessman named John Challinor booked an Australian Cessna 210 registration VH-MDX to fly from the small town of Proserpine to Bankstown, a suburb of Sydney, with a refuelling stop in Coolangatta.

Challinor owned the company that the Cessna 210 was registered to. He left Sydney on his motor yacht on the 31st of July, just over a week before the incident, and arranged for Michael Hutchins fly the Cessna 210 to Proserpine to meet the yacht crew there and take them and some others back to Sydney. Hutchins arrived in Proserpine and spent the night on the yacht. The following morning (the 9th of August), Hutchins refuelled and departed for Coolangatta with four passengers on board: Noel Wildash, Ken Price, Rhett Bosler and Phillip Pembroke.

There are two sets of rules for flying: Visual Flight Rules (VFR) and Instrument Flight Rules (IFR). If you are flying VFR then you are flying in visual meteorological conditions (VMC). This means that the weather must allow for a minimum level of visibility, for example, you cannot fly through clouds and you must be able to see the ground. VFR pilots are responsible for visual contact with other traffic: that is, they need to be able to see and avoid other aircraft. The big benefit of flying VFR is that you can choose any flight path you like, within airspace restrictions. You will often find that you can get a more direct route flying VFR than IFR.

If you are flying IFR, you may fly without requiring visibility of the ground or other traffic. IFR was initially referred to as "blind flying", as the view outside of the window is not relevant.

Instrument meteorological conditions (IMC) are specifically weather situations that are below the minimums prescribed for flight under Visual Flight Rules. IFR flights often take place within controlled airspace and require filing a flight plan. The routing is not completely at the pilot's discretion and thus if the weather clears up, it is often the case that pilots will convert their flight to VFR in order to be able to fly more directly to their destinations.

The Cessna VH-MDX was approved for IFR operations but not for flight into known or forecast icing conditions, as it was not equipped with suitable de-icing equipment. It was in good condition, having been serviced from new, and had just completed a 100-hour inspection.

They arrived at Coolangatta. An experienced pilot was operating the refuelling pumps when the Cessna taxied in under high power, he said about 1500 rpm. Five people came out of the aircraft, one of whom he knew well. He said that they looked a bit scared and that the pilot, Hutchins, was pale and looked tired. They all went to the Clubhouse but, soon after, Hutchins grew impatient to get away again.

It was a windy day, making flying bumpy and unpleasant. The pilot mentioned a problem with the aircraft's gyros or the electrics. The witness suggested that they stay overnight in Coolangatta but the pilot refused and picked up the local weather forecasts for their continuing flight.

The next leg was planned *Night VMC* (visual meteorological conditions), which means that they expected to remain in visual conditions and in sight of the ground.

The weather forecasts indicated a strong west-south-westerly airflow over northern New South Wales, with considerable cumulus cloud up to 6,000 feet to the east and over the coast. The freezing level was expected to be between 4,000 and 7,000 feet above mean sea level, and moderate icing was forecast in cloud above that level. A SIGMET (forecast of significant weather which may affect aircraft safety) was current, indicating occasional severe turbulence existed below 12,000 feet to the east of the mountains.

The Cessna departed Coolangatta and proceeded along the coast "without recorded incident" to their waypoint at Taree. From there, they'd planned to fly inland via Singleton and Mt.

McQuoid in order to avoid controlled airspace and the military restricted areas surrounding Williamtown.

As they overflew Taree, the pilot, identifying himself as VH-MDX, contacted Sydney Flight Information Service 5 (FIS 5) to report that they were cruising at 8,000 feet and expected to fly overhead Singleton at 19:30 local time, in about 40 minutes. The Cessna's call sign was quickly shortened to Mike Delta Xray.

Sydney Flight Information Service 5: Mike Delta Xray would you prefer a clearance via overhead Willie if it's available?

By Willie, he meant Williamtown and what he was offering was a direct route crossing over the airport through controlled airspace. It's effectively a shortcut and the pilot confirmed that yes, he'd prefer that. Sydney Flight Information Service contacted Williamtown Tower and then spoke to the controller at Sector One to get clearance for the aircraft to cross.

Sydney FIS 5: There's an aircraft following, a Mike Delta Xray night VMC 210. He was at Taree at five zero . . .

Sector One: Before you go on, we're not night VMC so clearance would not be available in controlled area.

Sydney FIS: It won't?

Sector One: It won't be available in my airspace, anyway.

The airspace in Sector One did not have the weather conditions to allow for the night visual flight. However, they agreed to check with Williamtown Approach to see if it was possible for the Cessna to fly low level along the coast to stay visual.

Sydney FIS: Approach, you have Mike Delta Xray, a Cessna 210. He's overhead Taree at this stage. Sector One advises his airspace is non-VMC. Would there be a clearance available for that aircraft coastal?

Williamtown Approach: I'll check on the weather and let you know.

Sydney FIS: OK then and if you could advise the highest level that he could expect.

Sydney FIS called the Cessna back to let them know the options.

Sydney FIS: I have checked you with Sydney Control and they advise their airspace high level is non-VMC. A clearance coastal at a lower level may be available, I will advise. So would you prefer to take that or track now via Craven, Singleton?

Mike Delta Xray: I prefer to go coastal.

That is, the controller hoped that Williamtown Approach would approve the Cessna following the coastal route below the bad weather and the pilot has agreed that this is the better option. However, a few minutes later, the pilot called back.

Mike Delta Xray: Rather than wait for the clearance, we'll track via Craven, thank you.

This meant that he's decided to take the slower route rather than continue to wait, clearly eager to get to his destination. Sydney FIS called Williamtown to let them know that the Cessna has turned before entering the controlled airspace and instead was following the inland route which avoids it.

Sydney FIS: OK, he couldn't wait, he ended up virtually on the boundary so he took off back to Craven.

Williamtown Approach: Was it that critical, was it?

Sydney FIS: It was that close, yes.

Williamtown Approach: He was running out of gas or something, was he?

Sydney FIS: No, he just didn't want to hang around. He was virtually in controlled airspace and he didn't want to hold in the area, so he's tracking down to Craven.

Williamtown Approach: Which way is he going? Craven-Singleton or something?

Sydney FIS: Yes, he was going to go Craven-Singleton.

Twenty minutes later, the pilot contacted Sydney FIS to report that they were overhead Craven at 8,000 feet and experiencing "considerable turbulence and quite a lot of down draught".

Sydney FIS asks him to standby, as he was dealing with other flights in the area. He also spoke to them about the turbulence and clouds at different altitudes.

The pilot called back.

Mike Delta Xray: Sydney, Mike Delta Xray is in the clag, in turbulence and would request a clearance to ah 10,000 from 8,000.

In the clag means "in cloud", usually low cloud or fog. He was asking if he could climb to 10,000 feet, presumably to get above the turbulence.

The controller contacted another aircraft to check the weather, who confirmed that there was no cloud above 8,000 feet. He passed this information to the Cessna but with a warning that the westerly winds were about 76 knots.

The pilot's next call made it clear that something was wrong. "Just to compound a little problem, I lost my AH and DI and if I could get 10, I'd appreciate it and also a radar steer to Bankstown."

This call meant that he'd lost his artificial horizon (AH) and his directional indicator (DI), both critical for navigation and instrument flying. He was hoping to climb to 10,000 feet and that the controller could use his radar display to give the Cessna directions towards Bankstown.

The controller responded immediately.

Sydney FIS: No traffic at one zero thousand. Report cruising one zero thousand. Can you maintain a rate of climb without your artificial horizon?

The controller was verifying that there were no other flights known to him at 10,000 feet and to report back once he's levelled out, making sure that the pilot could climb safely without an artificial horizon, which is what indicates the aircraft's attitude to the pilot. Without an artificial horizon and out of sight of the ground, it is easy to become confused about whether the aircraft is straight and level.

The following exchange is the controller trying to work out just how bad the situation is. The ADF is the automatic direction finder; this is an electronic navigation aid which allows the pilot to navigate towards radio beacons in instrument flight. If the pilot is in visual meteorological conditions, that is, free of cloud and in sight of the ground, then these instruments aren't critical.

Sydney FIS: Just to confirm your ADF and VOR on board the aircraft are operating normally.

Mike Delta Xray: My ADF is going all over the place.

Sydney FIS: Roger. Just confirm in VMC at this time.

Mike Delta Xray: Negative.

He wasn't in visual conditions. It doesn't matter how often I read that exchange, I feel sick every time.

Sydney Flight Information Service didn't bother to respond to that call; they went straight to Sector One, declaring that *Uncertainty Exists* and asking for radar identification.

An uncertainty phase declares that *Uncertainty Exists* as to the safety of the aircraft and its occupants. It is a precursor to *Alert Phase* (apprehension exists) which, if the situation does not resolve updates to *Distress Phase* (reasonable certainty).

Sydney FIS: Uncertainty phase declared Mike Delta Xray 0926 in IMC VFR. We've got an aircraft who's in IMC on climb to one zero thousand, without an artificial horizon on track Craven Singleton with a wonky ADF. I'll see if he's got a transponder, or which he has, if I can get him to squawk, what code for you, for us, thanks, if we can identify him.

Even in the transcript, the stress in the controller's voice comes across. A transponder (transmitter-receiver) is part of an identification system which emits a signal (or squawk code) which helps air traffic controllers to identify the aircraft.

Sector One was able to identify the position of the Cessna (thirty-six miles north of Singleton on the Mt Sandon-Singleton track). But the pilot had a new problem: the aircraft wasn't climbing. He called to say that he was struggling to reach 8,500 feet and asked for help routing to West Maitland.

Sydney FIS: Mike Delta Xray, present heading?

Mike Delta Xray: Mike Delta Xray is averaging somewhere around 220.

Sector One: 220, tell him I don't know what it's like for cloud. He's in cloud at the moment, is he?

Sydney FIS: Yes, mate.

Sector One: And he's lost his artificial horizon.

Sydney FIS: And his ADF by the sound of things.

Sector One: And his ADF.

Sydney FIS: Yes, he's got problems, this boy.

They gave the Cessna a heading to fly towards West Maitland, the closest airfield where the Cessna could land. The Sydney controller was trying to find out what cloud was like over Williamtown when the pilot called back.

Mike Delta Xray: We've picked up a fair amount of ice and I can just make out a few towns on the coast. I'd appreciate it . . . Oh hell, we just got in a down draught and we're down at about a thousand a minute.

The aircraft was unable to climb as the ice accumulated on the wing and the windy conditions then pushed the aircraft down. Then the next calls showed just how much drama was happening in the cockpit of the Cessna.

Sydney FIS: Mike Delta Xray, roger. Is the aircraft equipped with pitot heating?

Mike Delta Xray: It's a single (engined) and we'll try to continue our flight plan.

Sydney FIS: Roger. The lights are on at Maitland, the lights are on at Maitland.

Mike Delta Xray: Say again Maitland?

Sydney FIS: The lights are on at Maitland, if you wish to divert and make a landing at Maitland.

Mike Delta Xray: No, we thought we had a . . . just to compound things, we thought we had a cockpit fire but we seemed to resolve that little problem. West Maitland, but would appreciate it if you could leave the lights on for a while.

By "leave the lights on" the pilot meant at the airfield in West Maitland, keep the runway lights illuminated so that he would have a better chance of visually identifying it.

The controller asked the aircraft to "squawk ident" with a code of 3000. This involves pressing a button on the transponder which will make the aircraft flash or blossom on the radar controller's screen. The pilot did so but his problems were getting worse.

Mike Delta Xray: We're squawking 3000 ident and we're up and down like a yo-yo.

Sydney FIS: Roger, we're looking for you.

Mike Delta Xray: Sydney, MDX. We're having a little bit of a problem in that our standby compass is swinging like blazes.

Sydney FIS: Roger, are you able to maintain a gyro heading?

Mike Delta Xray: Negative, we've lost the AH and DI, the vacuum pump's gone.

Sydney FIS: MDX Roger Sydney.

Mike Delta Xray: And we're picking up ice.

Sydney FIS: And your present altitude?

Mike Delta Xray: Seven and a half.

Sydney FIS: Roger and if possible, could you give us some idea of your present endurance when available?

The controller was trying to find out the aircraft's fuel situation: how long can the Cessna stay in the air and how far can it go from here. If the fuel situation wasn't critical, the priority had to be to get the aircraft away from terrain and out of icing conditions. But the pilot was no longer in a position to answer.

Mike Delta Xray: We're having strife up here, we're . . .

Mike Delta Xray: We're losing a hell of a lot of . . .

Mike Delta Xray: We're down to six and a half

Sydney FIS: Mike Delta Xray, roger, Sydney. Your lowest safe in that area is six thousand, at this time if you continue towards the coast, towards Williamtown, Sir.

Notice how the controller offered nice and clear information and was no longer asking questions. His priority now was to support the pilot in any way he could: the aircraft needed to stay above six thousand feet to remain clear of terrain and it would be safest to continue flying towards the coast.

But there was no response. The controller called out again.

Sydney FIS: Mike Delta Xray.

Sydney FIS: Mike Delta Xray, Sydney.

Mike Delta Xray: Five thousand!

Sydney FIS: Mike Delta Xray, Sydney.

Sydney FIS: Mike Delta Xray, Sydney.

Sydney FIS: Mike Delta Xray. Mike Delta Xray, Sydney.

Nothing more was heard.

Around the same time, a NASA instructor was conducting a Night/VMC dual training flight in the local area. He diverted to Singleton due to "a wall of cloud" lying on a line to Nelson Bay and heard the final exchanges between Sydney and MDX.

This is from the investigation notes:

> He remembered thinking that the pilot's voice was very casual when commenting that his aircraft was going up and down like something or other and detailing other problems he was having.
>
> The voice became more panicky, however, and on the last call—which was short and said only "Sydney—5000" or something like that, it was nearly screaming.

He heard no calls from the aircraft after that.

The last known radar position of the aircraft was recorded as over Barrington Tops, about a hundred kilometres from Maitland Airport, a national park described in the search report as "the most heavily forested, rugged, inaccessible part of New South Wales".

Sydney Air Search and Rescue immediately diverted a number of commercial flights into the area to carry out a visual search. The aircraft were in the vicinity within ten minutes of the last transmission but they were unable to locate any trace of the Cessna. A full-scale search was in place by the next morning, despite gale-force winds and temperatures below freezing. However, in the rough tree-covered terrain, if the fuel did not ignite, there would be no visible scar, which they knew would make it difficult to locate the crash site.

The search continued for nine days.

From the search report:

> During the period of the search fixed wing aircraft flew 80 sorties totalling 191 search hours and helicopters flew 109 sorties, totalling 175 search hours.
>
> In addition, large ground search parties comprising Police, Forestry, Water Board, Bushwalkers, State Emergency Services personnel supported by 4WD vehicles and trail bikes searched a large part of the most probable area.

The extreme cold at the higher parts of the Barrington Tops and the strong westerly winds made the search dangerous both on the ground and in the air.

> Assistance of the RAAF was made available to photograph the complete search area, subsequent analysis failed to reveal any significant information. Action to utilise Satellite information from "Landsat" and the USAF. also resulted in nil information.

> Ground search by Police and volunteers also failed to provide any information as to the whereabouts of the missing aircraft.

The search ended on Tuesday, the 18th of August 1981, after 413 hours of air search failed to find any evidence of the crash.

The Air Traffic Controller at Sydney FIS that night later posted about what happened on a blog dedicated to collecting information about the crash:

> I was the ATS officer on the Sydney Sector (FIS 5) who had the misfortune to be on duty when these events occurred. It was one of the worst nights of my life.
>
> You may like to know that I was also rostered on the same sector the next day when the search got underway in full with daylight, from memory I think there were 22 aircraft including helicopters involved, I remember afterwards being kept so busy as it stopped one thinking about the events of the night before. They (the search aircraft) found a few older wrecks but never MDX or any indication of the crash site.
>
> There had been numerous accidents where pilots had inadvertently overstressed the aeroplane and pulled the wings off, so it may well be that the wings are in one place or several places and the fuselage body in another and it would be badly compacted either way, so really anybody looking for the aircraft would probably only see perhaps a wingtip or wing and a bit of tail.
>
> —Missing Plane Over Barrington Tops (http://vhmdx.blogspot.com/2011_08_01_archive.html)

The Bushwalkers Wilderness Rescue Squad were involved in the original search and they have never given up. It's been almost forty years but they have continued searching through the area on foot, collating information and tracking the area, attempting to find the crash site.

I spoke to Mark Nolan, a corporal in the Australian Army who is also a bushwalker and a pilot. He's been obsessed with the mystery for years, driven, as he puts it, by wanting to know the end of the story. Mark and the Bushwalkers have used modern technology to limit the area where Mike Delta Xray is likely to have crashed. Working with the New South Wales Police Rescue Squad, they continue to hope to find some remnant of the Cessna 210.

I also heard from Damien Pembroke, whose father was on that plane, after I highlighted the crash and search on my website, Fear of Landing.

He wrote:

> My father was on that fateful flight. His girlfriend was flying above on a commercial flight, pregnant with my little brother (subsequently named Philip). Obviously he never met his father and it is our sincere hope that the plane is found and the lost souls put to rest. My father has no gravestone but a plaque at the nursing home he built which is still owned and operated by my eldest brother and myself.
>
> We would all love some closure after decades of failed searches and fading hope. All the best of luck to the men and women who are sacrificing their time and energy in this noble cause.
>
> We truly appreciate all your individual efforts.
>
> — https://fearoflanding.com/

The Bushwalkers search continues to this day, with support from the National Archives of Australia, the Airways Museum and Civil Aviation Historical Society, the Department of Transport, the Royal Australian Air Force Air Traffic Controllers and the New South Wales National Parks and Wildlife Service. Mark Nolan told me that he remains confident that the Cessna 210 will be found; it is simply a question of when.

A very different mystery occurred two years later when Korean Air Lines 007 disappeared. There's no question as to what happened: the passenger jet was shot down by a Soviet SU-15 fighter plane and crashed with 269 civilians on board. The question is, what was it doing in Russian airspace in the first place?

1978

KOREAN AIR LINES SHOT DOWN BY SOVIET MILITARY (TWICE)

IN ORDER TO MAKE any sense at all of the mystery of Korean Air Lines flight 007, we have to look at a previous flight, Korean Air Lines flight 902, which was disturbingly similar. Both Korean Air Lines flights were shot down by Soviet military, just five years apart. In both instances, the aircraft were travelling via Anchorage and ended up flying off course and into Soviet military space. And in both instances, there's some question as to how the aircraft ended up off course in the first place.

At least in the case of Korean Air Lines flight 902, the crew lived to explain what had gone wrong. Korean Air Lines flight 902 was a scheduled passenger flight from Paris to Seoul with a stop at Anchorage, Alaska to refuel. The aircraft was a Boeing 707 and carried 12 crew and 97 passengers.

These days, a flight from Europe to Korea would overfly Russia. However in 1978, Cold War tensions were high and there were no agreements in place to allow commercial aircraft to transit through Soviet airspace. Also, the US and NATO had repeatedly been caught using reconnaissance aircraft to spy on the USSR. The routing for Korean Air Lines flight 902 was typical for its time, departing Paris to the north and then routing over the UK and the Norwegian Sea. The flight would cross the north-east corner of Greenland to continue across the Arctic Ocean to Anchorage, Alaska.

The Canadian Forces Station *Alert* was a waypoint on this route, located on the north-eastern tip of Ellesmere Island, the northernmost permanently inhabited place in the world. CFS Alert is named after the Arctic explorer HMS Alert whose crew charted the coasts of Ellesmere Island over the winter of 1875–1876 while the ship was packed in ice. The station was of strategic importance during the Cold War due to its location, situated marginally closer to Moscow than to Ottawa. From 1956, the station housed "High Arctic Long Range Communications Research", signals intelligence aimed at intercepting radio signals from Russia.

KAL Flight 902's flightplan (straigh path, Paris to Anchorage to Seoul) and deviation from plan (curve at "X", having turned southeast when over Ellesmere Island)

In 1978, aircraft navigation systems were somewhat more complicated than today, as there was no access to GPS or other modern location systems. Worse, the Boeing 707 did not have an inertial navigation system (INS), which was already in use in other aircraft at the time (and still is today). Instead, they needed to use magnetic headings to follow their route. And that close to the North Pole, well, what's north and what's south can be somewhat open to argument. What's clear is that the flight crew made a mistake as they calculated (or failed to calculate) the magnetic variation and ended up making a slow arc to the right, away from their planned route towards Anchorage. By the end of the arc, the Boeing 707 was flying over Spitsbergen in the Svalbard archipelago to cross the Barents Sea when they should have been continuing across the Arctic Ocean.

From 30,000 feet, the Barents Sea looked quite similar to the Arctic Ocean and the flight crew had no idea that instead of flying towards Anchorage, Alaska, they were flying directly towards the Russian-Finnish border.

When the Boeing 707 appeared on Soviet radar, it was less than 400 km (250 miles) away from USSR territory. Initially, the Soviet military thought it might be one of their own aircraft which was misidentifying itself (using the wrong IFF code); who else would so blatantly fly straight at them? But by the time the Boeing 707 flew over Russian waters near the Kola Peninsula, it was clear that this couldn't be a Soviet aircraft. The Kola Peninsula, in the far northwest of Russia, is almost completely in the Arctic Circle and bordered by the Barents Sea to the north and the White Sea to the east and southeast, to the West is the Finnish border.

The Kola Peninsula was also where the USSR hosted a number of naval bases and military command centres as well as a large number of bomber and reconnaissance aircraft. When flight 902 went astray, the USSR was conducting military exercises there, around the closed city of Severomorsk. At the time, the Soviet Union had over 40 closed cities: classified locations which did not appear on maps and were guarded with barbed wire and towers. A high level of security clearance was required to enter the city, and residents in the local area simply treated the cities as if they weren't there. Some of those closed cities from Soviet times, including Severomorsk, still restrict foreign visitors from visiting to this day.

The command staff were contacted to inform them that an unknown aircraft which wasn't responding to radio signals was flying towards Severomorsk at a speed of 900 km/h and an altitude of 10,000 metres.

The military scrambled a supersonic twin fighter jet, the Sukhoi Su-15, to intercept the unknown aircraft. The Mach-2 interceptors with onboard radar could fly to a ceiling of 60,000 feet and carried two air-to-air guided missiles, which it could shoot down from above its target.

The commander of the Sukhoi Su-15 fighter made visual contact and the commander identified the unknown aircraft as a Boeing RC-135, a type of reconnaissance aircraft based on the Boeing 707 design. The Sukhoi commander also reported that he could see a red maple leaf on the Boeing's tail. It's easy to imagine what his superiors thought of this information, which implied that it was a Canadian aircraft, presumably spying for NATO.

The design on the tail was actually a stork flying across a red circle, which was the Korean Air Lines logo at the time. If anyone had bothered to check, they would have found that Canada's military did not have any Boeing RC-135s, thus the aircraft could not have been Canadian reconnaissance.

The Sukhoi fighter swiftly caught up to the aircraft to intercept.

There are international guidelines as to how to intercept, and every pilot is taught them, so that they will recognize when they are being intercepted. The intercepting aircraft (in this case the fighter jet) is to approach the aircraft on level from behind and then pass the aircraft on the left. Once ahead of the aircraft, the interceptor waggles its wings, which is a signal to watch and follow the interceptor. The aircraft waggles the wings in response to show that the signal has been received and understood. Then the fighter jet leads the way to the closest airport (for landing) or to the border (to lead the aircraft out of the country which it has flown into without authorisation).

In the cockpit of Korean Air Lines flight 902, the captain finally realised that something had gone wrong when a Soviet fighter jet appeared alongside him. He later said that the Sukhoi fighter appeared on his right, the wrong side for an interception, but its existence alone meant that they were very, very lost. The captain says he that turned his landing lights on to signal that he had seen the Soviet fighter and attempted to contact him, or anyone, three times by radio but received no response.

According to the Soviet commander, the Sukhoi flew alongside the airliner and dipped its wings, but the Boeing did not respond. Nor did it make any attempt to land at the nearest aerodrome as was required. There's no mention of the landing lights or any attempt to communicate. Instead, the Boeing made a 90° turn to the right, heading directly for the Finnish border.

At this close range, the Sukhoi commander also saw that the design on the tail wasn't what he'd thought. He contacted his superiors to say that he could see Chinese characters on the tail and that the maple leaf might be an airline logo. A moment later, he corrected that to say that the maple leaf was actually a large red stork with open wings. He repeated the information, stating outright that this was a civilian aircraft and not military at all.

The aircraft was at 30,000 feet flying towards the safety of Finnish airspace. At full speed, it would be outside of Russian airspace within six minutes, presumably with data collected from the Soviet bases. The pressure was on to make a decision.

The military staff on the ground were convinced that the sudden right turn towards Russian airspace must have been deliberate. They may have thought it was a spy plane disguising itself as a civilian aircraft or that the Sukhoi commander had misinterpreted what he saw. They certainly didn't want the aircraft to simply escape.

The Sukhoi commander was given instructions to shoot down the intruding aircraft.

The then-commander of the 21st Corps of the Air Defence of the USSR later justified his decision to *Pravda Report.*

> If we hadn't taken those measures, we wouldn't have accomplished the combat mission. The Soviet Union was conducting large-scale exercises at that moment. The aircraft would have disappeared in six minutes. We all would have been expelled from the party and discharged from the armed forces. I ordered to destroy the aircraft that invaded Soviet airspace. The pilot asked whether he had to shoot the plane down. I repeated to him that it should be destroyed.

The Sukhoi commander launched an air-to-air missile, a Molniya R-60 missile with infrared homing, at the passenger airliner. It missed. He fired again and this time his missile found its target, striking the left wing, destroying the outer engine and breaking off a 4-metre long piece (13 feet). The debris from the wing punctured the fuselage, causing a rapid decompression in the passenger cabin and killing two passengers.

The unpressurised Boeing 707 immediately went into an emergency descent to reduce the chances of hypoxia as the captain made a broadcast on the international emergency frequency, which was picked up by Finnish radio controllers. It's worth noting that the missile hit the *left* wing, so by now, at least, the fighter was on the appropriate side for the intercept.

The Sukhoi lost sight of the Boeing as it descended through cloud. Low on fuel, the fighter jet returned to base, while another Su-15 sped to the location to replace the jet and find the aircraft.

The Boeing had also disappeared from Soviet radar and they had no idea where the aircraft was. However the ground team were able to track the radar image of the broken wing, which they took to be an enemy missile or possibly a drop of spy equipment. Another Sukhoi Su-15 was scrambled to that location.

Inside the Boeing, the flight crew knew they were down to three engines and that the fuselage had been breached. With no GPS, no electronic flight navigation, they still didn't know where they were or that they were so very close to the Finnish border. Once they broke clear of the clouds at 5,000 feet, the captain searched the icy terrain below for a flat place to land. The sun was setting and they had very little time. He made a number of attempts to land but broke off each time as they approached the hostile landscape. After forty minutes of searching for a safe landing spot, dusk was settling. They were out of options.

The commander of the Soviet aircraft made visual contact with the Boeing again as it circled the area. He claimed that the aircraft broke off looking for a safe place to land and continued flying towards Finland. He transmitted to the pilots in English but received no response. According to him, he spotted the frozen lake and flew towards the Boeing, forcing him towards the lake to land.

The Korean Air Line captain said none of this at the time, simply that he discovered the flat ice large enough for the Boeing and successfully landed on the frozen Korpijärvi lake, in Russian territory but just 140 km from the Finnish border.

Although the Sukhoi commander immediately reported the location of the Boeing, it took two hours for the Soviet military police to reach the landing site. The scene there was shocking, with a report at the time saying that as they entered the aircraft, the smell of blood, alcohol and human fecal matter almost overwhelmed then. A KGB investigator recalled the scene to *Pravda Report.*

> "It was something unreal," KGB investigator Valery Desyatkov recalls. "It was all in the wild of Karelian taiga. There was a small frozen lake and a huge airliner on it. The passengers were evacuated and we entered the aircraft. On the left side of the plane there were not less than a hundred shrapnel holes. Oxygen masks were hanging above each seat. Blood was everywhere, but it was not because of the wounds—it was because of the pressure drop. When the plane began to descend sharply, people had blood flowing from their noses and ears."

There were a dozen injuries but no further deaths. Soviet helicopters took the passengers to Kem, a town on the shores of the White Sea. The flight crew was held in Murmansk and questioned as to the reality of their "mission".

After a few days, the passengers were taken to the US consulate in Leningrad and then flown from there to Helsinki. The South Korean government are said to have paid $100,000 for their catering expenses while they were stuck in Russia and the passenger flights back to Seoul.

The flight crew were detained as a part of the investigation into the incident. The USSR declined to cooperate with any other bodies and refused to provide the data from the black boxes.

The aircraft was disassembled and taken for examination by the Soviet Air Defence. They found no spy equipment but were interested in many aspects of the aircraft, including the emergency radio broadcast capability and the fuel drainage system.

The captain and the navigator eventually pled guilty and applied for pardon from the Presidium of the Supreme Soviet, the collective head of state of the USSR at that time, at which point they were released. The investigation concluded that the rushed decision was caused by the fact that the aircraft hadn't been detected and intercepted until it had already entered Soviet airspace. However, other than that, investigators stated that they found no wrongdoing and that, under the circumstances, the response of the Air Defence was correct.

From the *Pravda Report* article:

> "There were representatives of many nations on the plane, but after the crash we became one big nation. Maybe it will be useful to put many high-ranking politicians on one plane and then arrange an air crash for them," one of the surviving passengers, Karlheinz Schwacken of Germany said.

The commander of the Sukhoi now works as a security guard in Petrozavodsk. Korean Air Lines is now known as *Korean Air* and uses a stylized Taegeuk as their logo, which could never be mistaken for a maple leaf. Flight 902 from Paris to Seoul still exists, however it is now an eastbound flight with no need to refuel in Anchorage.

But these changes came later. It was only five years after the shoot down that a disturbingly similar accident happened over Russian territory, this time with much more tragic results.

1983

The situation was still in everyone's mind when another airliner strayed into Soviet territory on the 1st of September in 1983.

This time it was a Korean Air Lines Boeing 747, flight 007 from New York City to Seoul, again with a stop in Anchorage, Alaska for refuelling.

The Cold War had escalated to a new peak and tensions were even higher than in 1978. Communications between Moscow and Washington were at an all time low, with then-President Reagan referring to the USSR as *an evil empire* and using the information picked up from their reconnaissance to justify the costs of his "Star Wars" missile defence project.

At the time, US military aircraft were constantly testing Soviet defences. In April of the same year, US aircraft repeatedly flew over military installations on closed islands and the Soviet military was held responsible, with many Soviet military officials reprimanded or even fired for allowing the critical surveillance to take place. Moscow passed a new law which defined Soviet borders as sacred and authorised local commanders to shoot down intruders without needing the OK from their superiors.

The Kamchatka Peninsula was on high alert as there was a significant missile test scheduled for that day. In addition, a US Air Force RC-135, the same military version of the Boeing 707 that KAL902 was mistaken for, had been flying around the area, probing Soviet responses.

The US knew that new radar had been installed in the area. Primary radar emits a pulsed beam of radio waves. Objects within the radius of the beams, especially metal objects like aeroplanes and large ships, reflect back energy. The radar system then measures the time between the outgoing pulse and the return of the reflection, which means the radar display can show the direction and range of the target. The original radar systems were wartime air defence units, surveillance systems which let a controller know that there were large metal things within the radar radius, along with how far away they were and which direction they were heading. The benefit of primary radar is that the response from the aircraft is involuntary; as the pilot, you can't simply decide that you no longer wish to respond to primary radar.

The US wanted to know how powerful the newly installed radar was, so the USAF reconnaissance aircraft was probing the area and purposely pushing limits in order to discover the limits of the Soviet air defence system. Each time they neared the Soviet airspace, they monitored Soviet radio communications, which told them when they had been spotted. The USAF RC-135 was flying in wide circles east of the Kamchatka Peninsula, purposely moving in and out of the Soviet's radar range.

On the 31st of August, Korean Air Lines 007 departed John F Kennedy International airport 35 minutes behind its scheduled departure time for the trans-Pacific flight to South Korea. There were 246 passengers and 23 crew members on board (3 flight crew, 14 cabin crew and six deadheading crew travelling to Seoul). The first leg of the flight was without incident and the aircraft landed at Anchorage International for refuelling. They departed again at 4 am local time and crossed the International Date Line, making it the 1st of September.

Their route was the oceanic track R-20, a route with 10 waypoints, which passed very close to Soviet-monitored airspace.

Anchorage ATC contacted the crew to confirm the flight plan:

> Korean Air 007 heavy is cleared to Seoul via the Anchorage eight departure then as filed climb and maintain flight level 310; departure frequency 118.6, squawk 6072.

This means that the flight was cleared via a specific route (as filed) at flight level 310 (31,000 feet), and that they should change frequency to speak to departures and set their transponder to 6072, which would show on radar displays, allowing the controllers to identify the aircraft. Of course, squawking an identification number only works for radar controllers who are talking to each other and sharing information.

The aircraft climbed to 1,000 feet and turned to the left for its westbound flight to Seoul. The autopilot was engaged in HEADING mode two minutes and nine seconds after take-off.

The next instruction was for the aircraft to turn to heading 220° and follow that heading to the BETHEL navigational waypoint and then follow the transoceanic track R-20 to Seoul.

The BETHEL waypoint was 346 miles (557 kilometres) from Anchorage. The aircraft navigation would be in heading mode until it reached BETHEL, at which point the flight was in range of the R-20 route and the system would automatically switch the autopilot to Inertial Navigation System or INS.

The autopilot on the Boeing 747 had four control modes: HEADING, VOR/LOC, ILS and INS. The HEADING mode was simple: the crew entered a heading, for example 220°, and the autopilot would follow that magnetic course until a new heading or a new mode was selected. In VOR/LOC mode, the flight crew chooses ground-based beacons and the aircraft uses them as waypoints to follow a specific course, like a dot-to-dot drawing. The ILS mode works similarly but also includes a vertical component, used for descending for a guided approach to an airfield. The INS mode, Inertial Navigation System, was used when the flight was not in range of the ground-based beacons and so VOR/LOC mode wouldn't work. Instead, the flight crew entered a list of imaginary waypoints that the autopilot would attempt to follow without external aids or references, that is, it had no external way of confirming whether it had reached the waypoint where it expected to be.

Once the aircraft was within 7.5 nautical miles of the route programmed in and flying in the right direction, the INS mode would attempt to fly from waypoint to waypoint, using gyros and three computers to calculate the change in latitude and longitude. Presuming the system was set up correctly, using INS mode was generally accurate within one nautical mile of the intended destination; easily within the range of being able to correct using VOR/LOC or even ILS mode once the aircraft was back in range of ground-based beacons.

For the oceanic route to Seoul, the Boeing 747 was out of range of beacons and other ground-based navigational aids for most of the flight, which is why INS was not just convenient but absolutely necessary.

The flight crew programmed in the 10 waypoints for the R-20 airway, which would take them from the Alaskan coast to the Japanese coast, at which point the Boeing would be back in range of the navigational beacons it needed. This route took them past Soviet airspace with a clearance of about 17.5 miles (28 km).

However, before they reached BETHEL, the aircraft began to deviate north, flying slightly to the right of its intended route. At Carin Mountain, a navigational waypoint on the way to BETHEL, it was five miles north of where it should have been. Half an hour after take-off, the flight appeared on civilian radar at Kenai. It was 5.6 miles north of where it should have been. This deviation from the published route continued without anyone apparently noticing, the distance from the route increasing steadily.

Korean Air Lines contacted ATC to say that they had passed BETHEL waypoint and estimated that they would reach the next waypoint, NABIE, at 14:30 UTC. However, according to King Salmon military radar, the flight was actually passing north of the beacon, 12.6 nautical miles off course.

How did the aircraft manage to fly off course? It's hard to know. The official investigation believed that the crew could have introduced an INS error of about 10° at Anchorage before starting the final leg of their flight. Another theory is that they entered the wrong heading when flying towards BETHEL, trying to account for the true heading vs. the magnetic heading. The other theory is that they intentionally flew slightly to the north of their route: it would not have been the first time that a Korean Air Lines skirted closer to the Soviet border in order to shave some time off the flight and they'd already suffered a 40-minute delay.

Or they may have intentionally decided to overfly Soviet airspace in order to pass information back to the US reconnaissance, believing their status as a commercial airliner would keep them safe from reprisal.

In any event, when Korean Airlines 007 reported reaching the BETHEL waypoint, they were actually just over 12 miles north of it, but either no one at King Salmon radar noticed or they didn't feel it was their place to mention it.

Now you'll recall that the navigation system could only intercept the transatlantic route using INS if they were within 7.5 nautical miles of it. If the flight crew set up the autopilot for INS mode and did not notice their deviation, then the display would show INS mode (with an amber light instead of green, showing as "ready to initiate") but the Boeing would still be flying in HEADING mode, flying in a straight line corresponding to whatever the last heading was that the flight crew entered.

This means that it's possible that the flight crew set up the autopilot for the INS route, expecting it to kick in once they were in range of the route at BETHEL and then somehow never noticed that INS mode had not engaged. However, if that was the case, then not only did they not notice at the BETHEL waypoint, but somehow the flight crew managed not to notice *for the next five hours* as Korean Air Lines flight 007 continued in a straight line without ever reaching any of the programmed waypoints while the display continued to show INS mode with an amber light (instead of the green to show that INS was engaged).

That is the conclusion that the official investigation came to: the flight crew made a simple mistake and then never noticed that the INS mode had not engaged. But if this is the truth, it's not just the flight crew who never noticed. The aircraft had also crossed the border of the North American Air Defense buffer zone, a military area north of the R-20 route which was off limits to civilian aircraft. None of the military radar personnel highlighted the deviation into military airspace. Everyone was asleep at the wheel . . . or it was an intentional deviation and known to US personnel.

In the cabin, the passengers did not notice anything amiss. It was dark and they were asleep, and maybe the pilots were too. Certainly, they continued to fail to notice that they were off route, continuing to report regularly to ATC, ticking off the planned waypoints, apparently never noticing that they were further and further from their route each time.

By now, they were no longer flying towards South Korea; the Boeing was making a beeline towards Siberia. While still over international waters, the flight caught the attention of the Soviet military.

This time, the Russians did not rush their response. They tracked the aircraft for over an hour, trying to determine if it was a civilian aircraft or a military one.

Another Korean Air Lines flight, KAL015, was on the same route to Seoul having refuelled at Anchorage. They were correctly following the R-20 airway and reporting the waypoints to ATC.

Around that time, Korean Air Lines 007 attempted to report the NABIE waypoint, some 200 miles west of the Alaska coast. By now, flight 007 was about 100 miles off track and about to enter Soviet airspace over the Kamchatka peninsula. They found that they were unable to reach ATC and they asked for KAL015 to please relay the message that they were at NABIE. Theoretically, KAL015 was just a few minutes behind on the same route. The flight crew discussed the communications failure but put it down to a problem with the radio, rather than realising they were out of range. They tried using the high frequency radio, which has a longer range, but still never considered that the aircraft was out of range of ATC communications

Three times, the flight crew asked KAL015 to relay messages to ATC. They also chatted to KAL015 about the headwinds that they were experiencing. The flight crew of the other aircraft said that no, they were experiencing strong tailwinds. Again, the flight crew discussed the anomaly in the cockpit but failed to draw any sensible conclusion as to the different flying conditions.

The USAF reconnaissance aircraft was also in the area and should have noticed the civilian aircraft's deviation from the airway. They should also have overheard the Soviet chatter about the aircraft, since a primary reason for being at that location was to intercept military communications by radio. But again, there was no attempt to contact flight 007 nor any record of the USAF crew attempting to tell anyone about the passenger jet which was entering the Soviet airspace that they were monitoring.

Korean Air Lines used high frequency radio to contact ATC with an updated ETA for the next waypoint, NEEVA, showing that the crew was awake, monitoring instruments and calculating the details of the flight. However, there is nothing on the cockpit voice recorder which shows any awareness of their situation.

Flight 007 was now 185 miles off course and nearing the Kamchatka Peninsula, which lies between the Bering Sea and the Sea of Okhotsk. At the time, the southern edge of the peninsula held a large naval base and was home to the Soviet Pacific nuclear submarine fleet. This was prohibited airspace, closed even to Russian civilian aircraft, and the peninsula closely guarded, with no land link by road or train.

The Boeing 747 overflew it.

The Soviets could no longer believe that this might be a civilian aircraft. Two MiG25 jets were scrambled to identify and intercept the unknown aircraft.

One military captain's disbelief was recorded on radio:

> Two pilots have just been sent up, command at the command post. We do not know what is happening just now. It's heading straight for our island [Sakhalin] . . . this looks very suspicious to me. I don't think the enemy is stupid. Can it be one of ours?

Local command scrambled another two MiG-25 jets, four of them now in the air and ready to deal with the intruder.

However, the jets had very little fuel—a deliberate policy, to prevent pilots from being tempted to defect to foreign soil once they were in the air—so all four fighters were forced to turn back to refuel before they made visual contact with the Boeing 747.

As the Boeing 747 continued on its dangerous route, it flew out of Soviet airspace into the relative safety of the Sea of Okhotsk, international waters. The military had lost their chance.

The conversation between the Soviet generals was tense.

General Kornukov: The fighter from Sokol is six kilometres away. Locked on, orders were given to arm weapons. The target is not responding to [requests to identify itself]. He cannot identify it visually because it is still dark, but he is still locked on.

General Kamenski: We must find out, maybe it is some civilian craft or God knows who.

General Kornukov: What civilian? [It] has flown over Kamchatka! It [came] from the ocean without identification. I am giving the order to attack if it crosses the State border.

The Boeing 747 continued in a straight line and twenty minutes later, it flew into Soviet Airspace, continuing straight towards Sakhalin Island and the Soviet's secret military base

The Soviet military couldn't believe what they were seeing. Although they were already convinced this was the RC-135 surveillance aircraft or a new one brought in for espionage, never before had the US Air Force been so blatant. The radar operators reclassified the aircraft from unidentified to military.

The generals did not want the embarrassment of missing this second chance to intercept the intruder. They scrambled three Sukhoi Su-15 fighters.

The radar controllers reclassified the target from military to combat, which meant that the commanders of the aircraft were able to engage the enemy if they decided it was necessary.

The commander of the Sukhoi Su-15 recalls that he was surprised to be sent to his fighter jet this early in the morning; it was much too early for the American surveillance planes, he thought, because they didn't usually appear until close to lunchtime. He received the clearance to depart and sped towards the radar target at 600 mph, catching up to the Boeing 747 in ten minutes. He saw the aircraft through the clouds and although at the time he claimed that all of the unknown aircraft's navigation lights were turned off, he later told journalists that it wasn't true, that he could see the lights through the clouds. The commander said he could tell that the aircraft was an airliner but it was hard to make out detail in the dim dusk light. He thought it might be a civilian aircraft modified for military use.

He received a confusing array of orders: destroy the intruder, intercept and force it to land, fire warning bursts.

Meanwhile, in the cockpit of the Boeing 747, the Korean flight crew finished their meal and chatted about currency exchange options at the domestic building of the airport.

It's no longer clear whether the commander of the Soviet SU-15 hailed the Boeing 747 on the emergency frequency, which is generally monitored in the cockpit of commercial aircraft. In 1991, when interviewed about the incident, he said that he never attempted to hail them, that it was a lie made up for the media after the event. However, the transcripts show that the commander reported directly to his superiors that he had the target in sight but "the target isn't responding to the call", contrary to his later claim that his attempt to hail was made up after the event. In any event, it's clear that contact with flight 007 was not established. From the cockpit voice recorders, the Korean flight crew seemed oblivious, showing no sign that they were aware of the fighter jet.

They contacted Tokyo control ATC and asked to climb to 35,000 feet, probably for the fuel savings of flying at a higher altitude.

The Tokyo controller initially asked them to maintain their current cruise level, which was 33,000 feet. The Captain complained to his first officer again about how bad the radio reception was.

The Su-15 commander flashed his lights and then, following the command received from ground, he fired a burst of 200 bullets at the Boeing 747. This was a warning shot across the bow, to signal to the flight crew the immediate need to land. He received no acknowledgement; from his point of view there was no sign that the pilots of the flight would allow themselves to be intercepted.

Directly after he fired on the airliner, the Tokyo controller cleared Korean Airlines 007 for FL350. As the flight crew initiated the climb, the airspeed dropped; the aircraft naturally slowed down. The Soviet fighter pilot suddenly found himself passing the Boeing 747 and in front of it, in what the commander could only interpret as an evasive manoeuvre. He reported to his superiors that he had lost his attack position.

Commander: The target is decreasing speed. I'm going around it. I'm already moving in front of the target.

General Kornukov: Oh [expletive]! How long does it take him to get into attack position? He is already getting out into neutral waters! Engage afterburner immediately. Bring in the MiG 23 as well. While you are wasting time it will fly right out.

As the Boeing was about to leave Soviet territory for international airspace, the Su-15 commander received the clear order: Destroy the target.

In 1991, he told *Izvestia* about that moment:

> They [KAL 007] quickly lowered their speed. They were flying at 400 kilometres per hour. My speed was more than 400. I was simply unable to fly slower. In my opinion, the intruder's intentions were plain. If I did not want to go into a stall, I would be forced to overshoot them. That's exactly what happened. We had already flown over the island [Sakhalin]. It is narrow at that point, the target was about to get away . . . Then the ground [controller] gave the command: 'Destroy the target. . . !' That was easy to say. But how? With shells? I had already expended 243 rounds. Ram it? I had always thought of that as poor taste. Ramming is the last resort. Just in case, I had already completed my turn and was coming down on top of him. Then, I had an idea. I dropped below him about 2,000 meters . . . afterburners. Switched on the missiles and brought the nose up sharply. Success! I have a lock on.

He launched two air-to-air missiles, intent on stopping the aircraft from escaping into international airspace.

His account gives interesting insight to the discussions at that moment and he admits that some of the details may have been changed in the political firestorm that followed. But on this point he is absolutely clear:

> "We shot down the plane legally."

One of the missiles missed completely. The second missile burst (?) near the aircraft. The blast from the explosion pierced the fuselage, punching a hole into the cabin. As the cabin lost pressure, the yellow oxygen masks fell and an automated announcement warned everyone to put on their masks. The aircraft rolled to the left and began to descend. The flight crew desperately tried to regain control but it was hopeless. The Boeing 747, with 269 souls on board, crashed into international waters about 30 miles off the coast of Sakhalin Island.

When the Boeing 747 failed to report in for the next waypoint, the Tokyo Air Control Centre controller began to get concerned. When the aircraft was 30 minutes overdue, the controller began notifying other air traffic services and military units to see if they were able to establish radio contact with the flight. It was quickly established that the aircraft had disappeared.

Soviet military set up search and rescue missions within half an hour of the attack, while Tokyo was still calling on all frequencies hoping for an answer.

Initially the Korean government reported that the aircraft had made an emergency landing and that the passengers and crew had been rescued. Then the CIA announced that the aircraft had been found and a Japanese newspaper reported that the passengers and crew had been rescued. Various news media around the world repeated this before finally the truth came out. No one had seen any sign of the Boeing 747; at that point, the Soviet government claimed they had no idea what had happened to the aircraft.

Possibly this was the standard disorganisation and the inevitable fake news flow that frequently plagues the early hours after a major accident, when rumours are shared as fact and spread during the time when everyone is desperate for information. However, it did lead others to suspect later that the CIA may have deliberately started the false rumours, in order to buy time to cover up the espionage mission which had gone so badly wrong.

Although initially the Soviets claimed they had no idea what happened to the flight, they soon admitted they had shot down the "intruder" after it had ignored attempts at interception. The Korean Airlines Boeing 747 was clearly on a spy mission and over sensitive military areas, they said, having flown deep into Soviet territory for several hundred kilometres and ignoring and disobeying the orders of the interceptor fighter planes. Even the flight number, 007, was thought to be an in-joke, referring to the British spy James Bond.

The General Secretary Yuri Andropov said that it was clearly "a sophisticated provocation masterminded by the US special services with the use of a South Korean plane."

The government expressed regret at the loss of life but made it clear that it was the US and the CIA that were to blame, not the Soviet military.

Marshal Nikolai Ogarkov during his September 9, 1983, press conference on the shootdown of Korean Air Lines Flight 007

South Korea, as owner of the aircraft and thus with responsibility for an investigation, designated the US and Japan as search and salvage agents, which meant that the Soviet Union could not salvage the aircraft if it was found outside of Soviet territorial waters.

The United States, South Korea and Japan worked together to search for the wreckage.

The Soviet military, bolstered by civilian ships and divers in the area, searched separately.

Once it was clear there could be no survivors, the search and rescue was downgraded to a search and salvage mission focused on the most important source of information: the flight data recorder and cockpit voice recorder. It was the only way to know what had actually happened on the plane.

The Soviets searched their own waters and a small "high probability" area in international waters. The US claimed that the Soviet searchers were not working with them but instead disrupted the US and Japanese search teams by dropping beacons to sound false pings in the deep water in order to lead the others astray.

Certainly, the Soviets had the advantage of having the last known location of the Boeing. On the third day of the search, they found the wreckage of the aircraft, but they told no one. Civilian divers were sent to the scene two weeks after the disappearance, where they clearly saw the wreckage of the Boeing 747 on the seafloor, but they were sworn to secrecy, only breaking that silence in the last days of the Soviet regime.

The divers expected to find the remains of passengers trapped in the submerged wreckage but as they explored the depths, they discovered that the wreckage was completely demolished and in small pieces. There were no bodies.

One of the divers, Vyacheslav Popov, later told the press:

> I will confess that we felt great relief when we found out that there were no bodies at the bottom. Not only no bodies; there were also no suitcases or large bags. I did not miss a single dive. I have quite a clear impression: The aircraft was filled with garbage, but there were really no people there. Why? Usually when an aircraft crashes, even a small one . . . As a rule there are suitcases and bags, or at least the handles of the suitcases.

The divers found some personal items, a few items of clothing, wallets and shoes. More shoes were found washed up on the beaches of Moneron Island. The Soviets handed them over, not admitting that they'd found the wreck but simply stating that this was all they had recovered: 213 shoes. The photographs made international news.

In Japan, a small amount of human remains washed up onto the shore of Hokkaido, Japan: two partial torsos and individual body parts which were determined to belong to thirteen individuals.

What happened to the rest of the passengers and crew remains a mystery. Many Soviets initially believed this justified their belief that the aircraft was some sort of reverse Trojan horse, an empty civilian aircraft used for the most daring spy escapade of the century. Another theory was that the missile caused some sort of wind-tunnel effect in the fuselage, pulling out all of the passengers at high speed, the bodies disintegrating as they hit the water.

The Su-15 commander said that maybe crabs had devoured everyone. But even he didn't really believe it, not even eight years after the Korean Air Lines flight was shot down.

> You know, even now, I cannot really believe that there were passengers on board. You cannot write off everyone to the crabs . . .

Two months later, Soviet divers discovered the black boxes. Again, the government kept the find under wraps, continuing to claim that they had never found the wreckage.

Those recordings told them that there were at least some non-essential crew on board and that the pilots had not at any point discussed the fact that they were straying into Soviet airspace. But neither did the recordings explain what they were doing there in the first place.

The recordings, the only evidence of what had happened on Korean Airlines 007, were suppressed until 1991.

Meanwhile, the US government seemed to have secrets of its own. The NTSB had taken on the task of investigating the incident. However, almost immediately, the NTSB chief in Alaska received orders from Washington to send all of the documents relating to the NTSB investigation, originals and copies, to the State Department. The NTSB were told to stand down; instead the State Department would conduct the investigation, on the grounds that the crash of Korean Air Lines 007 was not an accident.

Politically, the situation was heating up. The Soviets conceded that the Boeing 747 was a civilian craft but continued to insist that the flight had deliberately been diverted into Soviet airspace in order to spy on the military installations and test the Soviet air defence in the area.

In a further inexplicable decision, the US State Department did not investigate the case. Instead, the US passed the investigation to the ICAO (International Civil Aviation Organisation).

> The ICAO Council adopts standards and recommended practices concerning air navigation, its infrastructure, flight inspection, prevention of unlawful interference, and facilitation of border-crossing procedures for international civil aviation.

This was unexpected—it wasn't (and isn't) normal for the US to relinquish jurisdiction once it had it, especially such a politically sensitive issue such as this one. Besides, the ICAO had only ever headed one accident investigation, so it did not have the experience or the resources that the US authorities had. Passing the accident to them for investigation was a very odd choice.

However, there's one interesting reason why the US government could have preferred the ICAO to run the investigation: the ICAO holds less power than the NTSB. The ICAO cannot subpoena people or documents; they can only ask the governments involved to supply evidence voluntarily. The ICAO has no authority to compel the governments to hand over evidence. This meant that the US government did not have to allow access to political documentation or military information which they considered to be sensitive.

The other inexplicable decision from the US point of view was the lack of military radar information. It seems unlikely, or at least very lax, that the Boeing 747 could have strayed into the US high surveillance area without being noticed, having crossed into the protected area where no civilian aircraft were allowed. The radar controllers must have seen that the aircraft was off course and worse, heading towards Siberia. The CIA was known to be watching the area and listening in on Soviet military radio chatter at the time, which means they should have been alerted very early on that the Soviets had spotted an intruder, one that the CIA supposedly knew nothing about. And yet again, there was no information that the RC-135 ever responded or made any attempt to stop the civilian aircraft from continuing into enemy airspace.

There's also the point that usually, in the case of an air disaster or crash, radar trackings from the Air Force are saved and made available as evidence. However in this case, the US Department of Justice explained that the tapes from the Air Force radar installation at King Salmon Alaska, located in a position where the Boeing 747 could clearly be seen to be off track, had been destroyed after the accident. Initially the Department of Justice stated that the data was destroyed 15 days after the shoot-down, but this was later revised to the statement that the tapes had been recycled with new data 30 hours after the incident. Either way, the aircraft was known to be missing within 30 minutes: 30 hours after the incident, the full search and rescue mission was in force. Erasing the tapes is *at best* gross incompetence.

The military radar details of the Boeing as it flew out of range of civilian installations would clearly have been crucial: it is hard to believe that the tape wouldn't have been pulled and preserved immediately.

The ICAO concluded their investigation with no access to the radar returns of the US military installations en route, no details from the CIA aircraft known to be on an espionage mission in the area and no idea that the black boxes from the aircraft had been recovered. They were, not surprisingly, unable to explain what had happened with any level of confidence.

The ICAO report concluded that the violation of Soviet airspace was accidental. They believed that the crew must have committed a navigational error, much like Korean Air Lines 902 had a few years earlier, despite the fact that the navigation system in the Boeing 747 was much more modern and improved. They put forward the theory that the autopilot had remained in HEADING mode instead of INS mode, conceding that the fact that the crew had not noticed nor performed navigational checks was a clear "lack of situational awareness and flight deck coordination."

The Soviets argued that the aircraft had not flown in a straight line but had been seen to change course on radar; however, as they were also unable or unwilling to show any radar tapes, they could not prove this.

The question remained as to how a commercial airliner could blunder so completely into what was described as "one of the most militarily sensitive and well observed areas of the Cold War" and why the airliner hadn't been tracked by US military long before it entered Soviet territory. The US offered no information or data as to what the land and sea radar arrays had tracked that day.

The R-20 airway which passed so closely to Soviet airspace was closed after the incident but the airlines objected, as it was the shortest of five corridors between Alaska and the Far East. The airway was reopened a month later.

Sukhoi Su-15TM by Greg Goebel

The Sukhoi Su-15 received the gruesome nickname "Boeing Killer", as both Korean Air Lines flights had been shot down by the same model of Soviet fighter jet.

It was clear that the navigational systems needed improvement. If the two aircraft, KAL 902 and KAL 007 had not gone off course, then they would not have entered enemy territory. In both cases, there was the possibility that the flight crew were never even aware that they were off course.

In Alaska, tracking procedures for aircraft departing Alaska were changed, including the important change that military radar installations were expected to work with civilian air traffic in their region.

Until this point, the Global Positioning System, a precision navigation system developed in the US, had only been available for US military use. After this tragedy, the second Boeing which was shot down in foreign airspace that the aircraft had no business entering in the first place, US President Ronald Reagan determined that the Global Positioning System should be made available to civil aviation operators, in order to ensure such a mistake could not be made again. GPS was made available for civilian use free of charge and to this day forms the basis of navigation systems for everything ranging from aircraft to ships to cars to smart phone navigation apps.

As to what really happened, the conspiracy theories were never quelled. The US insisted that the Soviet military had deliberately shot down a civilian aircraft in cold blood. The Soviet countered that the aircraft may have been civilian, which was very hard to deny by now, but insisted that the CIA had deliberately used the Korean Air Lines aircraft and asked the captain, whose background was in the Korean air force, to accidentally-on-purpose fly into the Soviet territory to test their defence responses and attempt to get closer to the secret military installations. It was possible that the first officer and the other crew never knew what had happened, but years later, Soviet officials still believed that someone had taken the decision to enter the restricted airspace, believing the civilian nature of the aircraft would render it safe from reprisals.

Some of the theories were more outlandish, including that the Soviets successfully forced the Boeing 747 to land and pulled most of the passengers and crew onto emergency floats, from where they were sent to prisons and labour camps. The fact that both South Korea and the CIA had reported that the flight had landed on or near Sakhalin six hours after Korean Air Lines 007 had been declared missing lent credence to this theory, but then one would expect some trace of those people to be found eventually.

A further theory was that the incident was a collaboration between the US and the Soviet governments. The loss of US military radar of the flight and the refusal of the Soviet military to release any details were, according to this theory, because the two governments had deliberately conspired to confuse the aircraft and send it off track. This was supported by the records of the Anchorage ARTCC controller who recorded the position of *all* the flights that night, except for two: KAL 007 and its sister flight on the same route, KAL 015. If he had, the deviation would have been caught from the start. Instead, KAL 007 was deliberately sent off track and then shot down . . . apparently in order to assassinate the congressman on board and other congressmen who were expected to be on the flight (but instead chose to fly on KAL 015). However, there's no clear explanation as to why these particular congressmen would have needed assassinating by either the US or the Soviet government, let alone why they would enter into a collaborative effort to kill them.

The oddest of the theories is that there was actually a major air battle that night which has been kept a secret. In this scenario, the USSR fought against the US and Japan in the night sky over the international airspace, in which multiple aircraft were shot down, including the CIA's RC-135 Boeing known to be spying in the area. This theory claims that the passenger jet was caught in the crossfire and was the only lost aircraft which the governments couldn't cover up; the rest held military personnel who were simply declared to have been lost in action without further explanation.

The aftermath of this mystery has been extensive, even though many of the details of the case have never been explained.

It's interesting that this was not the last incident of its kind. Another aircraft blundered into the same Soviet airspace two years later, this time a Japanese airliner whose crew left the navigation system in heading mode, similar to the error put forward by the ICAO investigation. This time, the Soviet military intercepted the flight and immediately established radio communications with the flight crew of the lost airliner. It was escorted out of Soviet territory and continued its flight to Japan without further incident.

More light was shed on the truth behind Korean Airlines 007 in 1991. Eight years after the accident, the political situation was very different: the USSR was struggling economically and militarily, in what we now know to be the final days of the regime. In a show of good faith towards South Korea, Boris Yeltsin released the flight recorders which had been kept secret for all this time. These did not offer any further details on how the navigation of the Boeing 747 had been set up but the cockpit voice recordings did prove that the flight crew never discussed an incursion into airspace or the existence of the fighter jet trying to intercept them; up until the sound of the missile exploding next to the plane, there was no sign of concern or awareness that anything was wrong.

Investigative reporters in Russia started an exposé of the Soviet version of events, interviewing the military staff who had been there at the time—the only witnesses to the actual event, as everyone on the aircraft had perished.

The commander of the Su-15 was also interviewed and made it clear that he still believed that the aircraft was empty. "He does not want these 269 bodies on his conscience," said the investigative reporter who interviewed him. "He desperately wants to believe that the plane was empty."

The ICAO reviewed its investigation in light of the new facts and released a new report. However, this report simply confirmed the original conclusion of an accidental intrusion, with the new detail that an undetected 10° longitudinal error was made at Anchorage gate when they inserted their current position in one or more of the INS units.

A 1993 official enquiry by the Russian Federation absolved the Soviet hierarchy of blame, determining that the incident was a case of mistaken identity.

Journalist Nicholas Daniloff published a memoir of his time in Soviet Russia as a War Correspondent, called *From of Spies and Spokesman: My Life as a Cold War Correspondent.* The book includes his recollection of a conversation with an ex-KGB Chief, who was 100% convinced that the Reagan administration had used the Korean airliner for an espionage operation:

> . . . It just shows what lengths the Reagan administration goes. It bolsters the feeling in some quarters here that the White House wants to destroy socialism as it exists in the Soviet Union today.

Daniloff also quotes a former Brezhnev aid speaking after the fact:

> If there had been the slightest recognition that this was a passenger plane, it would not have been shot down. In more peaceful times, the Japanese could have telephoned Khabarovsk [the Soviet Far East air control centre]. There is a direct line. They could have said, 'Hey you guys, do you know anything about this plane?' Or Khabarovsk could have called Tokyo to ask what this plane was doing. But nobody could make such a call in the current situation. No one would even think of it.

The secrecy and deliberate cover-ups at the time, many of which are now clearly documented, make it impossible to unravel what happened that day. Did Korean Air Lines 007 flight crew make an innocent mistake before appearing to deliberately fly over top-secret Soviet military installations? Or had the airline and the captain agreed to slightly change the routing of the flight to overfly Sakhalin Island, confident that the Soviet government would not dare fire at a second civilian airliner but would instead see the civilian airliner and simply escort them out? This was, to be fair, the Soviet reaction when a third aircraft blundered into their airspace.

The shoot-down of Korean Airlines 902 in 1978 may have been coincidence or it may have inspired the plot, surely not the craziest in cold war times. The banter in the cockpit could be proof that the flight crew had no idea they had gone so wrong, or it could be that the captain was keeping the conversation light while keeping the first officer from noticing that he'd modified their route to take them over Soviet territory, invisible to them in the dark.

This mystery was clearly enough to fill the minds of conspiracy theorists for over a decade. The 1990s seemed a quiet time, with disagreements and political issues but no true mysteries. But then in 2002, a small cargo aircraft crashed in clear weather on a routine flight. The wreckage of the Cessna was soon found, but covered with red scuff marks and with no trace of another aircraft. The NTSB declared the cause a mid-air collision, but no one has ever found the other aircraft, which seems to have been swallowed by a swamp.

2002

Night Ship Needed to Deviate, but from Whom?

I often praise the NTSB for thorough and balanced reports, but in this case, it's hard to believe how badly the investigation was bungled. It is not clear whether the first report or the second report should be trusted; both leave more questions than answers in their wake and, in the end, what the investigators actually discovered is unclear.

The fatal accident happened in Alabama on the 23rd of October in 2002. The aircraft was a Cessna 208B Super Cargomaster.

The Cessna 208 is a single-engined fixed wheel turboprop popular for short-haul regional flights. This one, registration N76U, was owned by Mid-Atlantic Freight, Inc.

The pilot was 54 years old and held an airline transport pilot certificate (ATPL) for single engine aircraft as well as being certified as a commercial pilot for multi-engine aircraft and helicopters. He'd flown around 4,500 hours, including as a pilot for the New York City Police Department. He had also been an instructor for Pan Am Flight Academy on the Cessna 208, the aircraft he was flying that night.

His medical showed that he was in good shape. He was experienced, competent and knew the route.

That day, he picked up 240 pounds of cargo at Mobile, Alabama and told the controllers that he planned to fly at 9,000 feet because "the radar's out", meaning the weather radar system on the aircraft.

He took off from Mobile Downtown Airport (BFM) in the early evening. After departure, the pilot contacted Mobile Terminal

Radar Approach Control (TRACON) to say that he was on frequency and flying at 1,000 feet and climbing to 2,000 feet.

Night Ship: Mobile departure, Night Ship two eighty two is with you at one thousand going to two thousand.

Controller: Night Ship two eighty two, Mobile departure. Radar contact. Maintain three thousand, turn right, join victor four fifty four please.

Night Ship: Roger, right turn, four fifty four.

This is all very routine. Night Ship reported in as he climbed away from the airport (at 1,000 feet climbing to 2,000 feet). The controller confirmed that he could see the aircraft on his radar display and cleared him to climb to 3,000 feet with a right turn (turning east) to join the airway known as Victor 454, a set route. Night Ship 282 confirmed that he had understood by repeating the key details: right turn and airway 454.

The weather was clear and although it was cold, the freezing level was reported as 11,500 feet, so there was little risk of icing.

A few minutes later, the controller contacted him again to let him know about another aircraft in the area, a FedEx DC-10 flying to Mobile, the airport that Night Ship had departed from.

Controller: Night Ship 282, traffic at 12 o'clock of you and seven miles southbound. Heavy DC-10 at four thousand.

In aviation, clock positions are used for horizontal directions, where the clock face is imagined to be lying flat with the pilot in the centre. So when the controller says that there's traffic at 12 o'clock, what he means is that there is someone directly in front when looking straight out of the cockpit. In this case, there was only one aircraft in the area, the Fed Ex DC-10 aircraft flying southbound at 4,000 feet (one thousand feet above Night Ship). When the controller made the call, the DC-10 was seven miles away and heading towards Mobile but there was no reason to believe that the two aircraft routes would cross.

Night Ship: Night Ship Two is looking, I'm IMC.

This was an acknowledgement of the traffic and to let the controller know he doesn't have the other aircraft in sight (he's looking out for it). He was also letting the controller know that he was in *Instrument Meteorological Conditions*, which is to say that he was flying through cloud and relying on instruments. Even with the DC-10 directly in front of him, it would be difficult to see it.

The DC-10 pilot said later that there was a layer of cloud starting at about 1,200 feet which topped out at 2,500 feet and then was clear at his level of 4,000 feet, with more layers above. So he was clear of cloud but Night Ship was presumably flying through the cloud tops of that layer below the DC-10.

There was no real issue here. The DC-10 was a thousand feet above Night Ship, enough vertical separation that he could pass over it without issue. The traffic advisory for Night Ship was actually just politeness. To be honest, the controller was probably telling Night Ship about the DC-10 just to explain why he hadn't yet cleared Night Ship for a higher altitude.

Controller: Night Ship 282, you're still IMC but that DC10 is 1 o'clock and two miles southbound at four thousand.

So, looking out from Night Ship's cockpit, the DC-10 was slightly to the right and still two miles away, still heading south, still at four thousand feet.

Night Ship: Roger. I got him above me right now.

With the DC-10 in sight, Night Ship initiated a gentle descent from 3,000 feet; not actually necessary but possibly instinctive as he saw the DC-10 above him.

Everything seemed completely normal until the next call, 16 seconds after he confirmed he had the DC-10 in sight.

Night Ship: I needed to deviate. I needed to deviate. I needed to deviate. I needed—

The transmission ended as the aircraft descended through an altitude of about 2,300 feet. The radar signal disappeared.

The DC-10 continued on its route at 4,000 feet, unaware of Night Ship falling out of the sky behind him.

The controller called out, alarmed at the pilot's words. He received no response. Almost immediately, he sounded an alarm. There was a US Coast Guard aircraft nearby who immediately diverted to Big Bateau Bay, Night Ship's last known location before it disappeared from radar. However, the low clouds and poor visibility kept him from finding the aircraft.

It took two hours for search and rescue helicopters to find the crash site. The aircraft, or rather the pieces of it, were submerged in a swamp located between Mobile and Spanish Fort, Alabama. The soft mud bottom of the swamp was 8 to 10 feet deep with the water ranging from four inches to three feet, depending on the tide. The locals referred to the swamp as "puff mud" because it was very soft and impossible to stand on. Airboats were needed to access the site and a barge was brought in to transport the larger pieces of wreckage to solid land.

Photograph of the fuselage in the swamp taken for the NTSB investigation

The Cessna had broken up on impact and the wreckage was scattered over a 600-foot area. Investigators rushed to the scene and collected all the "major components of the airplane" as well as the remains of the pilot. The main fuselage had broken into small pieces. The engine was broken in two, but the bent blades of the propeller proved that the engine was producing power when it crashed into the swamp; there was no sign of any mechanical failure. There was no obvious reason why Night Ship should have crashed.

They transported the recovered wreckage to Georgia, so that Atlanta Air Recovery could examine it. Then the wreckage was moved to the Safety Board's Academy in Virginia for further examination.

What they found were strange marks on the aircraft, red streaks on the lower airframe skin. Most of the red marks were surface scuffs, without damage to the white paint or the aluminium. But some of the aluminium on the back edge of the left wing strut was dented, which investigators believed was associated with the red marks. There were also red scuff marks inside the cargo pod near the fuel reservoir drain tunnel, inside the left-side pod door and on a fragment of the pod's interior corner.

The marks had a definitive direction of transfer, that is to say, the red marks had been transferred from something else onto the plane. Night ship was white, with blue and grey markings.

There was also a small piece of black, anodised aluminium embedded in the left wing.

Night Ship's maintenance staff in Mobile were quite sure that the aircraft did not have any red markings when it departed that evening.

The ATC controller confirmed that he'd continually tracked the left-to-right crossing movement of the DC-10. The aircraft never came near each other. He did not see any targets on the radar near the accident aircraft. The closest traffic was a helicopter which had been flying in the general area about five minutes before the accident but, again, the radar controller was quite sure that the helicopter did not cross paths with Night Ship.

The DC-10 was investigated the following morning but it was not red and it showed no sign of damage.

Wake turbulence from a heavy aircraft can cause a smaller aircraft to suffer or even flip; however the DC-10 was about 1.1 nautical miles ahead of the aircraft had 1,600 feet above it, so there was no way that the aircraft suffered from wake turbulence from its location behind and below the DC-10's flight path.

With no other explanation as to how Night Ship could have crashed, the investigators focused on the red marks, which appeared to have been made during flight. They were concentrated at the front of the aircraft, forward of the main landing gear, as if the aircraft had rubbed up against or collided with something painted red. Most of the marks were on the pilot's side but not exclusively. They also discovered the same marks inside the nose landing gear wheel. The scuff marks were of varying shades of red and some of the parts showed more than one red mark. Most of the marks were on the bottom of the aluminium airframe, near the cargo pod bays.

The two main streaks of red transferred material were in straight lines on the aircraft skin with small streaks parallel to them. It was easy to see that the bending and folding of the skin on impact happened after the streaks were left.

The wreckage pieces with red marks were catalogued and sent to various laboratories for further analysis, hoping to identify where the marks had come from.

The CEO of Mid-Atlantic Freight, the owner of the aircraft, was sure that Night Ship had collided with something. The split engine, he said, "was a big deal right there to me. I think most everybody is convinced that that happened prior to impact."

US Air Force, Navy and Air National Guard were all contacted regarding any flights in the area—if not an aircraft then perhaps a missile or a drone. However, there was no record of any launches that night and USAF officials pointed out that, anyway, the crash site was beyond their drones' range. The closest military activity was a proficiency flight which ended 90 minutes before the accident.

Normally in a case like this, it is possible to match the paint transfers to a source or at least a specific type of paint that could shed light on what had collided with Night Ship. They were tested against the cargo in the aircraft, which included a red cargo bag, which could possibly have transferred the red marks in the impact. But the laboratory reported that the samples didn't match. They also didn't match the red plastic pitot cover of the aircraft. A piece of a drone was tested, as well as the red paint of the barge which had towed the wreckage to shore. Even the red paint from a nearby lighthouse was tested and no, it was not related.

Completely flummoxed, the NTSB issued a report in 2005 which shows nothing but confusion.

> On October 23, 2002, at 1945, central daylight time, a Cessna 208B, N76U, call sign Night Ship 282, registered to Atlantic Aero, Inc., and operated by Mid Atlantic Freight, Inc. collided in-flight with an unknown object at 3,000 feet MSL and descended uncontrolled into swampy water in the Big Bateau Bay in Spanish Fort, Alabama, shortly after takeoff from the Mobile Downtown Airport, in Mobile, Alabama.

After three years of searching for a match, they still had no idea what Night Ship had collided with.

They discovered that there was an issue with radar coverage in the area caused by an equipment problem, which meant that they could not be sure who or what was in the area. They also could not find the origin of the black metal embedded in the wing, other than that it hadn't come from the aircraft.

The report confirmed that the various red streaks on the fuselage skin came from the same material and that whatever this material was, it was significantly different from the comparison materials that had been collected. That is, the red streaks were not from the cargo bag, not from the red pitot cover, not from the barge which towed it to shore nor the red stripe of the lighthouse, not from the drone submitted by the military. Nothing matched. The report concluded that it was not possible to identify the source of the red streaks.

An NTSB spokesman said he'd never seen anything like that. "[Investigators] don't know of any other accident that we have in our files that states 'collision with an unknown object.' "

Of course, there were theories. The CEO of Mid-Atlantic Freight believed that the other flying object had crashed. "I believe whatever hit it flew right through it and probably ended up in the Gulf of Mexico someplace or somewhere in the bay." Certainly, it would be possible to lose something as big as an aircraft in the eight feet of mud of the swamp. The pilot's sister believed the same and took to searching the area, hoping for a clue that the NTSB had missed.

Many still believed that it was a stray unmanned drone that the military didn't want to admit to. Others thought it could have been drug smugglers, who apparently frequently flew over the swamp region "under the radar" and would not have been known to the controller.

Some believed that the name of the aircraft was meaningful, that *Night Ship 282* was a code name rather than a call sign, and some even believed that it was out over the swamp that night for a planned rendezvous with a UFO.

The pilot's family believed that the aircraft was destroyed by wake turbulence from the DC-10.

With no answers from the investigation, the wreckage was released to the insurers.

This would be odd enough, but in the beginning of 2006, the NTSB suddenly published an update to the report. They had repossessed the wreckage from the insurers, which implied that some new piece of evidence had come to light. It had: the pilot's sister had come to investigators with the third propeller blade from Night Ship's propeller, which she had found in the swamp at the accident site.

The NTSB confirmed that all of the major components of the propeller assembly had been accounted for but offered no explanation as to how they'd missed the find in the first place.

Because it wasn't just the propellor blade. The pilot's sister recovered *more than 700 pounds* (over 300 kilos) of aircraft debris from the accident site, which NTSB investigators had missed. In response to public pressure, the NTSB reclaimed the wreckage from the insurers in order to process and examine it in the context of the new finds at the NTSB Academy laboratory facilities.

They then published a press release which announced they had solved the four-year-old mystery of the crash.

The final report had been revised. The publication with NTSB Identification: ATL03FA008 now had a notice at the top.

!! NOTE: THIS REPORT WAS MODIFIED ON JANUARY 10, 2006. !!

No further details of the revision were given but it was immediately clear that the details had been changed.

> On October 23, 2002, about 1946 central daylight time (CDT), a Cessna 208B Cargomaster, N76U,

> call sign Night Ship 282, operated by Mid-Atlantic Freight, Inc., **entered an uncontrolled descent from an altitude of 2,700 feet mean sea level** (unless otherwise indicated, all altitudes are reported as height above mean sea level) and crashed in Big Bateau Bay, Spanish Fort, Alabama, shortly after takeoff from Mobile Downtown Airport (BFM), Mobile, Alabama.

The initial reference to a mid-air collision had simply disappeared.

Now the original report did specify that there were a number of red items in the cargo, including the material of the cargo bag, as well as some baseball caps and audiotape packaging. In addition, the aircraft contained several red items, including red laminate electrical power distribution boxes, the pitot tube cover fabric, a tow bar, a tail stand, a fire extinguisher, engine hose material, a batter case, red-coated exterior engine plugs and plastic cockpit control knobs. In the original report, it stated that the red transfer marks did not match the cargo.

The Wright Patterson Air Force Base laboratory again gave a detailed explanation of how they had examined and compared 34 red-marked pieces of aircraft with 19 red reference items. However, this time, they revised the conclusion to say that the laboratory examinations indicated that *some* of the red marks on the fuselage were consistent with the tow bar, the tail stand, the fire extinguisher and the extinguisher bracket. Also, they said, three of the marks matched a postal service priority mail envelope. In all, they said they had accounted for 22 out of the 34 red streaks on the fuselage, which had been caused by items inside the aircraft.

It was clear, according to the revisions, that most of the red marks were caused by parts of the aircraft or its cargo. The report included an argument against an in-flight collision with another aircraft. And finally, the small piece of black aluminium found embedded in the wing had finally been positively identified: it was a fragment from the lighting dimmer in the cockpit.

The new version of the report explained that a sound analysis of the pilot's transmissions that night showed that there was no evidence of loud noises or anything that might imply an impact with another aircraft. The only change was the background noise increasing, which indicates that the cockpit area was still intact and that the airspeed was increasing. In addition, in the last of the transmissions, the overspeed warning activated.

There was, said the NTSB, no mystery at all.

The third propeller blade which the pilot's sister said she found near the instrument panel matched the others, in that it confirmed that the engine was running, as the blades were bent and twisted. But, also, the NTSB stated that the hub pieces of the propeller had fractures consistent with overstress separation.

And so, a new scenario was put forward. It was night and the moon was obscured by low clouds. Although the pilot had been visual between the layers of cloud and clearly had the DC-10 in sight for at least a short time, there were no visible horizon references between the layers of cloud, which could have confused the pilot.

Once the DC-10 was visually acquired by the pilot, it would have existed as a light source moving against an otherwise featureless background, and its relative motion across and rising in the Cessna's windscreen could have been disorienting, especially if the pilot had fixated on it for any length of time. Manoeuvring the aircraft during this search could have compounded the pilot's resultant disorientation.

A simulation showed that the pilot's view would show the DC-10 moving diagonally across his windscreen from his left to straight in front of him, with the DC-10 appearing to triple in size. The simulation showed that it was at this point, with the DC-10 in the centre of his windscreen, that the aircraft banked sharply before rolling through 90°. The investigators concluded that a combination of large control inputs must have taken place for the aircraft to impact in the final orientation and high ground speed.

> Probable Cause
>
> The National Transportation Safety Board determines the probable cause(s) of this accident to be: the pilot's spatial disorientation, which resulted in loss of airplane control. Contributing to the accident was the night instrument meteorological conditions with variable cloud layers.

Never before has a new report differed so wildly from the previous. When asked, the NTSB simply stated that the initial report should never have drawn such a conclusion. They offered no explanation as to how the original investigation, including the laboratory testing, could have gone so horribly wrong; simply stating that the new report was correct.

But the new report still didn't answer all of the questions. What did the pilot mean when he said that he needed to deviate? How was it that the pilot's sister, working on her own, was able to collect not just a stray aircraft part or two, but *700 pounds* of aircraft which the organised search and salvage had missed? And what about the remaining 12 red scuff marks, which were never positively identified and were not matched to any of the red items on board?

The CEO of the Mid-Atlantic Freight spoke to CNN about his reaction to the revisions.

> I've never seen a report like that. And it's very troubling to have something like this happen and not know what caused it. I know the family's upset, and understandably upset. It's just a great thing that this kind of thing didn't happen to an airliner with a bunch of people on it.

The NTSB website has no reference at all to the possibility of a mid-air collision; the previous version of the report is gone. However, it is still, of course, possible to use the Wayback Machine search engine to read the original report without the revisions. The Internet never forgets.

The case is closed but the story of the Night Ship crash remains a favourite both on conspiracy sites and aviation forums, with various theories as to what Night Ship might have crashed into and why it was covered up by the NTSB revisions.

However, there are even larger flying objects that have disappeared, like the Boeing 727 which was stolen from an international airport, never to be recovered.

2003

The Stolen Boeing

It shouldn't be so easy to lose an aircraft.

Especially a big old airliner, 47 metres (153 feet) long and 10 metres (34 feet) high, with a wingspan of 33 metres (108 feet)—twice the height of a giraffe and four times the length of a London bus.

The aircraft was a Boeing 727, registration N844AA, and it has not been seen in 13 years, despite a worldwide search by US security forces.

Boeing 727 registration N844AA at Chicago O'Hare International Airport on 21 May 1989. *(Photo by RuthAS)*

It was not a particularly exciting aircraft; in fact it was barely airworthy. Maury Joseph, the president of Aerospace Sales and Leasing, Inc, was the effective owner. In 2001, he owned three

727s which had been retired by American Airlines, all three in almost mint condition.

Maury Joseph sold N844AA to a South African entrepreneur, Irwin, for a million US dollars. Irwin wanted the 727 and a crew to fulfil a contract to supply fuel to diamond mines in Angola.

Joseph says he was paid $125,000 as a down payment. He removed the passenger seats from the cabin so that it could be installed with ten large fuel tanks. He agreed the aircraft could be taken to Angola but insisted that one of his employees travel with it, so that he could make sure the money came through. On the 28th of February in 2002, still carrying the American Airlines livery, the aircraft departed Miami for Luanda.

It's unclear what the details of the deal were but only two payments were ever made. Maury Joseph never got his money.

One of the original crew posted on the Professional Pilot's Rumour Network (PPRuNe) about their arrival:

> When 844AA first arrived in Luanda from the USA it was grounded by the local Fed's because it didn't have an HF radio. An HF radio taken from a Cessna 206 (or close to it) including the long coaxial antenna was installed on 844AA.
>
> It may be possible to identify the aircraft by inspecting the belly and identifying the holes drilled aft of the EEC door along the center line of the belly where the antenna from the 206 was installed. The first hole would be roughly 3/8″ diameter directly aft and close to the EEC access door and then approximately 8 more 1/8″ holes drilled approx. 4′ apart running aft along the belly. Attached to these holes were brackets that the antenna was attached to. So it is possible that on inspection from an experienced 727 mechanic or flight crew member and if these holes were not filled in, they may be able to identify these non conforming holes in the belly thus confirming that the aircraft is 844AA. By the way, after this bizarre installation of the HF antenna designed for a Cessna was installed on 844AA, the local Fed's signed it off.

> After it was approved by the authorities in Luanda, it was removed because we were well aware of the fact it was non-conforming, illegal and so on. It was the biggest laugh we had the whole time we were there. We had another option and that was to install an HF that was purchased by Mr Irwin and we found out after the fact that it was from an Angolan military aircraft. It was quickly returned as far as I know.
>
> —PPRuNe post

The director of Angola's civil aviation authority told the Associated Press that the aircraft had been grounded for about a year because it lacked the proper documentation verifying its legal conversion to a tanker. He also said in a radio interview that the aircraft was banned from overflying Angolan territory on account of a series of irregularities.

The original deal to supply fuel to Angolan diamond mines fell apart. Another cargo deal seemed to consist of only 17 flights before the crew walked out. Soon, Maury Joseph's employee (who was meant to ensure Aerospace Sales and Leasing, Inc got their money) was the only one of the original crew left. Joseph fired him in the spring 2002, as the money was never forthcoming and the employee kept making excuses for not bringing the aircraft back.

The aircraft stayed at Luanda, effectively abandoned.

Joseph eventually found a buyer for the engines, which had only had around a thousand cycles and were now the only part of the aircraft with value.

Ben Padilla was a freelance flight engineer who lived in South Florida with his fiancée and two children. He had worked for Maury Joseph before and was happy to take on the job to fly to Angola in April 2003 to pay the outstanding fines and hire local mechanics in order to get the aircraft airworthy. He presumed, correctly, that the South African entrepreneur hadn't paid any of the bills.

Padilla hired Air Gemini to work with him to restore the 727 to service in Luanda. Within a month, the aircraft was airworthy again.

Padilla hired a pilot and co-pilot from Air Gemini in order to deliver the aircraft to Johannesburg. Padilla had a private pilot's licence but no commercial licence and was not rated for airliners or jets.

The plan was that Maury Joseph would meet him there with the new customer for the aircraft. Padilla arranged with Air Gemini that, the day before the flight, he would take the aircraft from the hangar to the main runway, so that he could run all three engines up to full power for a systems check.

On the 25th of May, shortly before sunset, Padilla and his hired assistant, John Mikel Mutantu, boarded the aircraft. They ran up the three engines and then, without contacting the Air Traffic Control tower or any clearance, the aircraft began to taxi. The lights were off and the transponder was not transmitting as it "manoeuvred erratically" and entered the runway.

The aircraft went to full power and rumbled down the runway.

Mutantu, who had accompanied Padilla to help him with the aircraft, was not a pilot. Padilla was, but he had only a private pilot's licence; he had no experience with large jets. The Boeing 727 was set up for a three-man flight crew.

With lights off and no communication, it took off from the runway, turned southwest, and flew out towards the Atlantic Ocean.

No one ever saw it again.

The following morning, Joseph was waiting in Johannesburg for the delivery of the 727 when Air Gemini phoned him, demanding to know why another crew had flown the aircraft out of Luanda. Joseph must have been very confused about what had happened, but soon after the phone call, he contacted the US Embassy in South Africa to report the stolen plane. He also called his wife, still in Florida, and asked her to inform the FBI.

In the aftermath of 9/11, US intelligence were extremely interested in the 727 and immediately began an international search. President Bush was given daily briefings on the case.

It was no use. Padilla, Mutantu and the 727 had disappeared without a trace.

Padilla's family believe that someone was on the aircraft waiting to ambush Padilla and his helper. They believe that Padilla and Mutantu were killed or held hostage.

Some thought Maury Joseph arranged for the plane to be stolen in order to collect the insurance money. But Joseph says no insurance money was ever paid: in order to file a claim he had to prove that the aircraft had been stolen and, with no trace of the aircraft, he had no proof.

BEN CHARLES PADILLA

LUANDA, ANGOLA
MAY 25, 2003

DESCRIPTION

Age:	50 years old	**Hair:**	Brown
Sex:	Male	**Eyes:**	Brown
Height:	6'2"	**Race:**	White
Weight:	Unknown	**Complexion:**	Light
Remarks:	Padilla is a United States citizen from the state of Florida.		

THE DETAILS

On May 25, 2003, at approximately 6 p.m. local time, an airplane took off from DeFevereiro International Airport in Luanda, Angola, with neither clearance nor a flight plan, and has not been seen since. The plane is described as a 200 series advanced 727 jet with a tail number of N844AA, and a serial number of 20985. It is unpainted silver in color with a stripe of blue, white, and blue. The plane was formerly in the air fleet of a major airline, but all of the passenger seats have been removed. It is outfitted to carry diesel fuel.

Law enforcement officials believe that Ben Charles Padilla may have been on board the plane at the time it disappeared. The FBI is interested in locating Padilla, as he may have information as to the whereabouts of the plane.

IF YOU HAVE ANY INFORMATION CONCERNING THIS CASE, PLEASE CONTACT YOUR LOCAL FBI OFFICE OR THE NEAREST AMERICAN EMBASSY OR CONSULATE.

Robert S. Mueller III

ROBERT S. MUELLER, III
DIRECTOR
FEDERAL BUREAU OF INVESTIGATION
UNITED STATES DEPARTMENT OF JUSTICE
WASHINGTON, D.C. 20535
TELEPHONE: (202) 324-3000

FBI Wanted poster for Ben Charles Padilla

In 2005, the FBI closed its case, no closer to solving the mystery.

Journalist Tim Wright has spent a lot of time investigating the mystery and his articles in *Air & Space Magazine* are well worth reading: "The 727 that Vanished" and "When Airliners Vanish".

The aircraft might have crashed into the sea or it could have been hidden in some quiet jungle, or possibly every single piece of it was scrapped.

To this day, no one has heard from Padilla. The aircraft was never seen again and none of its parts were ever spotted, although many were looking.

In an intriguing coincidence, however, a wreck of a Boeing 727 *was* found over 3,000 kilometres away, in the middle of the Malian desert, and no one had any idea where that 727 had come from.

First, however, there's the most recent victim of the Bermuda Triangle, a Trislander which disappeared full of passengers without a trace . . . and without even an investigation.

2008

The Latest Bermuda Triangle Mystery

We tend to think about the mysterious disappearances within the Bermuda Triangle as being from a bygone age of travel: Mary Celeste, the USS Cyclops and Flight 19 (covered in volume 1). But the most recent perplexing disappearance in the Bermuda Triangle was surprisingly recent, in 2008.

The aircraft was a Britten-Norman Trislander, a three-engine aircraft built for island hopping. It departed Santiago in the Dominican Republic on the 15th of December in 2008, with a flight crew of one, and probably eleven passengers on board, although it is impossible to be sure. Half an hour after departing Santiago, the aircraft made a Mayday call and then disappeared from radar. Its last known location was about four miles (6.5 km) west of West Caicos Island.

From the beginning, media reports of this accident contradicted each other. Originally, it was reported that the aircraft was a standard scheduled flight with Linea Aérea Puertorriquena Inc (Puerto Rico Airlines, also known as LAP). It was correct that the Britten-Norman Trislander which departed Santiago that day was owned by the president of the company and that LAP was the operator.

However, LAP had no flight scheduled from Santiago that day and the pilot was not from the airline. The Trislander was not scheduled for any passenger flights that day. The only reason it was in Santiago at all was because the owner of the Puerto Rican airline had been contacted by someone interested in buying the aircraft. The owner set a price of $225,000 for the Trislander and hired a pilot to fly it to the Dominican Republic so that the potential buyer could take it on a test flight, which is standard procedure.

When the LAP pilot landed in Santiago, he found that the potential buyer was waiting for him with eleven other people. The buyer started to load the passengers onto the Trislander. Another pilot, who appears to have simply been being helpful, helped load the passengers for the flight.

The LAP pilot attempted to stop the loading, explaining that they could not take passengers on a test flight. However, the buyer insisted, saying the aircraft had already been purchased by Atlantic Airlines and was flying to Turks and Caicos Islands, a British Overseas Territory north of the Dominican Republic and east of Cuba. The flight plan had already been filed.

The LAP pilot was right to be unconvinced: Atlantic Airlines had not purchased the Trislander, nor were they interested in it, and they had no knowledge of the man claiming to represent them. However, the man masquerading as a buyer was able to commandeer the aircraft with the passengers on board and taxied straight to the runway, taking off at 15:30 as per his flight plan.

It is not clear what the LAP pilot did at this point but I suspect it involved a lot of strong language.

About 35 minutes into the flight, the US Coast Guard received a distress call from the Trislander, which, presuming his flight plan was correct, would put him somewhere north of the Dominican Republic and south of Turks and Caicos. But at that point, the Trislander disappeared from radar.

Bahamas Aviation Authority were immediately contacted. They had not heard from the Trislander and quickly confirmed that it had not landed at any of the seven airports on the inhabited islands.

The Trislander was lost, along with the eleven passengers. The LAP pilot and the other pilot who had helped load the passengers on the flight were taken into custody.

The Coast Guard and local authorities immediately set up a search and rescue operation based at Providenciales. One hundred searchers, using two helicopters and seven ships, scoured the area. However, as the sun set after 48 hours of searching, they gave up hope of finding any survivors. The searchers had covered a 5,300-square-mile area of the Atlantic but not located any trace of the Trislander and its passengers.

Things get a bit confused from here. A few days after the accident, Fox News reported that the pilot who took the Trislander was an ex-Navy cadet and that when LAP reported that the aircraft had been stolen, the Dominican Republic drug and immigration authorities already knew of the suspect, who was believed to have been involved in drug smuggling and human trafficking.

Another report said that the man had previously been in the Dominican Republic Armed Forces but was discharged for unlicensed flying, cheating and theft, although I was unable to find any details to back this claim.

What is clear is that the pilot was not a pilot. He had previously held a rotorcraft licence, for flying helicopters, which the Trislander is not, but that had been revoked earlier in the year for *another* offence of flying a plane without the proper certification, again a multi-engine aircraft. He briefly attended flight school in the US and the only paperwork he had on the day he stole the Trislander was to show that he was a student pilot. Not that anyone had asked to see it.

Meanwhile in the Dominican Republic, the police attempted to find out who the passengers were; there was no passenger manifest or any other reference to who was on board. They discovered that all eleven were paying passengers: they paid 8,000 US dollars *each* for tickets in the island hopper, a ludicrous amount for a flight to Turks and Caicos.

Relatives of the passengers told the Coast Guard that they understood that the flight was only refuelling in Turks and Caicos before continuing to its final destination of New York. However, the FAA had no record of an inbound flight nor any record of the passenger information and passport details having been filed. Then it came clear that the $8,000 payment from each passenger was simply a down payment, with the remainder of the ticket cost (another $5,000) to be paid on arrival in the US.

The flight takes on an entirely different light with that information. There was no confusion or misunderstanding: the unlicensed pilot had posed as a prospective buyer in order to steal the aircraft to smuggle eleven desperate Dominicanos into the US, possibly by landing in the Florida Everglades, and collecting a tidy $13,000 per person with no costs other than fuel.

But that, of course, does not mean that the mayday call was false. Why would the pilot call attention to himself and the stolen aircraft with a mayday call unless something had actually gone wrong?

But that's where the trail ends. The US accident authority, the NTSB, closed the file. Their website lists the accident but states that the official investigation was carried out by the British authority, the AAIB, and to contact them for the final report. However, the AAIB database has no record of the aircraft or the accident at all. When I contacted them to ask for a copy of a report, I was told there wasn't one.

> This aircraft disappeared and was initially presumed to have crashed. However the wreckage was never located and we suspect the aircraft did not crash. Consequently, there was insufficient evidence for AAIB to continue with an investigation, and hence no report was ever produced.

The passengers were never heard from again.

The only line of enquiry still open was the owner, who had, after all, lost a valuable aircraft as a part of this. It seemed like perhaps the insurance company must have at least followed up on where the aircraft had ended up.

However, this investigation only brought up more questions.

The owner of the Trislander was also the owner of the airline, Linea Aérea Puertorriquena Inc (LAP), mentioned above, but he also owned *another* airline, ApelAir, both airlines registered in Puerto Rico, an unincorporated US territory. In 2009, the year after the theft of the Trislander, the US Department of Transportation asked the owner to provide compliance information for LAP and a full accounting of any FAA enforcement actions and all details of the relationships between the LAP and ApelAir. This was because the FAA had revoked ApelAir's Air Carrier Certificate, issuing an Emergency Order of Revocation. LAP was owned by the same man and the current LAP employees were all former ApelAir employees, and the FAA's interest is clear: it seemed quite possible that this was simply the same airline with the same issues operating under a different name.

> . . . the Department is reviewing LAP to ensure that sufficient information is provided on the record of this proceeding to enable us to make a determination that LAP has, among other things, the managerial skills to support its proposed operations, the proper regard for the laws and regulations governing its services, that its aircraft and personnel conform to applicable safety standards, and that acceptable consumer relations practices will be followed.

What had happened was that the owner purchased an aircraft, a Douglas DC-3 built in 1942 registration N86553, which he requested be added to ApelAir's roster. The DC-3 had paperwork to show that it had passed its airworthiness test on the 22 of Feb 2007.

The DC-3 N86553 photographed by Jon Wickenden at the Vintage Flying Museum in May 2010

In January 2008, an FAA aviation safety inspector turned up to inspect the aircraft and he didn't like what he saw. The result was a 29-point list of problems, ranging from doors held in place with speed tape to missing screws in the stabilizer to disconnected smoke detectors and windshield wipers. One point in the list is “All instruments are not reliable” and another queries simply whether the onboard flight manual (required) on board is actually the flight manual for the aircraft. The DC-3 was not airworthy.

ApelAir were told that they must contact the Flight Standards District Office and show the corrective action taken in regards to each of these 29 items. Nothing was filed but a few months later, in May, an FAA aviation safety inspector followed up to see if the issues had been rectified so that the DC -3 could be added to the airline’s operations. After seeing the plane, he made a new list of issues.

- Nose forward antenna missing
- Left engine cowling out of alignment
- Left engine forward panel is attached with a rubber washer; also there is a hole adjacent to it
- Left upper fuselage engine spot light is missing two screws
- Entry door upper hinge screws corroded and also missing attached faring
- Right ending cowling at 7:00 has material missing
- Right engine left hand side rivets missing and panel has strip of unsecured metal
- Right engine fastener at the 8:30 position there is a hole in the metal adjacent to the fastener
- Impact damage noted on the left lower elevator.

Note: there are no duplicates between the first list and the second. This is not the list of items still to be dealt with after the first inspection; it is an *additional* list of issues with the DC-3.

Apelair was told again that they must contact the Flight Standards District Office to show that they had corrected the issues if they wanted to add the aircraft to their operations.

Six months later, on the 18th of December 2008, which was three days after the Trislander had disappeared—an important point—FAA inspectors visited the Apelair's "principal base of operations" and asked where N86553 was. The inspectors were told that the aircraft was on the other side of the field undergoing a pitot-static check. When the inspectors insisted that they wanted to see the DC-3, the story changed: the aircraft had been flown to St. Maarten for maintenance and so wasn't available for inspection.

Not surprisingly, the inspectors were unimpressed. They started checking flight logs and discovered that the DC-3 had been flying regularly from San Juan, Puerto Rico to Tortola on the British Virgin Islands, with records of flights in August, October, November and December of 2008. On the 18th of December, the day that the inspectors were there, they found that the aircraft that they'd come to visit was logged as flying from San Juan to Saint Lucia to Saint Vincent and the Grenadines (west of Barbados) and on to Grenada before flying back to San Juan. This was certainly not about maintenance. In fact, the DC-3 was carrying cargo for Avon Products, who had paid for the flights.

This was in an aircraft that was not a part of ApelAir operations, and which ApelAir was not authorised to fly, because the aircraft was not in airworthy condition.

In fact, ApelAir only had one aircraft on their roster, up until the 18th of December. That was N650LP—did you guess it? The Trislander.

After the 18th of December, ApelAir reported the Trislander as having been involved in a fatal accident. When the aircraft was not recovered within the required 80 days, the Trislander was removed from ApelAir's operations.

Now ApelAir was *at best* an operator without any aircraft. The FAA revoked ApelAir's air carrier certificate on the spot, with a letter that goes to great pains to make it clear that an aircraft not in airworthy condition doesn't count. They did not have to prove that ApelAir were flying the DC-3 illegally, Apelair did not have an aircraft and thus could not operate as an air operator, which was ground for the air carrier certificate to be revoked on the spot.

But of course, that wasn't all of it. The FAA were scathing.

> . . . you knowingly operated this DC-3 when it was not in an airworthy condition. You knowingly

> operated this aircraft for compensation or hire when it was not listed on your operations specifications. Despite your attempts to add the DC-3 to your operations specifications, there were too many mechanical problems with the DC-3 and it was not safe to operate in the air transportation system. Despite all of this you chose to operate the DC-3 contrary to the regulations and knowing that its operations were in violation of the regulations. Such a non-compliant attitude shows a disdain for the regulatory system and a propensity to operate outside of the boundaries of the safety required of an air carrier. Your choice to operate this DC-3 knowing that it was not airworthy, knowing that it was not on your operations specifications, and knowing that its operation was contrary to the FAR [Federal Acquisition Regulation] clearly demonstrates that you are not qualified to be the holder of an air carrier certificate. Whether your choice was based upon a profit motive or a desire for expediency, it was a conscious decision to circumvent the regulations. Accordingly, the public cannot risk having carriers such as you operate with such an attitude of non-compliance when such an attitude has a high degree of probability of resulting in loss of life and/or property.

In other words, the FAA was making it clear that ApelAir blatantly broke the rules and clearly didn't give a damn about following regulations. The operation risked people's lives operating an aircraft that was not safe to fly and as such, even if ApelAir qualified, it would not be fit to be an air carrier. Which sounds almost petty but it's hard to disagree.

This makes it clear why the FAA then turned their attention to Linea Aérea Puertorriquena, Inc (LAP).

But in response, LAP explained that they were appealing the FAA's decision to revoke Apelair's certificate. They said that the appeals hearing was set for October 2009 and argued that providing the requested information would affect the outcome of the appeal.

It's hard not to admire the bravado: if we tell you what we are doing now, you may not reinstate ApelAir as an operator, thus we would like you to wait. And it worked.

The FAA came back and basically said fine, in this case, we have no way of judging whether you are fit to be an operator and if your managerial competence and compliance disposition are up to scratch.

They agreed to wait until the ApelAir appeal but, in the end, made it clear that if the appeal was delayed or deferred, they would not wait any longer for answers.

> In light of the above, we direct LAP to provide the Department with a detailed description of the outcome of its pending appeal, together with a complete response to our June 22, 2009, letter no later than 14 days from the scheduled hearing dates.

The Trislander doesn't come up again until 2010, when the ApelAir appeal reached its conclusion. ApelAir admitted that the Douglas DC-3 aircraft had never been added to its operations specifications and had never undergone any validations tests or proving flights before the logged dates of its flights. However, it appealed against the revocation based on the fact that you cannot be an operator if you do not own any aircraft. ApelAir argued that the Trislander had been stolen, yes, but that customs agents were in the process of recovering it.

From the court document:

> Respondent also indicates that a Customs Enforcement Agent "reported that the aircraft landed in Providenciales, where the passengers disembarked, the aircraft was re-fueled and continued its flight to Cali, Colombia, where it is presently."

ApelAir could not give any further information, because the "process had been kept in confidentiality" in order "to prevent damage of the investigation."

The court documents further note that "[ApelAir] did not explain in its opposition why the owner of the aircraft earlier reported that the aircraft was involved in a fatal crash in the waters off the Bahamas."

That's a very good question.

As a final defence, ApelAir also argued that although the DC-3 had been flown on the dates logged, it had been operated not by ApelAir but by Linea Aérea Puertorriquena, as if that somehow helped matters. ApelAir claimed that under the circumstances, the revocation of the air operations was unfair and that the FAA had purposefully delayed the DC-3 being added to the operations specifications.

> This is a demonstration on how the force and government positions can be used to harm honest people that work for living instead of giving or receiving brides [sic].

So the Trislander, flown by a man whose only qualification was as a student pilot, may have crashed into the Atlantic. Or it may have flown to Florida and landed in the still of the night, smuggling its cargo of 11 Dominicanos into the US. Or it may have refuelled at Turks and Caicos and continued on to Colombia in some sort of drug running operation with eleven paying passengers on board. No one seems to know and more importantly perhaps, no one seems to care.

In 2017, El Aviador, a Dominican transport magazine, ran an article marking nine years since the Trislander vanished after departing the island. The article names the passengers who were lost on that day and that as of writing, the families left behind had not had any word.

> The relatives of the disappeared stated that, despite the time that has passed, they still hoped to find their relatives alive. [translation mine]

It's hard to believe that none of the families have heard back and that no one is looking but it also highlights how easy it is to disappear an aircraft.

Exactly the opposite happened the following year, when a Boeing was discovered which to this day has not been identified.

2009

MYSTERY MALI BOEING

THIS STORY IS DIFFERENT from the others in that it isn't an aircraft which has disappeared. It is, instead, an aircraft which appeared, suddenly and unexpectedly, in the middle of nowhere.

On the 2nd of November in 2009, the first report came in of a burnt-out Boeing 727 abandoned in the Saharan desert of Mali in West Africa. But whose aircraft was it and where did it come from?

Initially, it seemed that the Boeing must have crash-landed on the desert, a lucky escape by an aircraft in distress, although it was odd that there were no reports of a Mayday call or a missing flight.

Soon it became clear that the burnt-out wreck had in fact landed safely and intentionally on a dried out lakebed which had been used as a makeshift desert airstrip. There was no accident. Any damage to the aircraft happened after it had landed; the passenger jet had been deliberately set on fire and left there to burn.

The Boeing 727 is a mid-sized three-engine airliner which carries 150–189 passengers with a range of 5,000 km (2,700 nautical miles). Almost two thousand 727s were built over the period from 1963 to 1984. The initial aircraft cost $4.25 million (US dollars) but by 1982 they cost $22 million each. In the early 1990s, the two-engine 737 swiftly overtook the 727 in popularity for short haul flights and is now the best-selling jet commercial airliner. By July 2013, only 109 Boeing 727s were in commercial service.

This particular Boeing 727 was flying under a Saudi Arabian registration, HZ-SNE. That registration had been flagged by

Guinea-Bissau for safety and registration violations. The initial investigation was hampered by confusion as to who had the authority over the incident.

The three-week delay in the investigation of the crashed plane was documented in US embassy cables:

> The deputy director of the Malian National Civil Aviation Authority stated that although the incident was clearly in his jurisdiction, he was not given authority to investigate until three or four weeks after the 727 had been discovered, as the initial investigation was placed solely with the DGSE, the Malian intelligence service.
>
> In a meeting with PolOff on November 25, the Deputy Director of ANAC, Issa Saley Maiga, stated that notwithstanding statutory jurisdiction for investigating aviation accidents, his agency was not given authority to investigate the incident until November 24, three to four weeks after the event. He said that until late November, responsibility for investigating the crash of the "drug plane" (as it has been called in the press) was placed solely with the DGSE.
>
> On December 17, Deputy Regional Representative of the United Nations Office Against Drugs and Crime (UNODC) Cyriaque Sobtafo explained that because the plane crash occurred in northern Mali, it was considered exclusively a matter for DGSE, and that not even the Drug Brigade of the Malian Judiciary Investigation Police was allowed to make inquiries. Sobtafo added that the Malian government had not shared any information from its investigation with UNODC.

Eventually, some facts were established. The point of the flight was clear: the aircraft was transporting cocaine and "other illegal substances". The UN Office of Drugs and Crime confirmed that the aircraft carried 10 tonnes of cocaine (22,000 pounds, 10,000 kilograms) to be taken to Europe from Mali, known for its smuggling activity. Nine jeeps, using forged number plates, met the aircraft and carried the cargo away. That's where the trail was lost.

It soon became clear that the Saudi registration documents were forged. The real HZ-SNE was a Boeing 727-200, serial number 22644, which had been operated by DHL. The aircraft had been destroyed in an accident in Lagos. However, international aviation data is not that easy to keep track of and the burnt-out Boeing had been able to masquerade as the perfectly respectable HZ-SNE for at least one flight.

The aircraft was a "ghost ship", history and provenance unknown. This makes the deliberate torching of the aircraft even stranger, having successfully "fallen off the radar" of aviation authorities.

But investigators had successfully traced its route. It had been seen under the false registration departing Venezuela, possibly stopping in Colombia, and then next seen passing through Cape Verde airspace before stopping in Guinea-Bissau.

It was already known that South American drug cartels had discovered that the European drug market was more lucrative and less secure than the North American market. At least three drug cartels were known to have organised drugs to be flown into West Africa and then transported to Europe. One of the drug traffickers claimed that he had six aircraft flying.

In 2008, many arrests were made related to large aircraft carrying drugs from Bolivia to Africa. The pilots and fuel had been paid by wire transfer and suitcases filled with cash. A bag containing €260,000 (£220,000 at the time or $290,000) was discovered at a hotel bar, apparently to pay a Russian crew to move a newly acquired aircraft from Moldova to Romania. A Gulfstream II carrying large amounts of contraband was seized in Guinea Bissau. In Sierra Leone, an aircraft carrying 600 kg (1,300 pounds) of cocaine was seized.

In recorded conversations related to the case, the trafficker stated that the gang had access to a private airfield in Guinea and was considering buying its own airport.

However, this only gave context to the contraband which had been flown into the Malian desert. It didn't explain where the 727 came from.

The only real evidence remaining was the burnt Boeing 727 and the fact that only drug trade profits could be high enough to be worth destroying the aircraft. Within a month, much of the aircraft was missing, scavenged by locals for aluminium, which they could sell for 1,500 CFA francs per kilo, about $2.50 US dollars or £2.00.

A 2008 United Nations report on the import of weapons found that the Democratic Republic of the Congo had twenty aircraft with obviously incorrect registration numbers and 89 aircraft whose manufacturing number (serial number) was missing or incorrect. Many aircraft "disappeared" from Russia after the dissolution of the Soviet Union.

The AeroTransport Data Bank, which tracks aircraft capable of carrying 30 passengers or more, has a special status for aircraft which appear neither to be flying nor stored: UFO, or ultimate fate obscure. Many of these have probably been scrapped but there's no question that some have been disappeared from the public records in order to use them for criminal activities.

My first thought was that the stolen Boeing could be the same Boeing 727-223 (registration N844AA) that had disappeared from Luanda in 2003, which we discussed in a previous chapter. However, investigators followed up on this and based on details of the wrecked aircraft it was proven that this was not the same plane.

The Civil Aviation Agency in Guinea-Bissau definitely had their eye on the aircraft flying as HZ-SNE, having flagged it for safety and registration issues at the time of its last flight. They were also investigating an aircraft registered in Guinea-Bissau as J5-GCU. In November, within days of the crash, they had declared J5-GCU as no longer airworthy and contacted the owner demanding the location of the aircraft within twenty-four hours. At the same time, they contacted the aviation authorities in Nigeria and Venezuela to say that they believed that J5-GCU was operating illegally in Venezuela with Nigerian crews and asked them to ground the 727 if it was identified. In December, they contacted the aviation authority in Mali to say that they had information that J5-GCU was operating flights from Colombia to Mali and asked the Malian ANAC for assistance in grounding the aircraft.

J5-GCU is currently shown as destroyed on an illegal desert airstrip 200km north of Gao in Mali. However, there's no proof that J5-GCU is the correct aircraft.

Another likely candidate is a Boeing 727-230F with serial number 21619. That aircraft was sold to a company called Africa Aviation Assistance, after having been transferred across three entities in four countries (and assigned four registrations in the process). Africa Aviation Assistance placed the aircraft in storage in Dakar in June, six months before the fraudulent HZ-SNE's flight.

Africa Aviation Assistance was shut down in July when it was discovered to be operating without an Air Operator's Certificate (AOC), which is required for any company which uses aircraft for commercial purposes. This was about the same time as DHL's Saudi-registered Boeing was destroyed in an accident. The timing was perfect for setting up an abandoned aircraft from a defunct company with the HZ-SNE registration from the DHL aircraft.

In June 2011, L'Agence France-Presse reported that three businessmen, one French, one Spanish and one Malian, had been arrested and charged with international trafficking in cocaine. There's a reference to having found the pilot of the aircraft, a Frenchman. Then in January 2012, in the final update of the story, *news24* reported that the Malian businessman had been freed.

> A justice ministry source confirmed the information but would not elaborate on the reasons behind his release.
>
> The bi-weekly newspaper "22 Septembre" said he was freed "following a demand from a group of young Arabs" who had been called upon to assist the army in fighting off Tuareg rebels who have launched an offensive in northern Mali.

And that's where the story ends. The rotting remains of the 727 still lie in the Malian desert, long since stripped of anything of value.

Those intrigued by the odd story couldn't know that the biggest mystery of them all was on the horizon, or rather, that a huge jet was about to disappear over one. I'm talking, of course, about the disappearance of Malaysian Airlines flight 370.

2014

MH370

On the 8th of March, 2014, Malaysia Airlines flight 370, a scheduled passenger flight from Kuala Lumpur, Malaysia to Beijing, China, departed Kuala Lumpur normally. The as-the-crow-flies distance is 4,392 kilometres (2,745 miles). This overnight flight standardly departs Kuala Lumpur at 00:25 local time, with an expected arrival in Beijing six hours later, at 06:35. Both Kuala Lumpur and Beijing are eight hours ahead of UTC. All times given here are in local time, in the early hours of the morning.

The Boeing 777 was registered as 9M-MRO. It was twelve years old and had the capacity to take 282 passengers (35 business seats and 247 economy seats).

There were 227 passengers on board. The seven-page passenger manifest shows the name, nationality and age of each of these passengers, ranging from passenger #162, Wang Moheng, Chinese, age 23 months, to passenger #92, Lou Baotang, Chinese, age 79. Little Wang Moheng was returning from his first trip abroad, a family holiday to Malaysia. The twelve crew members were all Malaysian citizens.

In South East Asia, all conversation between controllers and pilots is in English. The official transcript of the pilots of Malaysia Airlines flight 370 (MAS 370) and the air traffic controllers (ATC) at Beijing started just after midnight at Kuala Lumpur International, when the flight crew contacted ATC Clearance Delivery for their route clearance to Beijing.

The first officer spoke on the radio until take-off, at which point the captain took over the communications with air traffic control. This means that the first officer was almost certainly the

Pilot Flying: he had been assigned to be the flying pilot for that sector and was due for a check flight on his next duty assignment.

The Boeing 777 took off at 00:42 local time. As per normal procedure, Kuala Lumpur Area Control Centre (ACC) contacted Ho Chi Minh ACC on the phone and told them that, based on the filed flight plan, Malaysia Airlines flight 370's estimated time of arrival at waypoint IGARI was 01:22. Kuala Lumpur ACC requested FL350 (35,000 feet) for the flight's cruise altitude, which Ho Chi Minh ACC was happy with.

The IGARI waypoint is important because it is the point on the map where responsibility for the flight is passed from Kuala Lumpur ACC to Ho Chi Minh ACC. When the Kuala Lumpur radar controller sees the aircraft over IGARI waypoint on the radar display or when the flight crew report that they are over IGARI, the controller tells the flight crew to contact Ho Chi Minh. There's no "electronic handoff" between Kuala Lumpur and Ho Chi Minh and they do not have a system for notifying each other of the transfer of control. Once Kuala Lumpur notified the flight crew that they should contact Ho Chi Minh, control is considered to be transferred. Under normal circumstances, this is fine: the flight crew contact Ho Chi Minh ACC and carry on with them; if for some reason they can't get through, they contact Kuala Lumpur again to say so. Usually, it is very straightforward, especially in the quiet early hours.

The Boeing 777 reached its initial cruise altitude and levelled off. The flight was uneventful until Malaysia Airlines flight 370 approached the IGARI waypoint.

The radar controller saw that the aircraft was reaching the edge of his Flight Information Region (FIR) and instructed the flight crew to contact Ho Chi Minh on frequency 120.9. The captain responded at 01:19:30 with "Good night, Malaysian Three Seven Zero." This was the last communication from the aircraft.

This isn't a perfect readback; usually the pilot would repeat the frequency they are changing to, to confirm they have it right. However, it's not uncommon to simply make it clear that you are leaving the frequency without verifying the details, especially on a route you know well.

Voice sample analysis found no evidence of stress or anxiety in the statement, although on the previous two instances where the flight was transferred to a new controller, the captain did read back the frequency before changing.

The timing was almost exactly as filed on the flight plan. The estimated time for the transfer of control was 01:22. The *actual* transfer of control was 01:19:30. Radar recordings show that the aircraft passed over IGARI at 01:20:31.

At 01:20:36 the secondary radar symbol of Malaysia Airlines 370 disappeared from Kuala Lumpur's radar display.

In the chapter about Korean Air Lines 007, we discussed **primary radar** as a surveillance system which lets a controller know that large metal things are within their radar radius. However, primary radar has two clear negatives. It requires an extremely large amount of power to ensure returns from a target, especially at a distance. It's also very difficult to correlate a specific radar return with a particular aircraft. Originally, friendly pilots flying a known route would identify themselves by giving their distance from a predefined point so that the controller would know approximately where they were. Sometimes the controller would ask the pilot to turn and then watch the radar display for a heading change so that the aircraft could be clearly identified on the radar display.

Clearly, a better system for identifying friendly aircraft was needed, which is where **secondary radar** comes in. The aircraft has a *transponder* installed on board which responds automatically with identifying equipment. The transponder was developed in World War II under the code-name *parrot* which is why the four-digit identification code broadcast by the aircraft's transponder is known as a *squawk*. Within this system, the radar ground station sends an interrogation out to a wide range and all aircraft in the area with transponders respond with a reply signal. This signal is much stronger than a primary radar reflection, so the range of secondary radar is much greater than primary radar. The signal also carries additional information, which can include the aircraft identification and altitude. Modern air traffic control systems rely on secondary radar in order to monitor and direct traffic over a large area.

So four seconds after Malaysia Airlines flight 370 passed over the IGARI waypoint, the aircraft disappeared from the radar displays at Kuala Lumpur, Ho Chi Minh and Bangkok, which means that the transponder was either turned off or failed.

No one reacted.

Malaysia Airlines flight 370 had stopped communicating and had disappeared from secondary radar displays. That means that no one could see that it had also diverted from its planned routing and was now turning back towards Malaysia.

The Boeing 777 did appear on primary radar returns, still in use by the military because those do not rely on aircraft wishing to be seen. The Malaysian military returns showed that at 01:21:13, the aircraft turned right and then began a constant left turn to heading 273°. You can see the planned route (red line) and the diversion (dotted black line) on the map below.

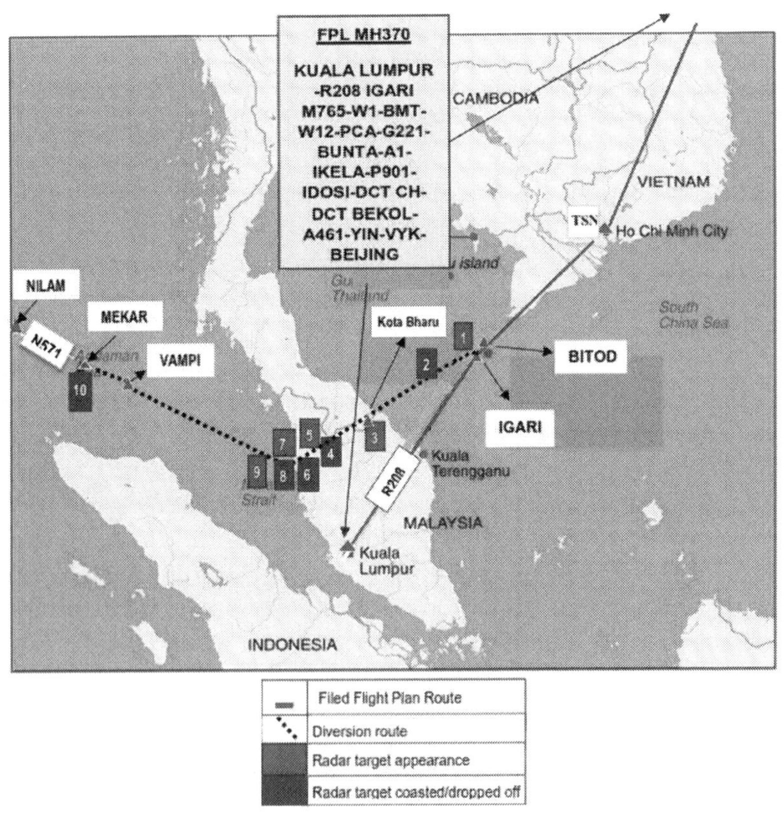

Diversion from Filed Flight Plan

Initially, Malaysian military returns showed that the Boeing 777 climbed to over 40,000 feet, which was taken by many to mean that whoever was in command of the aircraft was attempting to depressurise the aircraft and knock out the passengers and crew. However, the data as collected, showing a peak of

58,200 feet and a low of 4,800, is impossible. The altitude changes shown in these radar returns are quite simply not possible in a Boeing 777. The problem is that altitude returns in primary radar (in use by the military) are not to be trusted. This is another reason why commercial aviation relies on secondary radar, which is based on the aircraft sending information using its transponder, including altitude. In this case, we are reliant on primary radar, because the transponder either failed or was turned off. But it is important to remember that primary radar is limited in scope and that altitude cannot be identified consistently from primary radar returns.

As a part of the official investigation, the team ran through a number of flight simulations in order to recreate how Malaysia Airlines flight 370 initially diverted from its flight path. They knew that the aircraft made a left turn just past waypoint IGARI. Using radar returns, they were able to set up entrance and exit waypoints to reconstruct the flight path for that section of the flight which they knew took the Boeing 777 two minutes and ten seconds to achieve. With that information, they were able to test multiple configurations to attempt to find out more about the state of the aircraft as it made the turn.

The simulations showed immediately that, although the manoeuvre could be done using the autopilot and flight management systems, it could not be completed in under three minutes. This is because the maximum bank angle using the LNAV (lateral navigation) is 25° and in order to complete the manoeuvre in less time, a steeper bank angle was needed—the simulation which came closest to following the known path of the aircraft involves a steep turn with a bank angle of 35° and an indicated airspeed of 250 knots. In a Boeing 777, turning at this angle and speed would cause multiple bank-angle warnings and the stick-shaker would activate halfway through the turn: it could not be done using automated systems.

This tells us an extremely important point: the aircraft was under manual control when it turned. It was not following a programmed route. The autopilot was disengaged.

Another important point was that when they recreated the turn in the simulator, they confirmed that the manoeuvre could be performed by a single pilot.

After the aircraft levelled out again, the flight path followed a set of waypoints, almost certainly using the on-board navigation system (LNAV or heading mode). That is, someone hand-flew the aircraft to make a very sharp turn and then set up the navigation system once they were heading back.

The Boeing 777 continued south of Penang where it turned towards waypoint MEKAR. This turn could easily have been completed by turning gently using heading mode. Throughout this, there were no rapid altitude and/or speed changes.

There are some reports and articles which claim that the aircraft circled Penang in what's been described as a "farewell flight". This never happened. After the initial rumour surfaced in *The Weekend Australian,* which claimed that the aircraft "avoided Thai military radar, then turned, after circling Zaharie's home island of Penang," the Australian Transport Safety Bureau published a press release to clarify that MH370 passed by Penang and the radar data shows that it did *not* circle the island. The radar returns show no sign of the farewell flight and the investigative team found no evidence that the aircraft was evading radar, Thai or otherwise.

The next and final turn to the south is the one we know very little about. Ten nautical miles north of MEKAR, the aircraft disappeared from radar at 02:22 local time and some time after that (shortly after it passed the southern tip of Sumatra) it changed course.

Now, we know that the aircraft did not actually crash until much later; the final "handshake" of the aircraft SATCOM system connecting to the Inmarsat satellite was at 01:15 UTC, which is 09:15 Malaysian local time. This means that almost eight hours elapsed from the time that the Malaysian Airlines flight 370 diverted off course to the last known evidence of the aircraft with power.

How did the Boeing 777 manage to fly so far and for so long without anyone noticing? Mostly because no one was looking for it.

Under normal circumstances, if an aircraft fails to make a position report when expected, then no later than three minutes after the estimated reporting time, the controller should:

- Confirm the time of last contact
- Request information from other Air Traffic Services units and likely aerodromes

- Notify the Rescue Coordination Centre that the Uncertainty Phase exists

Loss of radio contact with an aircraft under Air Traffic Services control is a trigger event and if contact is not established, then an Uncertainty Phase is declared, signalling that uncertainty exists as to the safety of the aircraft and its occupants. The aircraft was estimated to pass IGARI at 01:22, so it would have been possible to declare the Uncertainty Phase as early as 01:25 and certainly no later than 01:55. Within 30 minutes, the phase is updated to Alert Phase (apprehension exists) and then after at most a further 30 minutes with no contact, the phase is updated to Distress Phase (reasonable certainty). This means that Search and Rescue operations would have commenced before 3 am, not long after the aircraft had turned south.

But this didn't happen.

At 01:39 Ho Chi Minh air traffic control contacted Kuala Lumpur to ask about MH370, stating that the flight crew had not made contact and that the aircraft was last seen at the BITOD waypoint.

This was incorrect. The BITOD waypoint was the next point on the aircraft's planned routing, but the aircraft never made it that far: the secondary surveillance dropped just after IGARI. It would seem that the radar operator was only half paying attention and had not realised when it disappeared off the display.

Kuala Lumpur confirmed that the flight had not returned to the Kuala Lumpur frequency, which would be standard procedure if an aircraft is handed off and can't make contact on the new frequency. The Kuala Lumpur control called Malaysia Airlines 370 on their frequency but received no response.

Ten minutes later, Ho Chi Minh queried again, as they had had no verbal contact with Malaysia Airlines flight 370, despite repeated calls and requests to other aircraft to relay.

Twenty-five minutes had elapsed. This would have been a good time to set the Uncertainty Phase, or even, considering the aircraft had disappeared from radar and not been heard from since, jumping straight to the Distress Phase. Instead the two stations continued with their attempts to make contact with the aircraft, checking in with each other to see if anyone had heard from the flight crew.

The responsibility for alerting lies firmly with Kuala Lumpur, as the service who was last in contact with the aircraft.

At 02:00, the Kuala Lumpur radar controller asked a junior officer to inform the Air Traffic Services Centre Duty Watch Supervisor, who was in the rest area next door, that Ho Chi Minh air traffic services had queried the status of Malaysia Airlines flight 370, because they were unable to make contact with the flight crew.

The Duty Watch Supervisor returned to the Air Traffic Services Centre immediately. He contacted Malaysia Airlines Operations Despatch Centre and informed them that Ho Chi Minh had not established radio contact and did not have radar contact.

We know now that by this point, the Boeing 777 had overflown Malaysia, where nobody was looking for it, appearing only on military radar. One radar operator noticed it. He confirmed that the radar return was from a civilian flight and thus "friendly". He did not take any further action as he had no idea there was any cause for concern.

Meanwhile, at Malaysia Airlines, the Operations Despatch Centre reassured the Air Traffic Services Centre supervisor that everything was fine. The airline's flight following system showed that the aircraft was in Cambodian airspace. He said that he would try to use the ACARS system to contact the flight crew and request that they contact Ho Chi Minh.

The Duty Watch Supervisor, having fulfilled his obligations and reassured that the aircraft was still flying, returned to the rest area at around 02:30 until about 05:30.

The Kuala Lumpur controller contacted Ho Chi Minh to let the controller there know that Malaysia Airlines Operations confirmed that the aircraft was still flying and had been located somewhere over Cambodia.

Ho Chi Minh, to their credit, queried this, stating that Phnom Penh, whose flight information region MH370 would be overflying, had no information on the aircraft. The Kuala Lumpur controller knew nothing more.

At 02:35, Malaysia Airlines Operations Despatch Centre said he was only getting updates every 30 minutes but confirmed again that the Boeing 777 was still en route to Beijing as per its flight plan and had just updated to a location east of Vietnam.

Both controllers found this odd, as no one in Vietnam or Cambodia had seen or heard anything from the aircraft. They tried again to contact flight 370 on various frequencies and asked other aircraft to relay the message in hopes of getting through.

Kuala Lumpur asked the Ho Chi Minh controller if they were taking "Radio Failure" action, but the Ho Chi Minh controller didn't seem to understand the question. The Ho Chi Minh controller's English was poor and the investigative interviews with the controller had to be done with the aid of a translator. The Ho Chi Minh controller suggested that Kuala Lumpur contact Malaysia Airlines Operations, which Kuala Lumpur air traffic control had already done.

And so, they waited and they hoped that everything was OK. It wasn't.

At 03:30, someone at the Malaysia Airlines Operations Despatch Centre finally realised that they had made a big mistake. Malaysia Airline's flight following system, called Flight Explorer, is a computer-based system which tracks aircraft *based on the flight plan data* entered into the computer before departure. The system generates the flight profile and position of the aircraft and updates every thirty minutes. What it doesn't offer is real-time tracking. It shows you where the aircraft should be, not where it actually is.

The person on duty that night didn't really understand how the flight following system worked and admitted later that he had not been properly trained in how to use it. This was effectively confirmed when investigation team asked the Operations Despatch Centre for a copy of the flight following system's User Manual and it turned out there wasn't one in the Centre. Later, a copy of the manual was delivered to the investigators.

The Malaysia Airlines staff member on duty passed on the position reports for Malaysia Airlines flight 370 because he believed that the system was giving him actual positions. He didn't understand that the position reports were simply projections based on the flight plan. The computer only knew where the Boeing 777 had planned to go; it had no idea where the actual aircraft was.

And now, neither did anyone else.

The radar controller at Kuala Lumpur broke the news to the Ho Chi Minh controller and asked if he'd checked with Hainan, which was the next Flight Information Region (FIR) where Malaysia Airlines flight 370 would have been expected to check in. The Ho Chi Minh supervisor now got involved, asking Kuala

Lumpur to clarify *exactly* where the last known position of Malaysia Airlines flight 370 was.

Everyone on the planned route was contacted to see if the aircraft had maybe been in touch, including Sanya, Hong Kong and Beijing. No one had seen or heard anything from the flight.

At 05:30, the Duty Watch Supervisor returned to the Air Traffic Services Centre and informed the Kuala Lumpur Aeronautical Rescue Coordination Centre of the situation. Ho Chi Minh contacted Kuala Lumpur again, asking if there were any updates. And then at 06:10, the Kuala Lumpur controller contacted Ho Chi Minh, this time to ask if they, Ho Chi Minh, had initiated Search and Rescue procedures. They had not.

Finally, at 06:32 local time, Kuala Lumpur Aeronautical Rescue Coordination Center issued a Distress Phase (DETRESFA) message. The aircraft had been missing for five hours and eleven minutes and over four hours had past since the Distress Phase should have been declared.

By now, the Boeing 777 had been silently travelling south for four hours. It was still in the air but no one had the faintest idea where to look. Search and rescue operations headed straight for IGARI to search the South China Sea while Malaysia Airlines flight 370 continued to fly for almost another three hours over the Indian Ocean.

The relevant parts of the of the report's conclusion are as follows:

> Evidence shows that Flight MH370 diverted from the Filed Flight Plan route. The aircraft's transponder signal ceased for reasons that could not be established and was then no longer visible on the ATC radar display. The changes in the aircraft flight path after the aircraft passed waypoint IGARI were captured by both civilian and military radars. These changes, evidently seen as turning slightly to the right first and then to the left and flying across the Peninsular Malaysia, followed by a right turn south of Penang Island to the north-west and a subsequent (unrecorded) turn towards the Southern Indian Ocean, are difficult to attribute to anomalous system issues alone. It could not be established whether the aircraft was flown

> by anyone other than the pilots. Later flight simulator trials established that the turn back was likely made while the aircraft was under manual control and not the autopilot.

Note: KL ATSC is *Kuala Lumpur Air Traffic Services Centre* and HCM ACC is *Ho Chi Minh Area Control Centre.*

> KL ATSC operation was normal with no significant observation until the handover to Viet Nam ATC. Being the accepting unit, HCM ACC did not notify the transferring unit (KL ATSC) when two-way communication was not established with MH370 within five minutes of the estimated time of the transfer of control point (Establishment of Communications, page 11 of Operational LOA between DCA Malaysia and Vietnam Air Traffic Management effective 1 November 2001). Likewise, KL ATSC should have taken action to contact HCM ACC, instead, relied on position information of the aircraft provided by MAS Flight Operations. By this time, the aircraft had left the range of radars visible to the KL ATSC. It is noted that about one minute elapsed from the last transmission from MH370 and the SSR being lost from the radar display. The Air Traffic Controllers of both Centres did not initiate the various emergency phases as required then, thereby delaying the activation of the alerting and Search and Rescue operations.

The day after the report went public, Malaysia's civil aviation chief resigned, taking responsibility for the shortcomings of the Kuala Lumpur air traffic control centre.

But it isn't just a question of *how.* The report's conclusions also help us to narrow down the possibilities of what happened to Malaysia Airlines flight 370. The details of the initial manual turn is extremely important, because it tells us that the Boeing 777 could not have been controlled from the outside (as per the *Remote Control Boeing* and *Hacked Autopilot* theories) because the systems in place would not have been capable of making the 35° steep turn.

Someone in the cockpit of the aircraft made the decision to turn the flight around. That is a crucial piece of information.

A second more nebulous point is that the sequence of mistakes made by the controllers, the duty supervisor and the Malaysia Airlines Operations Despatch Centre could not possibly have been predicted. That is to say, it seems unlikely that someone would *plan* an operation which had Malaysia Airlines flight 370 going dark directly before diverting, with a goal of flying to the Indian Ocean. Under normal circumstances, the alarm would have been raised within an hour at most of the initial loss of contact, which would not have given the aircraft enough time to complete its disappearing trick.

That's not to say that the there was no malicious interference with the flight, either by the flight crew or by a passenger. However, it is hard to believe that a plot was formed which relied on no one taking any action for over five hours.

This case has filled the hearts and minds of the public since it first disappeared in 2014 and it was the initial inspiration for this book.

However, it's not the most recent mysterious disappearance of an aircraft. That dubious distinction belongs to a fighter jet which disappeared in 2016 and still has not been found.

1986

Sutlej Missing over Indian Ocean

The most recent mysterious disappearance was just a few years ago in July 2016, when an Indian Air Force aircraft vanished in the middle of a routine courier flight.

The military flight was flying from Chennai to the Andaman and Nicobar Islands, a federal territory of India.

The aircraft was an Antonov An-32, a Soviet-built twin-engined turboprop military transport plane developed and produced by the Antonov State Company, originally a Soviet aircraft manufacturer and now owned by the Ukrainian Defense Industry . The An-32 are known as *Sutlej* in the Indian Air Force, named after the Sutlej River, the longest of the five rivers that flow through the crossroads region of Punjab in northern India and Pakistan.

The An-32 needs less than 3,000 feet of runway to take off or land. It's easily able to deal with high elevations and hot conditions and so is extremely useful for the Indian Air Force. The An-32 is regularly referred to as the "workhorse" of the transport fleet.

However, in an odd foreshadowing of the modern disaster, thirty years earlier, in 1986, an Indian Air Force An-32 went missing over the Indian Ocean, carrying three crew and four passengers, under inexplicable circumstances, when the aircraft fleet was still being delivered.

On 25 March 1986, three Antonov An-32 transport planes departed Muscat, the capital of Oman, in a staggered formation for the Indian Air Force base at Jamnagar.

Initially, the Indian Air Force were using Douglas DC-3 Dakotas and Fairchild C-119 Flying Boxcars for their transport. In the 1980s, spurred by the developing relationship between Leonid Brezhnev and Indira Ghandi, the Soviet Union made the offer of new aircraft at "friendship" prices. The Ministry of Defence decided that the medium transport aircraft should be replaced with the new Soviet-built An-32, an upgraded and re-engined version of the An-26. The then Joint Secretary (Air) is said to have stated, "sign as many aircraft as you want, for after a few years even a car may cost more than them."

The Indian Air Force was the first customer of the An-32 and purchased 125 aircraft on a 20-year military credit arrangement with no interest liability.

The large order of aircraft allowed the Indian Air Force to re-equip eight squadrons with the An-32 as transport, bombers and para-droppers: the No. 12 Squadron "Yaks" in Agra, the No. 25 Squadron "Himalayan Eagles" in Chandigarh, the No. 33 Squadron "Caribous" in Sulur, the No. 43 Squadron "Ibex" in Jorhat, the No. 48 Squadron "Camels" in Chandigarh, the No. 49 Squadron "Paraspears" in Jorhat, the Paratroopers Training School in Agra and the Transport Training Wing in Yelhanka.

A modernised An-32 is today worth about $15 million US dollars. There are a total of 240 An-32 aircraft in use by military operators around the world and the Indian Air Force is still the primary user. Of the original 125 aircraft purchased by the Indian Air Force, 105 are still in service, and the fleet is currently undergoing modernisation—a long-term project which has been expedited in the aftermath of the second disappearance.

The brand new An-32 aircraft began arriving in 1984 with three years to complete the order.

On the 25th of March in 1986, the deliveries were still in progress and three new aircraft were on the last leg of their ferry flight, from Oman to India. They took off at ten-minute intervals, forming a staggered formation to fly to the Indian Air Force base at Jamnagar. Each aircraft carried three crew and four passengers for the two-hour flight over the Gulf of Hormuz and the Arabian Sea to Jamnagar.

The weather that day was "fair" and the route straightforward. The first of the three An-32s landed at the coastal airport after an uneventful flight. The next aircraft to land was the third of the formation. The middle aircraft, tail number K2729, was missing.

The two surviving An-32s had believed themselves to be within close proximity of each other throughout the flight, however they had no idea that the middle aircraft was no longer with them. There was no radio call or signs of distress.

The loss of the An-32 straight from the factory was, of course, an issue, as well as the pointless deaths of the seven souls on board. But on top of this, the Indian Air Force was also under scrutiny as they'd lost another An-32 just three days earlier, when a military flight on weather reconnaissance crashed into a mountain at nearly 19,000 feet while descending through cloud.

As a result of the political situation, the search and rescue operation was massive. And yet they turned up no results. The media reported: "it was as if the sea had gobbled up the entire aircraft and buried it deep in its watery grave."

No one had a clue what could have happened. The An-32 was on its delivery flight and should not have been at risk from any sort of physical failure. The pilots were experienced. The route itself was straightforward, and the weather was clear. There was no reason to suspect sabotage. And yet the plane was gone, disappeared out from under its two companions without a sound.

With no distress call and no debris, the case soon grew cold. The investigation gave up, citing the probable cause of the loss of the An-32 as simply "Unresolved".

The Indian Air Force later discovered evidence that on the same day, the US Navy had supposedly lost an aircraft and launched a separate search and rescue operation, which equally found nothing. The interesting point was that the missing plane had been based on an aircraft carrier known to be in the same area where K2729 was believed to have gone down.

Apparently, the US Navy aircraft also simply vanished without a distress call and the wreckage of that aircraft was never found. Since the two military investigations were both conducted separately (and the US investigation has never been confirmed by the Navy), the possibility of a mid-air collision was never seriously considered. If that was what happened, it could help to explain why both aircraft vanished so suddenly.

However, this theory poses as many questions as it answers. How was it that neither of the two An-32 in loose formation saw any sign of the US Navy aircraft? If there was a mid-air collision, why didn't the An-32 bringing up the rear see the explosion? How could two aircraft disintegrate over the calm seas and not leave any trace of debris visible on that fair day? And finally, why has the US Navy never officially admitted that an aircraft vanished in the Arabian Sea on that day, although there were published reports of two missing airmen lost at sea and presumed dead?

The mystery of An-32 was highlighted in the Indian press in 2014 when Malaysian Airlines flight 370 disappeared. They could not have known that another An-32 was about to vanish in similar inexplicable circumstances . . .

2016

There are still a hundred of the An-32s in service in the Indian Air Force: mid-life extension and upgrades of the fleet started in 2010 and a further forty upgraded aircraft had arrived from Kiev in the five years before the accident flight. Upgrading the An-32s has been a slow and ongoing process.

This particular An-32, call sign AF330, was part of the 33 Squadron in Sulur. On the 22nd of July in 2016, it was flying a routine courier flight, ferrying twenty-three passengers from Tambaram Air Force Station in Chennai to the Veer Savarkar International Airport at Port Blair. It's just over three hours flight time from Tambaram to Port Blair, which has a major Indian naval base as well as sea and air bases of the Indian Coast Guard and Indian Air Force.

The passengers consisted of eleven members of the Indian Air Force, two soldiers from the Indian Army, a member of the Indian Navy, a member of the Indian Coast Guard and eight civilians from Visakhapatnam who worked with the Naval Armament Depot.

The flight departed without incident at 08:30 local time, which was expected to land at Port Blare at 11:45 after the 3-hour 15-minute flight. The aircraft carried fuel for four hours.

At 9:12, 45 minutes after departing Chennai, the An-32 was 280 km (170 miles) east of Chennai, flying over the Indian Ocean. They were nearing the end of the range of the primary radar coverage from the Indian mainland and, as a military flight, they were apparently not squawking for secondary radar coverage. Another ten minutes of flight would have placed the aircraft into a known black spot, an area about 150–200 nautical miles (175–230 miles or 280–370 km) with no radar coverage from either Chennai or Port Blair.

But the flight never made it that far. The An-32 was still within primary radar coverage when the flight disappeared off of radar. It seems likely that because it was near the black spot, there was no real concern about the flight. After all, there had not been any distress calls or any mention of difficulties. The crew had been in touch with the controller just a few minutes before, simply noting that they were deviating to the right. The controller understood this to be to avoid some weather in view ahead but there was certainly no reason to believe that the aircraft was in danger.

An hour after it had been due to land at Port Blair, there was still no word and An-32 call sign AF330 was officially declared missing.

The aircraft was never heard from again.

The facts were few. Seven minutes before the aircraft disappeared off of radar, the crew told air traffic control: “We are deviating to the right”. Then, a few minutes later, the aircraft tilted to the *left* and descended rapidly, losing 23,000 feet in seconds.

The Indian Navy and the Indian Coast Guard launched a search party as soon as it was clear that the aircraft was missing, sending out twelve ships, five aircraft and a submarine. They searched the area where the radar coverage had been suddenly lost but found no sign of the aircraft.

The sea was very choppy and thick cloud cover in the area hampered the search but aircraft and ships all rushed towards the region in hopes of finding some trace of the aircraft and its passengers. The Air Force put all available assets into the search operation and the Indian Navy and Indian Coast Guard immediately began deploying air and surface vehicles to the region.

The following day, the search continued and by the third day, a further sixteen ships and six aircraft joined the search now spread across the Bay of Bengal—150 nautical miles east of Chennai.

The An-32 had two emergency locator transmitters but they did not work underwater. None of the An-32 fleet had underwater locator beacons as they weren't considered "primarily a marine/maritime aircraft". This meant that if the aircraft had crashed into the sea, which seemed likely, there was no signal to pick up.

The aircraft also carried four life rafts, each of which was fitted with a Personal Locator Beacon which would activate upon coming in contact with water. However, they only operate on the surface of the sea so could only be tracked if those on board the aircraft had managed to evacuate and remove the life boats. As it was, no signal from the personal locator beacons was ever picked up.

The military could only hope that they might find traces of the wreckage or at least some debris.

Indian survey ships scoured the seabed along with the submarine but with a water depth of 3,000-4,000 metres (9,800-13,000 feet), specialist equipment was needed to properly search the area.

The Indian Navy, known for their reluctance to ask for foreign support, quietly requested the help of the Russian Navy rescue ship *Igor Belousov* to help locate the missing aircraft. The brand new ship was designed for search, rescue and salvage of distressed ships and submarines. Its submersibles could dive as deep as 700 metres (2,300 feet) and lift objects back up to surface. The Russian Navy diverted the ship, which spent over 12 hours in the surface search zone. They never found any sign of the wreckage and reluctantly left to continue to the ship's original destination.

The Defence Minister also contacted the US to ask if any of their satellites had captured signals from the An-32 before its sudden disappearance. However, this required a satellite to be crossing the area at the time and even then, with thick cloud cover in the area, the chances were slim. The Indian satellites had not recorded any signals and neither, it seemed, had the US satellites.

With no recorded signals and no underwater locator beacon, the focus had to be to search for visual clues: debris, oil slicks or floating wreckage washed on shore. However, the search area could not be reduced down to a sensible level, which meant that thoroughly searching the area would take months, during which time the visible signs of the crash into the sea would be long gone.

The search and rescue operation is to this day India's biggest search operation at sea. More than 201 search and rescue sorties spent over 500 hours searching over an area of 217,800 square nautical miles, in addition to extensive searches on the coast in hopes of finding some debris washed up from the aircraft.

Antonov An-32 K2692 in Kiev taken by Oleg V. Belyakov —AirTeamImages

By the 12th of August, hope was fading. By now, the search aircraft had flown over 1,000 hours and at one stage, 28 ships had been deployed. Although it had been the most intense search ever in Indian waters, no sign of debris had been found. The Navy refocused its efforts from the surface to the seabed, hoping to find the sunken wreckage. They detected two dozen electronic transmissions but, as with the first month of searching for MH370, they were all unrelated. None of the signals were from the missing aircraft or its life rafts.

The National Institute of Ocean Technology and the Geological Survey of India both sent specialised surface vehicles to the point where the An-32 was last seen on radar, using multi-beam echo sounders to profile objects on the sea floor. Both ships also used sonar equipment meant to detect objects on the seabed. Neither ship saw any sign of anything that could lead them to the final resting place of the An-32. It had vanished.

On the 15th of September, almost two months after the aircraft had disappeared, the search and rescue mission was called off. The Indian Air Force declared that there were no chances of survival and everyone on board was declared dead. The family members were told to sign the "certificate of presumption of death" to start the legal proceedings for compensation.

Once the military gave up on the search, the chances of finding any answers were slim. The only thing they really knew was that for some unknown reason, the aircraft had abruptly turned left without warning before rapidly descending 23,000 feet.

Sabotage was deemed unlikely, with the Defence Minister explaining that everyone on board was from the "defence forces" and understood standard operating procedures which they had not initiated. This has not, of course, stopped speculation that the crash was the result of high-tech terrorism.

Another theory was that of faulty maintenance on the ageing fleet. Local press claimed that the An-32 was "not in the best condition" when it undertook that flight from Chennai to Port Blair.

The missing An-32 call sign AF330 had received a full overhaul at 1 Base Repair Depot (BRD) in Kanpur less than one year previous and had flown 279 hours since then. However, it had also had a large amount of maintenance in the weeks before its disappearance with logged reports of sluggish throttle movements, a hydraulic leak in the left-hand wing root (where the wing extends from the fuselage), and a pressure leak at the left-hand door.

If the pressure leak in the door had not been properly dealt with, it could have burst suddenly, causing an explosive decompression. Explosive or rapid decompression is caused by a sudden structural failure in a pressurised environment, where the speed of the decompression is faster than air can escape the lungs. In this instance, even if the structural integrity of the aircraft allowed for continued flight, it is quite likely that the passengers and crew would have had no chance to react.

A recurrence of the leak itself could have led to gradual decompression, where the decompression is slow enough that the issue goes unnoticed. In this case, there is much more time to react. If the leak was known, the pilots would have put on their oxygen masks and declared an emergency (in that order!), so that can be discarded as a possibility. Even if they did not know that the leak was slowly depressurising the aircraft, there are instruments in the An-32 to warn that the aircraft is depressurising, but it is possible that the effects of hypoxia were such that the crew and passengers disregarded thc warnings, as happened 10 years earlier in the case of Helios Airways Flight 522.

However in the Helios case, the aircraft continued to fly for hours after the flight crew had lost consciousness. If the An-32 had suffered a similar slow failure, there's no reason why the aircraft itself would not have continued in a straight line for some time, allowing it to come into radar range of Port Blair.

Another possibility is that the hydraulic leak was not correctly dealt with, which would mean that the aircraft became uncontrollable. However, as they were cruising at over 20,000 feet, even if the aircraft hydraulics had failed, there should be plenty of time to make a distress call.

None of these theories answers the question of what happened to AF330 in any satisfactory way.

In India, the focus shifted on beefing up the maintenance, repair and overhaul of the existing fleet. As most of India's defence equipment is purchased from foreign manufacturers, they have a very clear challenge when it comes to maintaining their fleet.

The Indian Air Force prioritised fitting underwater locator beacons onto those of the remaining An 32 fleet which were expected to fly over the sea, a project which was already in progress but had only been moving ahead slowly.

Originally planned to be fitted as an integral part of the black box, the Ministry of Defence decided instead to push forward with a stopgap effort, installing stand-alone underwater locator beacons in the aircraft as an emergency measure.

Unfortunately, the pressure to expedite the upgrading of the fleet has led to even more disappearances as a result of the conflict in the Ukraine.

Sixty-four An-32s in India have not been able to be upgraded locally because the Ukraine state-owned arms trading company, who had agreed to upgrade the 104 transport aircraft, is no longer supplying the Indian Air Force the engineers to do the work nor parts required to complete them.

Meanwhile, forty An-32s were sent to the Ukraine to have the maintenance done in Kiev. Only 35 were returned.

The remaining five An-32s? They have disappeared.

Initially, the Indian Air Force denied the reports, explaining that the five missing An-32s were not missing, they were simply stranded in a factory in Ukraine due to the geopolitical situation.

However an Indian Air Force official told *Defense News* that the five aircraft are now completely untraceable.

A diplomat from the Ukraine Embassy said that the Indian Air Force must resolve the issue of the missing aircraft directly with Antonov and that the Ukrainian government cannot help.

Antonov denied having anything to do with the missing aircraft, stating that they had not taken delivery of them.

In 2019, the Indian Air Force confirmed that all further upgrades to the AN-32 fleet will take part at the Indian Air Force's base in Kanpur, using equipment transferred from the Ukraine.

As a result, the Indian Air Force are missing seven Antonov An-32s. The circumstances are different but the fact remains that all seven have disappeared without a trace.

Conclusion

As the aviation industry shifts to the use of ever more precise navigation technology and satellite tracking, it seems that such disappearances will become rarer and rarer; I cannot imagine another volume of aviation mysteries within my lifetime. However, if you would still like more, there's bonus content: The Appendix contains a rundown of the many suspects fingered in the Dan Cooper case. And you can get an in-depth look at one of them, Richard McCoy, by subscribing to my announcement mailing list, where I'll post updates to mysteries covered in the two volumes, if there are any, as well as letting you know when my next aviation book is out. Sign up here or simply email me at sylvia@planecra.sh with a subject line of "Aviation updates".

It is difficult to imagine that we might never find out what happened, that it isn't possible for us to learn the truth. We don't like to think that we will never have the answers. I get a lot of email to this effect, insisting that the answer must be simple and must be known, because it's so crazy to think that we can't have the answers. And yet, as the decades go by and turn into centuries, it seems unlikely that any greater truth will make itself known. We can only give a moment of silence for all those who disappeared, with their aircraft, without a trace.

APPENDIX

THE SUSPECTS IN THE DAN COOPER CASE

HERE'S A LIST of some of the more fascinating suspects.

Walter R. Reca admitted in 2008 to Carl Laurin, a close friend, that he was DB Cooper. He gave his permission for his friend to record the details, to be released after his death. They spent six weeks discussing the heist, recording over three hours of information about the hijacking. Laurin says that the tapes included information never revealed to the public, including that the hijacker used superglue to disguise his fingerprints and that he offered money to the cabin crew member before he jumped.

Reca died at age 80 in 2014 and Laurin wrote a book documenting Reca's confession (*D.B. Cooper & Me: A Criminal, A Spy, My Best Friend*), which Laurin said proved that Reca was the true DB Cooper. Reca's niece appeared at a press conference with Laurin to state that Reca had also confessed to her that he had hijacked the Boeing 727.

Reca, born in 1933, was a war veteran. He served in the 82nd Airborne as a paratrooper, so he had the experience needed to pull off the heist. His description of the landing site included a café where he stopped to ask "a cowboy who had driven a dump truck" for directions to the café so that a friend could pick him up. Laurin was able to reconstruct his journey using the landmarks and was able to identify the landing site, the café and the cowboy, who confirmed that he'd seen a man that night who'd asked for directions. In 2018, a four-part documentary was released detailing the investigation, which concluded that Reca was the true DB Cooper. The producer said that all documents were examined by a certified fraud examiner and forensic linguist and they could find no discrepancies that eliminated Reca as a suspect.

However, Reca had also claimed that a few weeks after the hijacking, he was approached and blackmailed by the FBI: work as a covert intelligence operative for the US government or go to prison. He claimed that he was given a KGB identity card and various other aliases but Laurin was unable to offer any proof of this. Laurin claimed that the FBI covered up the truth and that is why they were unwilling to consider Reca as a serious suspect.

Lynn Doyle Cooper, a leather worker and veteran of the Korean War, died in 1999. Ten years later, his niece, Marla Wynn Cooper, contacted the FBI and the press to tell them that her uncle was the hijacker based on some odd events from 1971. She was eight at the time and recalled that her two uncles were planning something "very mischievous" which involved some expensive walkie-talkies. She remembers the timing because the family had all gathered at her grandmother's house to celebrate Thanksgiving. The following day, which was the day of the hijacking, her uncles arrived at her grandmother's but Uncle LD was unable to get out of the car and his shirt was bloody and torn. She overheard the two brothers say that they had hijacked an airplane and that their money troubles were over, but Uncle LD had been injured in a parachuting getaway. She'd quickly forgotten about this until years later, when a conversation with her parents jogged her memory. In 2011, an FBI agent confirmed to the press that they had a new suspect whom they had been investigating for over a year. "We do have a promising lead," he said at a press conference. "It is the most promising lead we have right now." Which, under the circumstances, was not saying much.

Marla Cooper handed over a guitar strap belonging to her uncle but the FBI were unable to recover fingerprints from it. They requested additional belongings from LD Cooper's family and were able to recover a DNA sample . . . but it did not match the partial DNA profile that they had from the hijacker's tie. However, there is still the question of whether the DNA found on the tie was definitely from the hijacker.

John List was a veteran of World War II and the Korean War and probably had paratrooper experience during his time in the military. In late 1971, the neighbours noticed that the lights of the List mansion, which had been continuously on for a month, were beginning to burn out without repair. The police broke into John List's home where they found the bodies of his wife and their three teenaged children laid out on sleeping bags, with organ music playing over the intercom. There was also a note from John List to his pastor, confessing to the murders and letting him know that the body of his mother, Alma List, was in the hallway in the attic, as she was too heavy to move.

The bodies had been there for a month; the killings had taken place just two weeks before the Cooper hijacking. List had stopped the newspaper and milk deliveries and told everyone they were going on a family trip. In the house, he tore himself out of every family photo and left all the lights on and disappeared.

He immediately became a suspect in the Northwest hijacking. His general characteristics matched descriptions given by the eyewitnesses and it seemed clear that a man on the run after having murdered his entire family had very little to lose. Could John List also be Dan Cooper?

In 1989, America's Most Wanted took an interest in the case and released age-progression photographs he FBI had produced of List, along with a life-sized bust representing John List 18 years after the murder and hijack. When the show aired, the police received 300 calls claiming to know where John List was, including one woman, who was so convinced her husband was John List that the FBI flew to her home to arrest him. As it happens, the woman was wrong and her husband had never murdered anyone. It's hard not to wonder what the dinner conversation was like at their house that night.

However, one of those callers identified her next-door neighbour as John List. It turned out she was right: police discovered John List under an assumed name, living a new life with a new wife. List immediately admitted to having killed his first family, saying that they were going bankrupt. He'd killed them out of love, so that they would not experience financial ruin and because he wanted to ensure their places in heaven. He was adamant, however, that he had not hijacked any planes and he definitely was not DB Cooper.

The FBI concluded that his fingerprints did not match any of those found on the Boeing 727 and, once again, the evidence linking the suspect to the case was all circumstantial. List was convicted of five counts of first-degree murder in 1990 and sentenced to five consecutive terms of life imprisonment without parole. He died in prison in 2008 at the age of 82.

Robert Lepsy was a married father of four who worked as a manager in a grocery store. In October 1969, he left work but never arrived at home. Originally treated as suspicious, the police discovered his car parked at a local airport with the keys in the ignition. Airport staff then confirmed that a man matching his description was seen boarding a flight to Mexico. The case was dropped as authorities concluded that he had disappeared voluntarily, and Robert Lepsy's family never heard from him again.

However, when the news covered the daring hijack in 1971, the family immediately reacted: the composite drawings of "DB Cooper" were the spitting image of Robert Lepsy and the clothing that the suspect was said to be wearing was similar to Lepsy's uniform at the grocery store. His daughter said, "When the composite sketch of DB Cooper came on the TV screen, everyone looked at each other and said, 'That's Dad!' "

The tie discovered on the plane was confirmed as being very similar to the one Lepsy wore for work. His daughter submitted a DNA sample to the FBI in 2011 but there is no record of the results nor any comment from the FBI as to how or why Lepsy was dismissed as a suspect. Lepsy was declared legally dead in 1976.

Duane Weber was another deathbed confession; in hospital in 1995 he admitted to his wife, Jo Weber, that he was Dan Cooper. At the time, she didn't recognise the name or what he meant, at which point he became agitated and upset, saying, "Oh, just let it die with me." The nurses sedated him and he died not long after. Later, Jo Weber realised that Dan Cooper was the real name (or the real alias) of the infamous hijacker known in the media as DB Cooper, whom she had of course heard of. That, she realized, was what her husband was trying to tell her.

This actually explained a lot, Jo Weber said. There were many things that had happened since their marriage in 1977 which she had not been able to explain. He had a knee injury that he said he got jumping out of an aircraft but he never gave any details. She'd once found he was keeping an old plane ticket from Portland to Seattle, but when she asked her husband about it, he wouldn't answer and the ticket later appeared hidden in his drawer before disappearing completely.

And there was an incident around the Columbia River, where the young boy found a bundle of $20 bills confirmed as from the hijacking. Duane Weber showed his wife around the area, pointing out a spot which, he told her, was "where DB Cooper walked out of the woods." When she asked him how he could know that, he joked that maybe he was there. He then stopped the car near the river and told her to stay in the car. He opened the trunk and then disappeared for a few minutes but she didn't know what he did or if he took something out of the trunk. A few months later, the package of $5,800 from ransom money was discovered buried in the sand of the river's shore, just a few miles downstream of where they had stopped.

The FBI collected Duane Weber's DNA in 2003 and excluded Weber as a suspect based on DNA evidence.

Jo Weber contacted me in 2010 to talk about the case after I wrote about it on the Fear of Landing website (fearofland-ing.com). She was the one to tell me that the FBI had created multiple composite images of Dan Cooper (known as composite A, B and C) as they attempted to reconcile the conflicting information from the eyewitnesses. I had used one of the later composites in my piece and she wanted to tell me that the original composite was a much closer match to her husband. She said that after her husband died in 1995, his possessions had been cleaned and handled by many people and then stored in a humid and hot attic, so the DNA samples collected by the FBI could not be trusted. She also said that when the evidence was returned to her, they left the detailed report in the box, which showed that the DNA wasn't actually tested until 2006 or 2007. Even if the DNA they retrieved was definitely Weber's, that didn't mean that the partial DNA sample they had on file for "Dan Cooper" was that of the hijackers. She said that no one ever saw the tie removed; it was merely found slung over the back of the seat where he'd been sitting. She still believes that the FBI never properly investigated Weber and that he should not have been ruled out based on the DNA evidence.

William Wolfgang Gossett was yet another deathbed confession, telling his sons in 2003 that he was actually DB Cooper. He fit the description better than most: he was 41 years old at the time of the hijacking and his physical characteristics matched those given by eyewitnesses: medium complexion, brown eyes, 5′10″ tall, 186 pounds and a smoker. He had served with the Marine Force Fleet where he was trained as a reconnaissance paratrooper.

William Gossett was obsessed with the Cooper hijacking and always said that he knew enough about the case to write DB Cooper's epitaph. One amateur sleuth also found evidence that Gossett could have written the letters sent to the newspapers in the aftermath of the hijacking which were signed as DB Cooper, but there was no evidence that the letters were actually written by the man who hijacked the aircraft.

One of his sons remembers his father having "wads of cash" shortly after the hijacking in 1971; he believed that Gossett lost the money gambling in Las Vegas. His sons said that when he confessed, he gave them a key to a Vancouver safe deposit box where he told them they would find the ransom money but no evidence was ever turned in of the contents. The FBI haven't treated Gossett as a serious suspect, as they found no evidence linking Gossett to the crime other than the statements he made to other people.

Kenneth Peter Christiansen was reported to the FBI by his brother, Lyle Christiansen. Kenneth Christiansen served in the US Army and was stationed in Japan, where he trained as a paratrooper. In 1954, still in the South Pacific, he got a job as a mechanic with Northwest Orient. Later he became a flight attendant and relocated to Seattle when he was promoted to purser (senior cabin crew member). He had a number of characteristics in common with the hijacker: in 1971 he was 45 years old, he smoked, he drank bourbon and he was left-handed—Cooper's tie clip was attached from the left side. In 1994, when Kenneth Christiansen was on his deathbed, he told his brother that he had a secret. "There's something you should know, but I cannot tell you." His brother then discovered after his death that he owned gold coins and a stamp collcction valued at over $400,000 and had another $200,000 deposited in his bank accounts, none of which could be explained on Christiansen's income. The brother also found a folder of news clippings about

Northwest Orient, which began at the time when Kenneth Christiansen was hired, and then stopped abruptly in 1971, just before the hijacking, even though Christiansen had continued to work for the company for some time longer.

The brother also pointed out that Christiansen had purchased his house with cash just a few months after the hijacking. He was resentful towards Northwest Airlines for the poor pay and a series of lay-offs in the year leading up to the hijacking.

The FBI stated that Christiansen was not considered a serious suspect, as the physical descriptions did not match those given by eyewitnesses at the time, and even that Christiansen may have had *too much* parachuting experience. One FBI agent said outright that the only piece of information that matched was that Christiansen and Cooper were both male.

Lyle Christiansen hired a private investigator to find out more, convinced that he could find a link to prove that his brother was in fact Dan Cooper. He also contacted a famous Hollywood producer in hopes of selling the film rights.

However, much of what he knew about Kenneth Christiansen turned out to be wrong. Christiansen had not paid cash for his house; he had a mortgage which took him 17 years to pay off. Shortly before his death, he sold much of his land, almost two dozen acres, for $17,000 an acre, which accounted for the cash in the bank. And the coin collection was actually worth only $30,000, not $400,000; his brother said that he had accidentally added an extra zero.

Barbara Dayton confessed to the crime in 1979. Dayton admitted to friends at the airfield where she kept her plane that she was Dan Cooper. She told multiple witnesses that she had staged the entire heist, hijacking the aircraft disguised as a man so that she wouldn't be treated as a suspect. She landed safely south of the Columbia River, she said, and hid the money in a nearby cistern. Dayton knew the area but also, unlike many of the suspects, she had motive: after getting her private pilot's licence in 1959, her dream had been to follow a career as a commercial pilot but she struggled with the theory in the written test and failed to understand the algebra required to pass, which she didn't think had much to do with the ability to fly.

Excluded by the FAA and struggling with finances, she often joked about robbing a bank. She also had the experience: Dayton was a transwoman and had served in World War 2, both with the US Merchant Marines and the US Army (the Air Force disqualified her because of an eye condition). After her transition in 1969, Dayton found it hard to get work. She told her psychologist that she was willing to take any kind of job (as long as it didn't require short sleeves, as her arms were covered in tattoos) but no one was willing to hire her. According to the notes published by her friends after Dayton's death, her doctor agreed that she had run into much employer prejudice and reported that she was understandably very depressed, as she had no source of income and was ineligible for welfare. He noted that she had considered suicide. Eight days before the hijacking, her files include another note that she was considering suicide.

However, two weeks after the jump, Dayton's files state that "the patient is doing well, not depressed" and notes that she was strangely unworried about finances despite an inability to get work. He wrote that "she seems reasonably happy and adapted to the circumstances." Shortly after, she got a job as a librarian at the University of Washington. Her friends, who have written a book about Dayton's life and adventures, believe that the change of heart was caused by the fact that she'd pulled off the perfect heist and now had enough money that she didn't have to worry about her future.

Dayton later denied that she was Dan Cooper, possibly because she realised the FBI were still looking for a viable suspect. The statute of limitations should have expired in 1976, three years before her confession, but following an indictment for "John Doe" the case was kept open and so anyone, even now, can still be charged with the crime.

In any event, the FBI dismissed her as a credible subject fairly quickly, not because Dayton was a woman but because she was too short; she stood a few inches shorter than most of the eyewitnesses remembered Dan Cooper as being. The money she said she'd hidden in the cistern was never recovered.

Dayton retired from the University in 1988 and moved to Nevada, where she gambled away her social security in Carson City casinos in an attempt to increase her income. She died in 2002, aged 76.

Ted E. Mayfield had served in the Special Forces and was both a pilot and a competitive skydiver, giving him more than enough experience to pull off such a heist. He also lived in the local area and was known to have been involved in various criminal activities, including armed robbery and transportation of stolen aircraft.

His pilot licence was revoked in 1967 for illegally carrying a passenger when he was still a student pilot. He reapplied successfully, and in 1972, a year after the hijacking, he obtained his commercial pilot's licence and opened the Pacific Parachute Center. His licence was removed again in 1982 for failing to disclose his criminal history as a part of his certification. It was never reinstated. He served time in 1994 for repeatedly flying without a licence. Mayfield closed the Pacific Parachute Center in 1994 when the FAA began investigating his operation as a result of the high number of deaths reported. In 1995 he was charged and convicted for negligent homicide: two of his skydiving students died when their parachutes failed to open and the case showed that the parachutes were improperly packed and maintained. In the twenty-two years that he ran his skydiving operation, thirteen people died, mostly from malfunctioning parachutes. Mayfield argued that skydiving was an inherently risky sport and the number of deaths was not unusual.

On the night of the hijacking, six callers reported Mayfield as a possible suspect. Mayfield argued that he had a cast-iron alibi: he claimed that the FBI called him for advice that night while Cooper was still in the air.

Two amateur sleuths fingered him for the crime again in 2006, questioning his alibi. The FBI agent in charge of the case said that the FBI had never called Mayfield. Mayfield called *them*, offering to advise the FBI on skydiving practices and possible landing zones in the local area. The files released on the case confirm this, showing no record of the FBI calling Mayfield: the first contact was Mayfield calling them, and that was just under two hours after the Boeing 727 had landed at Reno. The FBI ruled him out as a suspect early on as a result of this phone call but the sleuths argued that Mayfield, who had won many awards for skydiving accuracy, could easily have jumped to a known location where a car was waiting and arrived home within two hours after the plane had landed.

Mayfield stuck to his story that the FBI contacted him earlier and also claimed that the sleuths had talked to him before they went to the press and asked him to play along, saying they would all make a lot of money for solving the case.

Not one to rest on his laurels, 2010 saw Mayfield in court again, where he was sentenced for another three years probation for piloting a plane twenty-six years after his pilot's licence had been revoked. His radio had failed and he took off without permission, having attempted to interact with air traffic controls with light signals.

Mayfield died in 2015, aged 79, in an unrelated aviation accident.

Richard Floyd McCoy Jr. became a suspect when he hijacked a Boeing 727 in 1972, demanding $500,000 in cash and four parachutes. His jump near Provo, Utah was successful and he made it home with a bag full of cash.

He'd left behind quite a bit more evidence than Dan Cooper, including a clear fingerprint and a hand-written note that he'd handed to the cabin crew member and forgot to get back. Still, he might have got away with it if he hadn't told his friend that he'd come up with a foolproof plan for hijacking an airliner. He was arrested at home three days after the hijacking when police with a search warrant found $499,970 wrapped up in bank bands in a cardboard box.

McCoy's was the seventh hijacking involving parachutes in the five months following Dan Cooper's hijack and it is likely that he was yet another copycat: after the Cooper case was in the news he'd told the same friend that Cooper should have asked for more money and was well known to have been interested in the specifics.

Sadly, there isn't enough room to tell you all about this but I've written about McCoy's weird and wonderful story separately and it is available to anyone who signs up for the mailing list at http://eepurl.com/dlv7Lj.

Robert Rackstraw was a Vietnam War veteran who served as part of a helicopter crew. He was given two Distinguished Flying Crosses before being kicked out of the army in 1971 when they found he'd falsified his school records; he had never finished high school. He returned home "disillusioned and angry" five months before the hijack.

He shared the general features of the composite drawings of Dan Cooper. Accused of financial fraud (writing $75,000 worth of bad cheques), he fled to Iran in 1978, which is when the FBI became aware of him. While Rackstraw was training pilots for the Shah, authorities discovered rifles and explosives illegally stored in his warehouse and, more surprisingly, the murdered body of Rackstraw's stepfather, who had been shot twice through the head.

Rackstraw was deported from Iran back to the US where he was acquitted of his stepfather's murder but charged with illegal explosives possession, forgery and financial fraud. Released on bail, he faked his own death by renting a small plane and then radioing a Mayday call, telling ATC that his engine was on fire and he was ditching the aircraft and bailing out over Monterey Bay. Search and rescue found no sign of the wreckage but Rackstraw turned up soon thereafter at an airfield 360 miles south, where he was caught trying to forge federal pilot licences. The accident aircraft was also there, repainted and parked in a hangar. The FBI asked him outright if he was Dan Cooper. Rackstraw responded with a simple retort: "Could have been." He also told a journalist that his uncle taught him to parachute when he was 16. His uncle's name, he said, was Ed Cooper.

In 1979, the FBI eliminated Rackstraw as a suspect, saying they had only circumstantial evidence and they did not want to muddy the waters of his ongoing trial. Rackstraw made a plea deal and served a year in prison.

In 1980, a friend of Rackstraw, who had himself claimed to be the real DB Cooper, supposedly said that some of the ransom money was about to be discovered. He said that the money would wash up on the river so that investigators would think the hijacker had drowned. Friends insisted that the news of the $5,800 in twenty dollar bills hit the news a few days later.

In 2016, an author and filmmaker filed a lawsuit against the FBI for the full copies of the hijack case files under the Freedom of Information Act. He alleged that the FBI had suspended the active investigation out of embarrassment for their failure to develop sufficient evidence to prosecute Rackstraw and published a book (*The Last Master Outlaw*) attempting to prove that Rackstraw was clearly the man behind DB Cooper. The author claimed they had proof that the FBI had covered up evidence and lied for decades. By then Rackstraw was 72 years old and living in San Diego. He reportedly had told the author that yes, he had told everybody that he was the skyjacker. His lawyer also confirmed that he always enjoyed letting people think he was DB Cooper, in part, the lawyer said, to meet women. Rackstraw petitioned the judge to issue arrest warrants for the author and his team, charging them with “conspiracy to commit premeditated murder,” claiming they hired gunmen to ambush him.

In 2018, the documentary team led by the author claimed that they had cracked the code in the letters sent to national newspapers in December 1971, supposedly from DB Cooper, and that their results proved Rackstraw’s involvement. The team claimed that the FBI refused to acknowledge the findings because they didn’t want to admit that amateur sleuths had cracked a case that the FBI couldn’t. The author also claimed that Rackstraw cut a deal with the CIA, which was why the case had been dropped.

At this point, Rackstraw, 74 and living on a yacht called *Poverty Sucks*, finally denied any involvement with the hijacking, responding to the allegations with, “It’s a lot of [expletive].”

Image Credits

In Order of Appearance

The Mysterious Truth behind Foxtrot 94

Google Maps screenshot. Map data: Geobasis-DE/BKG, Google, Inst. Geogr. Nacional. Imagery: Data SIO, NOAA, US Navy, NGA, GEBCO, Landsat

Source: https://goo.gl/maps/ZYa8h7bhf1G2

Screenshot from BBC News article

Source: http://www.bbc.co.uk/insideout/yorkslincs/series1/alien-abduction.shtml

Who Was the Real Dan Cooper?

Snap on black tie, found on the seat after Cooper disappeared.

Source: https://archives.fbi.gov/archives/news/stories/2009/march/in-search-of-d.b.-cooper/cooper-gallery

Great Mull Air Mystery

Glenforsa Airfield taken by Keith Boardman in 2005

Attribution: Keith Boardman / Glenforsa Airfield / CC BY-SA 2.0

A UFO Hunter Finds What He's Looking For

Department of Transport Aircraft Accident Investigation Summary Report V116/783/1047

Source: https://recordsearch.naa.gov.au/NAAMedia /ShowImage.asp?B=10491375&S=8&T=P

Korean Air Lines Shot Down by Soviet Military (twice)

KAL Flight 902's flightplan (in blue, Paris to Anchorage to Seoul) and deviation from plan (in red, having turned southeast when over Ellesmere Island)

Attribution: Anynobody 2007/ CC BY-SA 3.0

Mahrshal Nikolai Ogarkov during his September 9, 1983, press conference on the shootdown of Korean Air Lines Flight 007

Attribution: Central Intelligence Agency/Public Domain

Sukhoi Su-15TM
Public Domain image by Greg Goebel

Source: http://www.airvectors.net/avsu15.html

Night Ship Needed To Deviate, But From Whom?

Fuselage photograph from the NTSB Docket

Source: https://dms.ntsb.gov/pubdms/search/document .cfm?docID=210703&docketID=35935&mkey=55956

The Stolen Boeing

Boeing 727 registration N844AA at Chicago O'Hare International Airport on 21 May 1989.

Attribution: RuthAS / CC BY-SA 3.0

FBI Wanted poster for Ben Charles Padilla

The Latest Bermuda Triangle Mystery

The DC-3 N86553 photographed by Jon Wickenden at the Vintage Flying Museum in May 2010

Source: https://www.flickr.com/photos/wickenden1967/

Malaysia Airlines flight 370

Diversion from Filed Flight Plan Route based on Civilian Radar

Source: Safety Investigation Report H370 (9M-MRO)

Sutlej Missing over Indian Ocean

Antonov An-32 K2692 in Kiev

Source: AirTeamImages
Attribution: Oleg V. Belyakov / CC BY-SA 3.0

References

The Mysterious Truth Behind Foxtrot 9

Dr David Clarke (27 June 1905) "Captain Schaffner's last flight", *Fortean Times.* Available at https://drdavidclarke.co.uk/secret-files/captain-schaffners-last-flight/ (Accessed 1 Apr 2018)

(16 September 2002) "Yorkshire Alien Abduction", BBC News. Available at http://www.bbc.co.uk/insideout/yorkslincs/series1/alien-abduction.shtml (Accessed 1 Apr 2018)

Tony Dodd (7 October 1999) *Alien Investigator: The Case Files of Britain's Leading UFO Detective,* Headline Book Publishing

Ian Black and Michael Schaffner (1 July 2014) "English Electric Lightning: High-speed Cold War interceptor in detail", *FlyPast* magazine

Who Was the Real Dan Cooper?

Bruce A. Smith (30 August 2015) "DB Cooper suspect, Ted Mayfield, killed in aviation accident", *The Mountain News.* Available at https://themountainnewswa.net/2015/08/30/db-cooper-suspect-ted-mayfield-killed-in-aviation-accident/ (Accessed 12 Oct 2018)

(13 February 1995) "Skydiving Operator Faces Charges Over Deaths of 2 Jumpers", The Seattle *Times.* Available at http://community.seattletimes.nwsource.com/archive/?date=19950213&slug=2104806 (Accessed 12 Oct 2018)

Bruce A. Smith (23 February 2012) “Suspects in the DB Cooper skyjacking—sketches, pictures and comparisons”, *The Mountain News.* Available at https://themountainnewswa.net/2012/02/23/suspects-in-the-db-cooper-skyjacking-sketches-pictures-and-comparisons/ (Accessed 13 Oct 2018)

Elizabeth McCracken (23 December 2008) “Wanted: John”, The *New York Times Magazine.* Available at https://www.nytimes.com/2008/12/28/magazine/28List-t.html (Accessed 14 Oct 2018)

Martin Andrade (1 December 2014) “Survival Probability Analysis of the D.B. Cooper Hijacking using Historical Parachuting Data”. Available at https://martinandrade.files.wordpress.com/2014/12/dbcooperfinalupdated.pdf (Accessed 21 Oct 2018)

Tyler Rogoway (22 April 2014) “When The CIA Proved That A Boeing 727 Can Perform Air Drops”, *Foxtrot Alpha.* Available at https://foxtrotalpha.jalopnik.com/the-cia-proved-that-a-boeing-727-can-perform-air-drops-1566155708 (Accessed 21 Oct 2018)

Great Mull Air Mystery

(9 July 1905) “Peter Gibbs’ Great Mull Air Mystery”, *Historic Mysteries.* Available at https://www.historicmysteries.com/peter-gibbs-great-mull-air-mystery/ (Accessed 26 Mar 2019)

(undated) “Series 8, The Great Mull Air Mystery”, BBC Radio 4 Punt Pi. Available at https://www.bbc.co.uk/programmes/p02zm886/p02zm98h (Accessed 26 Mar 2019)

David Howitt (undated) “Glenforsa Airfield History”. Available at http://web.archive.org/web/20160306155513/http://glenforsaairfield.co.uk/3.html (Accessed 26 Mar 2019)

Scott Macadam (7 June 1905) “The Great Mull Air Mystery”, Staffa Press (undated) "ASN Wikibase Occurrence # 18583", *Aviation Safety Network*. Available at https://aviation-safety.net/wikibase/wiki.php?id=18583 (Accessed 26 Mar 2019)

A UFO Hunter Finds What He's Looking For

James McGaha, Joe Nickell (1 December 2013) "The Valentich Disappearance: Another UFO Cold Case Solved", *Skeptical Inquirer*. Available at http://www.csicop.org/si/show/the_valentich_disappearance_another_ufo_cold_case_solved (Accessed 14 Apr 2019)

Danno (22 November 2012) "The Disappearaance of Frederick Valentich", *Beside the Yarra*. Available at http://marvmelb.blogspot.co.uk/2012/11/the-disappearance-of-frederick-valentich.html (Accessed 14 Apr 2019)

(27 April 1982) "Aircraft Accident Investigation Summary Report V116/783/1047", Commonweath of Australia Department of Transport

(23 October 1978) "UFO Enthusiast Missing After Reporting Craft", Toledo *Blade*. Available at https://news.google.com/newspapers?nid=1350&dat=19781023&id=6hFPAAAAIBAJ&pg=3318,4275388 (Accessed 14 Apr 2019)

The 38-year Search of Barrington Tops

Nev (31 August 2011) "Mike Hart", *Missing Plane Over Barrington Tops*. Available at http://vhmdx.blogspot.com/2011_08_01_archive.html (Accessed 2 Apr 2019)

(undated) "Bush Search and Rescue NSW (previously Bushwalkers Wilderness Rescue)", BSAR. Available at http://vhmdx.com.au/download/Dec-5-2014-Sensing-Presentation.pdf (Accessed 14 Apr 2019)

ATSB (14 November 2015) "Cessna 210M, VH-MDX, near Barrington Tops, NSW", Australian Transport Safety Bureau

Korean Air Lines Shot Down by Soviet Military (twice)

Jan Paradowski (22 May 2015) “Forgotten Flight 902”, *The Bad Pilot’s Blog.* Available at http://thebadpilotsblog.blogspot.com/2015/05/forgotten-flight-902.html (Accessed 10 Jan 2019)

Chris Sherwood (3 June 2008) “The Korean Boeing”, *English Russia.* Available at http://englishrussia.com/2008/06/03/the-korean-boeing/ (Accessed 10 Jan 2019)

Daniel Morley (20 April 2017) “A Forgotten Soviet Shoot-Down: The Story of Korean Air 902”, *Airline Geeks.* Available at https://airlinegeeks.com/2017/04/20/a-forgotten-soviet-shoot-down-the-story-of-korean-air-902/ (Accessed 20 Jan 2019)

James Albright (3 July 2013) “Korean Air Lines 902 Accident Case Study”, Code7700. Available at http://code7700.com/accident_korean_air_lines_902.htm (Accessed 20 Jan 2019)

Dmitry Sudakov (20 April 2018) “USSR shot down Korean passenger Boeing 40 years ago”, *Pravda.ru.* Available at http://www.pravdareport.com/society/stories/20-04-2018/140819-korean_boeing-0/ (Accessed 20 Jan 2019)

Michael Dobbs (26 May 1991) “Soviet Journalists Attack KAL Story”, *Washington Post.* Available at https://www.washingtonpost.com/archive/politics/1991/05/26/soviet-journalists-attack-kal-story/a0fab253-91f4-47e9-ada0-85d5b263d1df/?noredirect=on&utm_term=.e2f5c65409ba (Accessed 20 Jan 2019)

Asaf Degani (26 June 1905) *“Taming HAL: Designing Interfaces Beyond 2001”,* Palgrave Macmillan. Available at https://books.google.ee/books?id=DMQWDAAAQBAJ (Accessed 24 Jan 2019)

Night Ship Needed To Deviate, But From Whom?

NTSB (undated) "ATL03FA008", National Transport Safety Board. Available at https://web.archive.org/web/20050314184209/http://www.ntsb.gov/ntsb/brief2.asp?ev_id=20021029X05400&ntsbno=ATL03FA008&akey=1

Sara Kehaulani Goo (11 January 2006) "NTSB Solves Riddle of Small Plane Crash in '02", *Washington Post.* Available at http://www.washingtonpost.com/wp-dyn/content/article/2006/01/10/AR2006011001688.html??Noredirect=on (Accessed 14 Apr 2019)

(15 April 2004) "NTSB: 'Collision with Unknown Object' Killed Mobile Pilot", *Aero News Network.* Available at http://www.aero-news.net/index.cfm?do=main.textpost&id=c8886b93-36c4-4dca-a0dc-a5f40806f6c8 (Accessed 14 Apr 2019)

AIN Staff (24 July 2007) " 'Red Marks' confound accident investigators", *AINonline.* Available at https://www.ainonline.com/aviation-news/2007-07-24/red-marks-confound-accident-investigators (Accessed 14 Apr 2019)

NTSB (10 January 2006) "NTSB Identification ATL03FA008", National Transport Safety Board. Available at https://www.ntsb.gov/_layouts/ntsb.aviation/brief2.aspx?ev_id=20021029X05400&ntsbno=ATL03FA008&akey=1 (Accessed 14 Apr 2019)

The Stolen Boeing

Tim Wright (1 September 2010) "The 727 That Vanished", *Air & Space Magazine.* Available at https://www.airspacemag.com/history-of-flight/the-727-that-vanished-2371187/?no-ist= (Accessed 8 Apr 2019)

Tim Wright (1 October 2014) "When Airliners Vanish", *Air & Space Magazine.* Available at https://www.airspacemag.com/flight-today/when-airliners-vanish-180952793/?all&no-ist

(Accessed 8 Apr 2019)

(1 September 2010) "The 727 that Vanished: N844AA", *Professional Pilot's Rumour Network*. Available at https://www.pprune.org/african-aviation/427014-727-vanished-n844aa-2.html (Accessed 8 Apr 2019)

The Latest Bermuda Triangle Mystery

NTSB (undated) "NTSB Identification ERA09WA113", National Transport Safety Board. Available at https://www.ntsb.gov/about/employment/_layouts/ntsb.aviation/brief2.aspx?ev_id=20081230X20609&ntsbno=ERA09WA113&akey=1 (Accessed 14 Apr 2019)

(19 December 2008) "Lawyer: 'Bermuda Triangle' Plane Stolen by Human Trafficker", Fox News. Available at http://www.foxnews.com/story/2008/12/19/lawyer-bermuda-triangle-plane-stolen-by-human-trafficker.html (Accessed 14 Apr 2019)

AIN Staff (19 December 2008) "Authorities: Pilot of Missing Trislander Stole Aircraft", *Aero News Network*. Available at http://www.aero-news.net/index.cfm?do=main.textpost&id=d279ebc7-27ed-44f1-a5f1-715482318d0a (Accessed 14 Apr 2019)

(undated) "Registration Details for N650LP", *Plane Logger*. Available at https://www.planelogger.com/Aircraft/Registration/N650LP/676841 (Accessed 14 Apr 2019)

Simon Hradecky (19 December 2008) "Crash: Linea Aerea Puertorriquena TRIS near Providenciales on Dec 15th 2008, airplane missing after distress call", The *Aviation Herald*. Available at http://avherald.com/h?article=411d3d2b (Accessed 14 Apr 2019)

(15 December 2017) "A 9 años de la desaparición del avión N-650 LP al mando de Adrián Jiménez", *El Aviador*. Available at http://elaviador.do/2017/12/15/a-9-anos-de-la-

desaparicion-del-avion-n-650-lp-al-mando-de-adrian-jimenez/ (Accessed 8 Apr 2018)

Office of Aviation Analysis (3 September 2009) "RE: Docket DOT-OST-2009-0053", US Department of Transportation

Federal Aviation Administration (22 June 2009) "Emergency Order of Revocation", US Department of Transportation

Mystery Mali Boeing

(14 December 2010) "US embassy cables: Three-week delay for Mali 'drug plane' crash investigation", The *Guardian*. Available at https://www.theguardian.com/world/us-embassy-cables-documents/246478 (Accessed 14 Apr 2019)

(23 January 2012) "Mali frees 'cocaine plane' suspect", *news24*. Available at https://www.news24.com/Africa/News/Mali-frees-cocaine-plane-suspect-20120123 (Accessed 14 Apr 2019)

Tim Wright (1 October 2014) "When Airliners Vanish", *Air & Space Magazine*. Available at https://www.airspacemag.com/flight-today/when-airliners-vanish-180952793/?all&no-ist (Accessed 8 Apr 2019)

Malaysia Airlines Flight 370

Sylvia Wrigley (25 April 2014) *The Mystery of Malaysia Airlines Flight 370.*

Malaysian Safety Investigation Team (2 July 2018) "MH370 Safety Investigation Report", Ministry of Transport Malaysia. Available at http://mh370.mot.gov.my/MH370SafetyInvestigationReport.pdf (Accessed 14 Apr 2019)

Sutlej Missing Over Indian Ocean

Soutik Biswas (16 August 2016) "The 'puzzling' disappearance of an Indian Military plane", *BBC News*. Available at https://www.bbc.com/news/world-asia-india-37081390 (Accessed 18 Mar 2019)

Air Marshal BK Pandey (27 July 2016) "Missing AN-32: sabotage cannot be ruled out", *Deccan Herald*. Available at https://www.deccanherald.com/content/560363/missing-32-sabotage-cannot-ruled.html (Accessed 18 Mar 2019)

Rahul Bedi (22 January 2019) "India, Ukraine to resume stalled An-32 upgrade programme for IAF", *Jane's 360*. Available at https://www.janes.com/article/85872/india-ukraine-to-resume-stalled-an-32-upgrade-programme-for-iaf (Accessed 18 Mar 2019)

Vivek Raghuvanshi (28 March 2015) "Ukraine Conflict Stalls Indian AF Upgrades", *Defense News*. Available at https://www.defensenews.com/training-sim/2015/03/28/ukraine-conflict-stalls-indian-af-upgrades/ (Accessed 18 Mar 2019)

(13 April 2019) "Record ID 19860325-1", *Aviation Safety Network*. Available at https://aviation-safety.net/database/record.php?id=19860325-1 (Accessed 14 Apr 2019)

Jimmy Bhatia (1 April 2014) "MH370: Rekindling Memories of IAF's AN-32", *India Strategic*. Available at http://www.indiastrategic.in/topstories3291_MH370_Rekindling_Memories_IAF_AN-32.htm (Accessed 14 Apr 2019)

ABOUT THE AUTHOR

SYLVIA WRIGLEY is a pilot and aviation writer who has been obsessing about aviation safety for over a decade. Her in-depth knowledge of plane crashes has brought a number of interesting opportunities, most recently discussing crash details on the Discovery Channel's *AirCrash Confidential*. She's published six non-fiction books on a range of aviation subjects. The latest, *Without a Trace*, tells the true stories of aircraft and passengers who disappeared into thin air.

Sylvia holds both German and US-American citizenship and speaks both languages. She emigrated to Scotland where she guided German tourists around the Trossachs and searched for the supernatural. She now lives in Tallinn, Estonia.

She's worked across all modern media including:

Newspapers

Contributor to *The Guardian, Piper Flyer, Forbes, BBC News* and many other reputable news venues.

TV

Aviation expert featured on the Discovery Channel series *Aircrash Confidential series 2 and 3*, the Russian Channel 1 News, French Channel M6 *Disparition du vol MH370* and NTV.ru Central Television program.

Web

Creator of and sole contributor to Fear of Landing, with associated social media connections.

Her website https://fearoflanding.com/ continues to be a successful reference for aviation accidents, investigations and history, with over 300,000 visits in 2018.

Books

Her series, *Why Planes Crash*, launched in May 2013. The first book of the series covers eleven accidents and incidents in 2001, including the disastrous runway incursion at Linate, the near miss over Tokyo, the Avjet crash at Aspen, the Twin Towers and American Airlines Flight 587 disintegrating over Queens. The series currently covers from 2001 to 2003.

You can also follow her on social media:

https://twitter.com/fearoflanding
https://www.facebook.com/fearoflandingdotcom

Made in the USA
Columbia, SC
06 February 2025

53365436R00207